Rationality and the Ideology of Disconnection

Rationality and the Ideology of Disconnection is a powerful and provocative critique of the foundations of Rational Choice theory and the economic way of thinking about the world, written by a former leading practitioner. The target is a dehumanizing ideology that cannot properly recognize that normal people have attachments and commitments to other people and to practices, projects, principles, and places, which provide them with desire-independent reasons for action, and that they are reflective creatures who think about what they are and what they should be, with ideals that can shape and structure the way they see their choices. The author's views are brought to bear on the economic way of thinking about the natural environment and on how and when the norm of fair reciprocity motivates us to do our part in cooperative endeavors. Throughout, the argument is adorned by thought-provoking examples that keep what is at stake clearly before the reader's mind. To anyone who wishes to grasp what matters in the now highly charged debate about rational choice theory, this book is indispensable.

Michael Taylor is a professor of political science at the University of Washington in Seattle. He has taught previously at the University of Essex in England and at Yale University. He was for many years a leading practitioner of rational choice theory and published two influential books on cooperation in the absence of centralized coercion: *Anarchy and Cooperation* (later revised as *The Possibility of Cooperation*, 1987) and *Community, Anarchy, and Liberty* (1982).

T0349203

Contemporary Political Theory

Series Editor
Ian Shapiro

Editorial Board

Russell Hardin	Stephen Holmes	Jeffrey Isaac
John Keane	Elizabeth Kiss	Susan Okin
Phillipe Van Parijs	Philip Pettit	

As the twenty-first century begins, major new political challenges have arisen at the same time that some of the most enduring dilemmas of political association remain unresolved. The collapse of communism and the end of the Cold War reflect a victory for democratic and liberal values, yet in many of the Western countries that nurtured those values there are severe problems of urban decay, class and racial conflict, and failing political legitimacy. Enduring global injustice and inequality seem compounded by environmental problems; disease; the oppression of women and racial, ethnic, and religious minorities; and the relentless growth of the world's population. In such circumstances, the need for creative thinking about the fundamentals of human political association is manifest. This new series in contemporary political theory is needed to foster such systematic normative reflection.

The series proceeds in the belief that the time is ripe for a reassertion of the importance of problem-driven political theory. It is concerned, that is, with works that are motivated by the impulse to understand, think critically about, and address the problems in the world, rather than issues that are thrown up primarily in academic debate. Books in the series may be interdisciplinary in character, ranging over issues conventionally dealt with in philosophy, law, history, and the human sciences. The range of materials and the methods of proceeding should be dictated by the problem at hand, not the conventional debates of disciplinary divisions of academia.

Other books in the series:

Ian Shapiro and Casiano Hacker-Cordón (eds.)
Democracy's Value

Ian Shapiro and Casiano Hacker-Cordón (eds.)
Democracy's Edges

Brooke A. Ackerly
Political Theory and Feminist Social Criticism

Clarissa Rile Hayward
De-Facing Power

Continued after the index

Rationality and the Ideology of Disconnection

Michael Taylor
University of Washington, Seattle

CAMBRIDGE
UNIVERSITY PRESS

CAMBRIDGE UNIVERSITY PRESS
Cambridge, New York, Melbourne, Madrid, Cape Town, Singapore, São Paulo

Cambridge University Press
32 Avenue of the Americas, New York, NY 10013-2473, USA

www.cambridge.org
Information on this title: www.cambridge.org/9780521867450

First published 2006

Printed in the United States of America

A catalog record for this publication is available from the British Library.

Library of Congress Cataloging in Publication Data

Taylor, Michael, Ph.D.
Rationality and the ideology of disconnection / Michael Taylor.
    p.   cm. – (Contemporary political theory)
Includes bibliographical references and index.
ISBN 0-521-86745-2 (hardback) – ISBN 0-521-68704-7 (pbk.)
1. Rational choice theory.   2. Social choice.   3. Social ethics.
4. Human ecology.   I. Title.   II. Series
HM495.T38   2006
302′.13–dc22   2006002126

ISBN-13   978-0-521-86745-0 hardback
ISBN-10   0-521-86745-2 hardback

ISBN-13   978-0-521-68704-1 paperback
ISBN-10   0-521-68704-7 paperback

Contents

Preface

I intend this book as a contribution to the overthrow of a radically reductive and dehumanizing but deeply entrenched way of thinking. It is entrenched most completely in the discipline of economics – it is part of what *defines* neoclassical economics – and because of this has come to have enormous influence on how public policies of all kinds are made, and in this way affects all our lives, especially here in the United States. It has also made roads into the thinking of people in a variety of other academic disciplines, especially political science, where it has, for example, largely framed the discussion of when and why people are disposed to do their part in promoting common interests – a subject that is of fundamental importance in the study of politics because a great deal of governmental and other political activity and organization would not be necessary if most people were generally willing to do their part in advancing shared interests, and because, at the same time, democratic governance would not work well if most people were *not* generally prepared, without being coerced, to do their part in certain cooperative endeavors. Some environmentalists, too, among them even some well-known biologists, have fallen under the sway of the economists' version of this way of thinking, or at least have become willing to make selective use of it when they believe it will serve their purposes in the short run: they say, for example, that we should preserve biodiversity because it *pays* to, and in general to save the environment we must appeal to the businessperson's bottom line and the consumer's famous pocketbook.

At the foundation of this way of thinking about the world – an ideology if ever there was one, as the whole of this book will make plain – is the idea that human beings are moved only by desires, that their choices are to be understood always as being the resultant of weighing or trading off desires.

What is wrong with this? Human beings make promises and agreements, explicitly and tacitly, and generally they feel bound by them. They help to create or enter into or find themselves in certain relationships, with particular other individuals and with groups, and it would not occur to them to act except as required by such a relation, in ways that, in fact, are constitutive of the relation. They commit themselves to social practices and abide by the norms that define such practices, and again generally it would not occur to them to do otherwise. They make moral judgments, judgments of right and wrong, and then feel bound by them. Many people see (and many more in the past once saw) themselves as links between past and future generations or even as in part constituted by those links, and this may be bound up with a deep attachment to a particular place (for place – one to which humans can be attached – is never just a matter of physical location and physical objects, but is something made significant by human history, by events); and again, as a result of such attachments people can feel bound to act in certain ways.

In these and other ways we humans create for ourselves reasons for action that have force at the time of choice whether or not we want (in an ordinary nontautological sense of desire that I shall later try to make clear) to do that action. We create for ourselves what John Searle calls desire-independent reasons.

Human beings are conscious *of* themselves. They are self-reflective. They think about what they are: they have descriptive self-conceptions or self-understandings. They also think about what they *ought* to be – about the kind of person they should be, and how they should live their lives: they have *normative* self-understandings. They endorse or set for themselves *ideals* – moral ideals or the ideals (or standards) associated with and in part constitutive of the attachments and commitments to people, practices, projects, and places that I mentioned previously.

Although they may not be articulately held or consciously deployed or aimed at, these ideals directly provide us with motivating reasons to act. In some cases they also structure or frame the way we see a choice situation and determine what other considerations in that situation provide reasons for action: they may totally silence or exclude some reasons (such as a generally operative desire for pecuniary gain) or they may diminish their reason-giving force. When a person's ideals structure or modulate her choices in these ways, I shall say that they form her *identity*. So a person's identity is the part of her normative self-understanding that structures and modulates her choices.

These connections we make to the world and their capacity to move us directly and to structure the way we see and make our choices are a large part of what makes us human. If economists and other Rational Choice theorists take account of them at all, they misrepresent them; they do not understand them for what they really are. In fact, they *cannot* accommodate them in their theories, because those theories are committed to understanding human action solely in terms of *desires* (or *preferences*). They take the idea of desire to be primitive and foundational; they lump together as "desires" several different sorts of things (or simply assume that if someone chose something he must have wanted it, that he must have been motivated by a desire); they take it for granted that these desires can be balanced or traded off against one another – that they are, as it were, all on the same level and can all be put into a single utility function to be maximized; and they assume (tacitly, because the possibility seems not even to occur to them) that there are no desire-independent reasons, hence nothing that can structure those desires, nothing that can silence or suppress them or diminish or qualify them in any way.

Thus, although economists and other Rational Choice theorists sometimes talk about altruism, commitment, community, social approval, and those self-assessing but highly social emotions, guilt and shame, the subjects of their theories are not truly social. Moved only by desire, by what they want or prefer, they also are not rational, for reason's only role in these theories is to guide people (not motivate them) as they try to get what they want. Rationality (I shall take it) requires at least the capacity to consider and be moved by reasons, including those provided by our ideals, by our normative self-understandings. (For this reason I shall capitalize the initials of Rational Choice whenever I am referring to the model of choice assumed by Rational Choice theorists, whose practice *denies* rationality to its subjects.)

In these ways, Rational Choice theory denies its subjects capacities and dispositions that are an important part of what makes us human. It denies them also – and in many cases (as we shall see) denies much else besides – to real human beings when it is put into practice: when it advocates and legitimates public policies and projects that are predicated on the premise that humans are moved only by their wants, and especially when the further assumptions of the normative part of neoclassical economics ("welfare economics") are added, assumptions that together imply that the value of anything to anybody is fully replaceable, so that anyone can be compensated for the loss of anything.

In Part One of the book I sketch (in Chapter 2) the general argument about ideals and identities, desires, and the structure of reasons, after first (in Chapter 1) trying to soften the reader up a little with some discussion of several examples of choices, made (with one exception) by real people, that cannot be explained or understood by the Rational Choice model without being radically misrepresented and trivialized. Some of these choices (involving, for example, the rejection by poor people of fabulous sums of money) are extraordinary, but I hope to convince the reader in the rest of the book that my argument applies to the more mundane choices we make every day.

Economists don't just use the model of Rational Choice to explain social behavior; they *idealize* a world in which it holds, a world in which there are no desire-independent reasons, no framing or structuring ideals (provided, for example, by attachments or connections of the kind I discuss in Part One), no normativity, and no moral motivation. This is the world of the Market Ideal, the economist's utopia, where anything people care about is a commodity, where everything of value is owned and consumed as a private good, where every "resource" is put to its "most productive" or "most highly valued" use, where all problems, including environmental problems, are *defined* as the failure of markets to produce efficient allocations of resources. In Part Two of the book I shall look at what happens in this world of the Market Ideal to the individual human being, her communities, and her natural environments.

Economists proudly proclaim their commitment to the principle of "consumer sovereignty" – the principle that people's *wants* or *preferences*, as expressed by the choices they make in markets, must be respected; they must not be judged. But normal people certainly judge their *own* preferences, and economists are repeatedly told, when they conduct "contingent valuation" surveys, that social choices about public projects and policies should *not* be made on the basis of what individuals want (especially wants they express as isolated buyers in markets), and it would seem that the respondents who reject these surveys think that such decisions should take account of their *judgments*, their beliefs about what *ought* to be done, which perhaps they can discover or develop in a process of public *deliberation*. (Contingent valuation surveys are conducted when there is no market – as there is not for whooping cranes, Grand Canyons, or stratospheric ozone layers – in which people's values can, so the economist claims, be inferred from the choices they make – from what they are willing to pay for things.) Economists reject this: consumers are sovereign but human beings apparently are not. Economists deny their subjects the distinctively human capacities and dispositions that I describe in Part One of the book – above all to endorse and be moved by ideals that determine the reason-giving force of other considerations – and insist instead that they think and choose according to the neoclassical version of the Rational Choice model. All this, as I hope to make clear, is far from being a merely academic matter.

In Part Three of the book, and with further help from T. M. Scanlon's account of moral motivation and *What We Owe to Each Other*, I bring the general argument of Part One to bear on a topic that is fundamental for all the social sciences, namely whether, why, and when people will do their part in mutually advantageous cooperative endeavors. I believe the norm of fair reciprocity must play a central role in our understanding of these things, but not in the way proposed by economists and other Rational Choice theorists. They have recently come to recognize that people seem to cooperate more often than is predicted or explained on Rational Choice assumptions (in one-shot Prisoners' Dilemma games, for example) and that people seem to be disposed to conform to a norm of fair reciprocity. But in trying to explain why this is so, they have once again resorted to the standard model according to which choice is always, in effect, the outcome of a competition of unstructured, comparable desires. On the Rational Choice account, cooperation and noncooperation are *both* explained by the balance of benefits and costs; there is only one sort of motivation at work. If people are recognized as caring about the fairness of outcomes, this is represented as just another desire or preference, to be balanced against other desires in a utility function. Or it is assumed that the norm of reciprocity or fairness plays the role merely of a shared belief that enables people to coordinate their actions to select an equilibrium – helping each person to maximize his utility in the light of what he expects others to do. In either case, the norm has no motivating power of its own. The essential characteristic of a norm – its normativity – is therefore ignored or assumed away. I shall argue instead that, *first*, doing your part in a cooperative endeavor (from which you will benefit even if you do not contribute) is a part of most people's normative self-understanding, and that the norm of fair reciprocity therefore provides, in the right conditions, a motivating reason to act, one that structures or modulates other reasons for or against doing your part in cooperative endeavors; but *second*, this moral motivation can be deactivated or demobilized and replaced by Rational Choosing when people are not recognized as fully human beings – beings with the capacities and dispositions I described in Part One – but are instead treated as if they were in fact specimens of *Homo economicus*, radically asocial animals manipulable or movable only by incentives. (In other words – I am not denying – people *sometimes* act like *Homo economicus*.)

Readers familiar with the work of the philosophers Thomas Nagel, Bernard Williams, Joseph Raz, Elizabeth Anderson, and T. M. Scanlon and the criminologist John Braithwaite will recognize my special debt to them. For many years I practiced what I here attack. But almost from the beginning I had my doubts. For a while my response to these doubts was a version of the argument that Rational Choice theory applied only in certain domains, or only to certain sorts of choices, essentially those in which a great deal – in terms of the benefits and costs specified in the explanation in question – turns on the individual's choice. But, if it is not a tautology, this argument is shown to be wrong by examples of the kind I discuss in Part One, and the general argument I make there implies that it is beside the point. For some years I spent much of my time seeking out and thinking about difficult cases for the Rational Choice approach, even while continuing to defend it (in a retrenched domain). It was not until, belatedly, I came to see the sometimes devastating consequences (for human lives, for communities and cultures, and for the natural environment) of government decisions made on the assumption that people think and choose in the way assumed by economists and other Rational Choice theorists that I decided I should write this book. But in finding my way out of the Rational Choice way of thinking, I was helped enormously by the work of the philosophers I have mentioned, and the form in which I now express my views derives largely from their work. (They are not, of course, to be blamed for anything here. Nor is anyone else mentioned in this Preface.) I was helped too, at an early stage, by another philosopher, Michael Smith, who kindly took some time, while I was a visitor at the Australian National University, to introduce me to the arguments for and against the (neo-) Humean theory of motivation, of which he is perhaps the most able defender.

Originally this book included a short essay on some novels of Patrick White, especially *The Solid Mandala*. His work has been important to me. I have learned as much about identity and integrity from his writings as from anyone's.

I have many other debts. It is a little embarrassing for me to realize that I first tried out an earlier and eventually rejected version of some of the arguments presented here in a public seminar on commitment, identity, and rationality that I gave at the University of Washington as long ago as early 1991. In the same year I had interesting discussions with several members of the Tribal Council of the Yakama Nation (in Washington State) and I am most grateful to them. (Those discussions left me uncertain about the motivations at work in the Council decision that I had gone to talk with them about, a decision of a kind I discuss in the first chapter that follows, and so I decided not to include any account of it here.) In the following school year, gratefully spent at the Center for Advanced Study in the Behavioral Sciences at Stanford, I divided my time between doing Rational Choice explanation and thinking about what was wrong with it and whether I could go on defending it. Soon after that I had interesting and useful discussions with a group of people who were fighting to prevent the mountain they lived around – Buckhorn Mountain in north central Washington – from being taken apart by a multinational corporation bent on developing a cyanide leach-heap gold mine there; they were most hospitable and their company most enjoyable. Some of the arguments here I tried out at a conference in Stockholm and at a seminar in the sociology department at the University of Stockholm; at both of them I received useful comments, especially from Richard Swedberg. The argument I make here about cooperation in hierarchies and an earlier version of the argument about the activation and deactivation of the norm of fair reciprocity went into a paper entitled "Good Government: On Hierarchy, Social Capital, and the Limitations of Rational Choice Theory," which was eventually published in the *Journal of Political Philosophy*, and I am grateful to the publisher of that journal for allowing me to use a few paragraphs of my article. A draft of that article was circulated at a conference on social capital convened at Cape Cod in 1994 by Robert Putnam; I had some useful discussions about it with several participants, particularly Jane Mansbridge. It was also presented around that time to a conference at the Center in Political Economy at Washington University.

I am grateful for their help to Julius Kincs and Xila MacLeod and to several other people in and around Alto in Portugal whose names I did not learn and especially to Robin Jenkins, who did the study of Alto that I discuss in the first chapter. I discussed my visit to Alto and made some of the arguments presented in this book at a seminar in the School of Economic and Social Studies at the University of East Anglia (at Norwich in England). I thank Edwin Lyon, archeologist at the U.S. Army Corps of Engineers' regional office in New Orleans (assertively built right on a levee of the Mississippi), and Kirsten Lahlum, Librarian at the Corps' regional office in Portland, Oregon, for helpful discussions and for making documents available to me. I am grateful to the many people, not already mentioned, whose writings I have put to work (I hope without distortion) for my own purposes – especially John Berger, Boyce Richardson, Wendy Espeland, and Edward Lazarus. I hope I have made all due acknowledgments in my notes. And lastly, I thank the people who have discussed this work with me or commented on earlier versions of all or parts of the book, especially John Braithwaite, Gardner Brown, Eugene Hunn, Jim Scott, Sara Singleton, Eric Alden Smith, and, most of all, Alan Carling. To Alan Carling I owe many improvements to my text, though I fear I have not adequately met all of his penetrating challenges to my argument. To Gardner Brown I would like to say that if the cost-benefit analyses that have been used to justify many of the large dams and other projects in the United States had been conducted by him, the world would be a better place. (See the chapter on him – "Dr. Brown Flies the Eel" – in Ted Simon's book, *The River Stops Here.*)

I have learned from many people, and I thank them all.

Part one

Attachments, reasons, and desires

... & is he honest who resists his genius or conscience only for the sake of present ease or gratification?
William Blake

"A memorable Fancy"
Plates 12–13 in *The Marriage of Heaven and Hell*

1   Attachments: five stories

1.1.   "The world has left the earth behind"

In his luminous fictional trilogy, *Into Their Labours*, John Berger describes in the first two volumes, *Pig Earth* and *Once in Europa*, the world of a small peasant village in the French Alps, a village that until very recently must have been fairly remote from big cities, as it begins to come apart with increasing contact with the wider economy and market mentality of the outside world, and, in the final volume, *Lilac and Flag*, the scattering of its children to the big cities.[1]

In the village and the country around it we see, as we move through the first two volumes, an older peasant mentality, the mentality of a culture of survival and intergenerational continuity with (as Berger says in his Introduction) a "profound suspicion of money," collide with a mentality that is still fairly novel to most of the villagers, a mentality that some would call capitalist, though it is wider than that and which, for now, we can call the market mentality as long as we remember that it is not confined to societies in which economic transactions are governed largely by competitive markets.

On three occasions in the trilogy someone refuses to sell something. Marcel, of *Pig Earth*, refuses to sell his old cider press. In *Once in Europa* Odile's father refuses to sell his farm to the owners of the factory complex that now completely surrounds the farm and is poisoning the land and mutilating its own workers. "The owners first doubled, then trebled, the price they were prepared to pay him. His

---

[1]   John Berger, *Into Their Labours* (New York: Pantheon, 1992).

3

reply remained the same. My patrimony is not for sale" (p. 277). And finally, in *Lilac and Flag*, Sucus, the migrant worker searching for home and love and a little security in the alien city, refuses to sell his knife, though he is desperate for money, because the knife was his father's.

Let us go back to Marcel. Not everyone in the village is like Marcel. He is the only one left who still plants new apple trees – grown from seedlings that had sprouted from the *marc* (the residuum from pressed cider apples) that he buried each year in a corner of his garden. He doesn't expect his children to stay on the farm. But he continues to work with effort and care, though the farm will end with him, because it is, he thinks, "a way of preserving the knowledge my sons are losing," and he plants the trees "to give an example to my sons if they are interested, and, if not, to show my father and his father that the knowledge they handed down has not yet been abandoned. Without that knowledge, I am nothing" (p. 67).

One day, Marcel is pressing apples for cider, when one of those sons, Edouard, returns from work. Earlier that day, Marcel has observed Edouard at work trying to sell some sort of wonder-soap to women in the market, an activity that in Marcel's eyes is fraudulent. Edouard, whom we've already seen exasperated with his father for refusing to buy a tractor – for refusing the twentieth century – now casually tells Marcel that he could sell the ancient oak cider press, which has the date 1802 carved on it and has probably been in the family for generations, as an antique. There's a dealer he knows who would pay a lot of money for it; in turn the dealer, he says, could sell it to a bank or hotel, where, Edouard tells his astonished father, it would become . . . *décor*. To this proposal, Marcel's only response is: "The world has left the earth behind."

Berger has nothing more than this to say about Marcel's response. But it is clear that Marcel lacks interest in selling the cider press for half a million francs, though not because he thinks that he should be paid more for it. To him it is ridiculous, unseemly, almost incomprehensible that it should become décor in a bank's lobby (where the bank no doubt expects it to lend an aura of solidity, reliability, permanence, and integrity). It has never occurred to him to sell it, and it is to him an alien thought that the press is merely potential money.

With that money he could no doubt buy another, equally effective press, and have much money to spare. But the cider press – this particular cider press – has a significance or meaning for him that no other press could have. It is not just an old, familiar, and reliable friend; it *connects* him to his past life – to among other things the annually enacted routines of picking apples with his wife, and planting apple tree seedlings from the *marc* and making cider and *gnôle* and drinking them with family and friends; it is a link between past generations and his own living family and, he forlornly hopes, future generations; it represents and collects significance from the ancient culture, the knowledge and customs, that have sustained him and his ancestors.

All this is compromised when the press is thought of in terms of the money it would fetch, or when it is thought of as interchangeable with some other press, or as serving the extraneous purpose his son suggests for it. (We should note here parenthetically that if Marcel did voluntarily sell the press to, say, a bank, it would then, as our twentieth-century neoclassical economists like to say, be finding "a more valued use," perhaps its "most productive use," and that, say the economists, would be good. We'll return in Part Two to this mad way of thinking). To sell the press – and especially to outsiders beyond the peasant's world who will not even continue to use it as a cider press, to a hotel or bank moreover, which in peasant (and some other) minds represent the very forces that are gradually destroying the whole way of life that has given Marcel's own life meaning – is, in the mind of someone who thinks like Marcel, to *de-mean* his past life, to *disconnect* and alienate him from his culture (while contributing to a new one he cannot respect), to rupture the continuities that give meaning and some measure of dignity to his life.[2]

---

[2] *Into Their Labours* is in part about losing one's *home*, about being an emigrant, especially from the country to the city. But I should add that Berger, who writes elsewhere of the twentieth century as "the century of banishment," does not believe that it is possible "to return to that historical state in which every village was the center of the world. The only hope of recreating a center now is to make it the entire world. Only worldwide solidarity can transcend modern homelessness...." *And Our Faces, My Heart, Brief as Photos* (New York: Pantheon, 1984), p. 67.

1.2.   "The meeting point of two worlds"

I do not know how close John Berger's fictional world is to the French mountain community in which he has lived for many years, but the collision of two worlds that is the subject of his trilogy is of course something that has taken place – in differing ways and at different times and speeds – all around the world. Let us look at this collision as it occurred in one small place – a hamlet called Alto in the Serra de Monchique in southern Portugal – as described in a fine book by Robin Jenkins.[3] Here, in Western Europe, less than an hour's drive now from the Algarve coast, with its swarming tourist hotels and night clubs, a way of life that had gone on largely unchanged for a thousand years did not begin seriously to give way until the 1950s and was still in the process of collapsing when Jenkins lived there in 1976.

The precipitant of this destruction was the building of a road, of only twelve kilometers, connecting Alto to the town of Monchique and thence by existing roads to the larger towns and cities of Portugal and the wide world beyond. Before this road was built in 1951, there was little movement of people or goods into or out of Alto and the surrounding country because the only link with the outside world was by rough donkey tracks – a thousand years old – to Monchique, a journey of three hours on a donkey or two hours on foot. Cork, medronho (the local firewater), and sweet chestnuts were the only things exported from Alto and, aside from a little iron for tools and donkey shoes from the mines of Aljustrel, seven days away to the north, and salt, rice, almonds, and cigarettes and a few other manufactured goods, all of which required donkey journeys of several days, the people of Alto were self-sufficient.

In a climate that is cool and wet in winter and hot and dry in summer, and on mountainsides whose natural vegetation would be only evergreen trees and scrub bushes, they had constructed and maintained over the centuries a series of terraces irrigated with water that they have tapped from springs by tunneling into the rocky hillsides

---

[3] Robin Jenkins, *The Road to Alto: An Account of Peasants, Capitalists and the Soil in the Mountains of Southern Portugal* (London: Pluto Press, 1979).

and stored in stone tanks. By these means they fashioned a "luxuriant environment," one that is no doubt biologically more diverse than the natural ecosystem, and were able to grow a great variety of food crops: potatoes, onions, carrots, cabbages, peas, and beans of several kinds; peppers, pumpkins, sweet potatoes, yams, tomatoes, maize, and peanuts; "oranges, lemons and tangerines, plums, cherries and nectarines, loquats, pomegranates and figs, and many varieties of apple and pear"; a few persimmon, mulberry, and grape vines. There were also olive groves, sweet chestnuts, willows along the streams – "carefully pollarded each spring for making baskets" – and on dry hillsides sometimes far from the village wheat and oats were grown, and there were stands of medronho trees whose berries are fermented and distilled into a spirit.

From the cork of cork oaks the people of Alto fashioned many things, including plates and cups and beehives. They made furniture and tools from local woods. They collected herbs for medicines and certain grasses for making string and sacks and for washing the dishes. They hunted a little.

Little entered the region, little left; nothing was wasted. Although the people of Alto utterly transformed their local natural environment, they were an *ecosystem people*: they lived for centuries within the constraints of their local ecosystem without degrading it, having indeed greatly increased its biological productivity. In their isolation before the coming of the road, their almost entirely self-contained economy, an economy governed by orally transmitted customs that encapsulated "the intelligence, trials and errors of generations because the local customs are a very precise reflection of what the local landscape, its soil and climate actually make possible," might very well have been indefinitely reproducible.

All this began to crumble with the coming of the road in 1951. By the time of Jenkins's sojourn there in 1976, the ancient subsistence economy had been penetrated and demoralized by the external capitalist order. Now, the biggest trucks could reach Alto and take out timber, and rich foreigners could easily scout the area for sites to build villas, and multinational corporations could come to prospect for uranium. Now it was easy for the literate to leave for work abroad and for the young to sample life in the cities. And before long the people of

Alto were no longer united by shared experience but divided between "those who remain illiterate peasants and those who are every bit a part of the modern world."

The road, of course, was not the force that turned Alto's world upside down; its role was to let that force in. Down the road came many things. The first effect was to make it possible and initially attractive for Alto's peasants to produce and export an agricultural surplus: chemical fertilizer was trucked in, potato yields were greatly increased, the surplus was sold and indeed had to be sold to pay for the fertilizer. Now more things that previously had been made or done in Alto were bought in Monchique – motorbikes, for example, replaced donkeys, whose manure had fertilized the terraces. Then the peasants discovered that increasingly large amounts of chemical fertilizer were needed to maintain the yields as their soils deteriorated with its use. And so they were drawn into a wider, capitalist economy and bound to it ever more tightly.

The road also brought the eucalyptus trees. Before the road was built, the only economic value of the arid mountain scrub all around Alto derived from the wild medronho trees, whose berries were used to make medronho, a spirituous liquor. But the fast-growing, nonnative eucalyptus grows well on this terrain, and those families in Alto that owned large tracts of mountain land were approached by large paper-manufacturing companies with offers of forty-year contracts. (Only large tracts of land are economically suitable for this purpose and the cost of clearing the mountainsides, bulldozing access roads, and planting the trees is beyond the means of even the local capitalists). From such a contract, with the company paying all the costs and doing all the work, the owner of 500 hectares of mountain land could sit back and earn an annual income (I calculate from Jenkins' 1976 figures) exceeding that of well-paid professionals in the capitals of Europe.

Four families in Alto had large enough tracts of land. Of these, three signed contracts. One family, that of Eloi and his wife Eulalia, both in their fifties, refused. It is this refusal that interests me. Before considering it, there is one more aspect of the eucalyptus plantations that must be noted. Eucalyptus trees drink enormous quantities of water and where they have been planted on the mountains around

Alto they are using the winter rainfall that would otherwise feed the mountain springs on which the peasants had always relied for irrigation. Below the eucalyptus plantations, the water is disappearing: some terraces can no longer be used for crops requiring irrigation and on others there is less and less water available even as more is required because of the use of chemical fertilizer in place of manure. The water supply of one of the contract signers is being dried up by the eucalyptus plantation on his own land; for the rest, their water is being taken by other people's trees. There is now aggressive competition for the dwindling water supply. Soon (wrote Jenkins) "the terraces will no longer be able to produce summer crops and the economic and ecological basis for centuries of stable agricultural production, already undermined by the excessive use of fertilizer, will be destroyed." This is a part of the background of Eloi's refusal to sign a contract for eucalyptus; it also illustrates a process – the effects on ecosystem people, on their intertwined local ecosystems, communities, and cultures, of integration into a much larger economic system – that I will come back to in Part Two.

But now let us look at Eloi's refusal. Eloi and Eulalia's lives were ones of almost unremitting manual labor and, with their refusal, would remain so. Their four children had turned their backs on this life on the land and had left Alto for good to live and work in the towns. When they returned to Alto each year they tried strenuously to persuade their parents to sign a contract with the paper company. The spreading eucalypt forest would in any case doom their parents' ancient way of life. They owned 600 acres of suitable mountain land whose only use to them was in the production of medronho. If they signed, they would be rich; they could look forward to a life of ease – in Alto, if they chose, or at a pleasant spot on the coast near some of their children – or they could continue to work on the land as long as that was possible. And if they did not sign away their mountain land their children would certainly do so as soon as they inherited it. Why did Eloi and Eulalia refuse?

Every year, in September, the couple make the trek over to their mountain land, several miles from Alto, to camp out for a month in a tiny cottage while they pick several tons of medronho berries, which are then carted off by donkey to be fermented in their vats.

They are joined, after some arm twisting, by their daughters and their husbands and their son and his wife, who all bring along *their* children. It is hard work. For Eulalia, though she doesn't drink and hates drunkenness, this is the best time of the year. "For a few brief weeks she can enjoy *her* family on *her* land, all working together in the traditional way. This is what her peasant life was all about – carrying on with the age-old traditions of work, keeping everything in good order, and above all, feeling that it was going to be left in good order for all the generations of family to come."

Of course, they make money from the sale of the medronho spirit, but it is a tiny fraction of what they would earn from the same land planted with eucalyptus. But they are not interested in becoming rich. They are not interested in the kind of life they could live with the secure income the plantation would provide. They prefer to continue to live the way they have lived their lives so far. But it is not just a matter of taste, or of preference – for a self-sufficient, unalienated life working the land they know so well. And it is not just a fear of the unknown, or a preference for the familiar or for a life filled by routine, by necessity even. Nor is it only the pleasure that Eulalia has of working with all her family every year at the medronho-picking season, or even of the couple's desire not to be among those who contribute to the destruction of the medronho tree and the ruin of Alto's centuries-old system of irrigation agriculture. It is also the satisfaction that they feel in continuing a set of ancient traditions, in being part of a process that has gone on for centuries and that they would like to see their children continue and pass on intact in their turn.

But Eloi and Eulalia's refusal is not, or not only, motivated by prospects of future preference satisfaction. (That is the only way the economists can see it, even if they admit more than a desire for profit or for things reducible to money or for the satisfaction of material wants.) The couple's refusal has also, I think, very much to do with the meaning, significance, and value of the way of life of which their lives and work have been a part and hence the meaning and significance and value of their own lives. To exchange their mountain land for money would be to devalue and demean the way they had spent their lives, to subvert the very meaning and significance of their lives and of the culture they had spent their lives helping to sustain and the centuries-old tradition in which their lives had been a link, rendering obsolete all the accumulated knowledge of how to live in that particular place on earth. To abandon all this for money, for a life of ease, and in doing so, moreover, to contribute to the demise of that way of life, would in effect be to say that their lives and practices were worth no more, meant no more, than this other prospective life or the money with which it would be purchased. To sign the contract would be to allow an adventitious and (from their perspective) arbitrary intrusion of an almost incomprehensible world beyond Alto – to break the intergenerational continuity and community and to tear the ecological fabric that they had helped to sustain and that sustained their lives and in large part made them what they were. It would break the thread of their lives.

1.3. "The money means nothing"

In 1971, the premier of the Canadian province of Quebec, Robert Bourassa, announced "the project of the century": a colossal hydroelectric scheme in which all but one of the great wild rivers draining into James Bay and others draining directly into Hudson Bay would be dammed or diverted. Some two dozen power stations would be constructed, with the power going to cities and industrial facilities far to the south. To accomplish this, thousands of kilometers of road and dozens of towns and airports would also have to be built. Thousands of kilometers of transmission lines would be stretched across the province. Vast tracts of low-lying taiga would be inundated; hundreds of lakes would disappear.

The project would be built in three phases corresponding to three watershed complexes, spanning an area roughly equal to that of France. The first phase would be the La Grande Complex, in which ten hydroelectric dams would be thrown across the La Grande River and its tributaries the Eastmain and Opinaca Rivers.

The government of Quebec thought of this vast area as essentially empty of human habitation. In fact it was the home of the Eeyou Aski, or Cree, and, in the north of the affected area, of Inuit people. The Cree and the Inuit had lived there, in place, for several thousand years, utterly dependent until very recently and still substantially dependent, as hunters, fishers, and trappers, on the healthy functioning of the ecosystems of this fragile, harsh, and unforgiving terrain. They were not consulted about the proposed project, which if completed would be one of the largest hydroelectric projects the world has ever seen, one that would transform their ancestral homeland, especially the rivers that are so central to their way of life as vital means of transportation and as sources and gathering places of a rich array of foods, and moreover would bring into the area for the first time large numbers of white men, their money, and their culture, further disorienting the younger Indians.[4]

The government of Quebec did not even bother to inform them of its plans. They first heard about it when one of them picked up a day-old Montreal newspaper in the town of Chibongamou.

[4] For a general account of the James Bay project see Sean McCutcheon, *Electric Rivers: The Story of the James Bay Project* (Montreal: Black Rose Books, 1991). For the views of the Cree on the project as construction began, their testimony in the Malouf court hearings (from which I shall be quoting), and an account of their culture and economy at this time, see the book (a book that everyone should read) by Boyce Richardson, *Strangers Devour the Land* (New York: Knopf, 1976). For the Cree's traditional hunting culture and economy, see Adrian Tanner, *Bringing Animals Home: Religious Ideology and Mode of Production of the Mistassini Cree Hunters* (New York: St. Martin's Press, 1979). When, in March 1989, Hydro-Quebec announced that it was reactivating its plan to move ahead with the next phases of the project, developing first the Great Whale watershed to the north, then the watersheds of the Nottaway, Broadbeck, and Rupert Rivers to the south, it was obliged under the terms of the James Bay and Northern Quebec Agreement to produce a report on environmental impacts. When the result, in thirty volumes, did not satisfy the Cree, a further study, more fully addressing the impacts on the natives, as they saw it, was conducted: see C. Scott and K. Ettenger, *Great Whale Environmental Assessment Community Consultation: Final Report for Wemindji and East Main*, 2 vols., and D. Nakashima and M. Roue, *Great Whale Environmental Assessment Community Consultation: Final Report for Whapmagoostui and Chisasibi*, 4 vols. – both of these reports prepared for the Grand Council of the Crees (of Quebec) and the Cree Regional Authority under contract with Hydro-Quebec (Montreal: Hydro-Quebec, 1994). For a considerably shorter report on some of these impacts, see Kreg Ettenger, " 'A River That Was Once So Strong and Deep': Local Reflections on the Eastmain Diversion, James Bay Hydroelectric Project," Chapter 4 in John M. Donahue and Barbara Rose Johnston, eds., *Water, Culture, and Power: Local Struggles in a Global Context* (Washington, DC: Island Press, 1998). On the social impacts, see Ronald Niezen, "Power and Dignity: The Social Consequences of Hydroelectric Development for the James Bay Cree," *Canadian Review of Sociology and Anthropology*, 30 (1993), 510–520.

The James Bay Development Corporation, a Crown corporation that had been given control of a newly created municipality of
133,000 square miles, began work on Phase One in 1971 – before carrying out any comprehensive assessment of environmental impacts
(which, the Corporation asserted, would be negligible) and apparently with no concern at all for the impact the project would have
on the native human communities. The Cree and Inuit, when they
learned of the project, objected. It was obvious – and later a scientific
team that surveyed the La Grande River area would concur – that the
project would have a devastating impact on the land and its native
inhabitants. But the provincial government was not interested even
in scaling the project back. Bourassa was dismissive of the natives
and their objections, and the Corporation continued to build roads,
airports, and construction sites. So the Cree and Inuit went to court.
They had, after all, never ceded these lands in any treaty; nor had
they ever been conquered in battle.

In seventy-eight days of hearings, conducted in French and
English, over the period December 1972 to June 1973, in the Quebec Superior Court in Montreal, Justice Albert Malouf, presiding,
patiently listened to a stream of native witnesses (speaking through an
interpreter) and their lawyers and scientists speaking on their behalf,
and of course to witnesses and lawyers for the James Bay Development Corporation and the government of Quebec.

The government witnesses told the Court that Quebec *needed* the
energy (though in fact the province produced a surplus of electricity, and much of the vast quantity of new energy the project would
produce would go south to the United States); they said that without
it the province would become a backwater, a museum (the premier
himself said) of "picturesque fishermen half living on government
handouts and some tourist attractions," and although (Bourassa continued) the people would have "birds and fresh water, and vegeta-
bles and animal reserves" they would have to give up their "tele-
visions, bungalows, electric kitchens, movie theaters, autos, planes,
modern apartments. . . . "[5] The government lawyers tried to persuade
the court that the natives were now really just regular Canadians, no

[5] Richardson, *Strangers*, p. 328.

longer living from the land and dependent on the bush for their sub-sistence but living off store-bought food, eating toast for breakfast and pork chops for dinner, riding about in skidoos, and generally participating in the market economy.

But the court also heard the natives. They had come down to Montreal out of their wilderness – to Montreal, an unhealthy place, as one of them put it, where "the cars do not make room for the people . . . and the people are scattered all over the sidewalks." They came out of another world. One of them, asked by the Court if he would tell the truth, the whole truth, and nothing but the truth, had first to consult at length with the translator, who then said to the judge: "He does not know whether he can tell the truth. He can tell only what he knows."[6]

And now, the Crown lawyers wanted to know the impact of the pro-ject on the natives and their land *in money terms*. A native witness, Job Bearskin, a Cree hunter, replied: "When you talk about the money, it means nothing. There will never be enough money to pay for the damage that has been done. I'd rather think about the land and when I think about the land, I think about the children: what will they have if the land is destroyed? The money means nothing." (The Crown lawyer: "I object to the contents of this reply, your Lordship".)[7]

Boyce Richardson, from whose wonderful book I have drawn these quotations from the Court's proceedings, sat once for an hour and a half with this Job Bearskin on the banks of the La Grande River, the great wild river at the heart of Phase One of the project that would be turned into a string of huge reservoirs:

> Job . . . talked about this person, this river, which had always helped the Indian so much. About its clean, good taste. About its good-tasting fish. About the many places he could camp along its shores. About the vegetation on the banks where the animals liked to feed and were easy to find and kill for food. About its utility as a highway, helpful to the Indian when he wanted to travel up and down the country. Nothing, in Job's experience, had ever been so helpful to the Indian as this river.[8]

---

[6] Richardson, *Strangers*, p. 46.
[7] Richardson, *Strangers*, p. 121.
[8] Richardson, *Strangers*, p. 162.

Justice Malouf agreed with the natives. In November 1973 he ordered work on the project to be stopped. But the developers appealed (while continuing to work, in defiance of the court order) and, within one week of the Malouf judgment and after just five hours of deliberation, the Quebec Court of Appeals reversed Justice Malouf – making no reference to Indian rights but asserting simply that the interests of "about 2,000 inhabitants cannot be compared with the interest of the people of Quebec." But of course the justices managed easily to compare the latter interest – the interest, I suppose the justices meant, of the several million Quebecois who were not Indians or Inuit – with the interest of the natives, and to deem it more weighty; or perhaps the native interest was assumed to be of no significance at all.

The Cree and Inuit were subsequently put under pressure to end their opposition and to come to a settlement. They were offered $100 million, together with a development corporation to handle this money, and hunting, fishing, and trapping rights, and reserved land. They rejected the offer: "the Indian lands are not for sale," they said, "not for millions and millions of dollars." "The money is really nothing. The land is the most important thing of all. It is what everyone here has survived on, and we cannot sell it. We cannot exchange money for our land. That way cannot be. In ten years, maybe, the money will all be gone."[9] When their leaders toured Cree villages to canvass opinion, the natives asked only about the land, not once about money.

But eventually, in late 1975, when it became clear to them that there was little hope of halting the project, they signed the James Bay and Northern Quebec Agreement with the governments of Quebec and Canada and with the corporations that would build and manage the project. (The Quebec government's and the corporations' incentive to settle was simple: after the Malouf decision, and knowing that the natives had good grounds to sue again because they had never relinquished title to the land, the government and corporations feared later costly delays, or worse.[10]) Under the settlement – and in "a great

[9] Richardson, *Strangers*, pp. 305, 308–309.
[10] McCutcheon, *Electric Rivers*, p. 55.

act of faith," as Boyce Richardson says – "the James Bay Cree and Inuit of Quebec" surrendered all their existing "claims, rights, titles and interests in and to the land in Quebec" in return for a range of promises.[11] They were promised, first, $150 million in cash, half to be paid to community organizations over ten years, the rest as royalties from the hydroelectric project, together with no less than 25 percent of any future royalties Quebec would earn over the next fifty years from any development in their territories; second, that certain modifications to the project would be made; and third, that northern Quebec (about two-thirds of the entire province) would be divided into (1) lands reserved for the exclusive use of the Cree (2,020 square miles) and the Inuit (3,205 square miles) – amounting in all to 1 percent of the total area – though the Crown reserves mineral rights, which, however, it cannot develop without the natives' consent, (2) lands, amounting to about 14 percent of the area, reserved for hunting, fishing, and trapping by the Cree (25,030 square miles) and the Inuit (35,000 square miles), which can, however, be developed by the province subject only to compensation in cash or with other land, and (3) the rest of northern Quebec, which would be surrendered and become available for development, though hunting, fishing, and trapping there would be subject to joint control by native and government representatives, as would environmental conservation.

Of course, there were those, especially other Indians and Inuit, who said the James Bay Cree and Inuit leaders had sold out. But these leaders had no choice about whether to make some sort of agreement with the government and the corporations, and they would have been mad, once this became absolutely clear, not to have tried to do the best they could for their people.[12] And it is quite clear that, until the inevitability of a deal was clear, they had no interest in giving up land, and their way of life, for money.

A postscript

Phase One of the James Bay Project was completed in December 1985. The environmental impacts have, as feared, been substantial – including mercury contamination of the fish – and the emotional

---

[11] Richardson, *Strangers*, p. 323.
[12] Richardson, *Strangers*, pp. 318–324.

effects of the project have been great, including a sense of loss of personal autonomy and of community.[13] (Mercury in a harmless form in the rock and soil is converted under the impact of flooding into toxic methylmercury.) After years of lobbying by environmental and other organizations, in 1989 the state of Maine cancelled its agreement to buy power from Hydro-Quebec (the James Bay developers), and in 1991 New York State cancelled its agreement. In November 1994, the premier of Quebec suddenly announced the indefinite postponement of the next phase of the project.

1.4. "This land . . . is part of us"/ "Stay with it; stay with it"

On a small reservation astride the Verde River, just above its confluence with the Salt River, to the northeast of the city of Phoenix in Arizona, live about 800 Yavapai Indians. At that confluence the Bureau of Reclamation (in the United States Department of the Interior) had wanted, ever since the 1940s, to build a dam as part of what would become the Central Arizona Project, one of the biggest and most controversial water projects in American history. The reservoir behind the dam (which came to be known as the Orme Dam) would inundate a large part of the Fort McDowell Reservation, the Yavapai's land. Many families would have to move; burial sites would be inundated. In 1981, after many years of planning and politicking, the Bureau offered the Yavapai (there were then about 400 of them) some $40 million for the required land. The offer was spurned. The Indians said that they would not part with their lands for *any* amount of money; the land was not for sale. Needless to say, some people thought they were merely bargaining.[14]

[13] Ettenger, "'A River That Was Once So Strong and Deep.'...."
[14] The quotes in the section title are from U.S. Department of the Interior, Bureau of Reclamation, *Final Report: Social Impacts and Effects of Central Arizona Water Control Study Plans* (Washington, DC: Government Printing Office, 1982) (hereafter *Final Report*), vol. 2, pp. 40 and 94. This report and a very fine book by Wendy Espeland – *The Struggle for Water* (Chicago: University of Chicago Press, 1998) – are my chief sources for this section. For readers who do not know why big dams and water diversion projects have been controversial, especially in the last few decades, and in

The Yavapai were in fact fiercely attached to this particular patch of land. They had been fighting for it, fighting to stay on it, almost continuously for 150 years. This long struggle, and more, was written on the land: "we remember with the land," they say.[15] Their first encounters with Europeans were with Spanish explorers in the late sixteenth century, but their problems with white men began around the middle of the nineteenth century, when miners moved onto their territory, which then encompassed a much larger area of what is now Central and Western Arizona. The miners were not friendly. The federal government built a number of army forts, and several small reservations for the Indians were established. The Yavapai resisted resettlement. More white settlers came. The Yavapai's situation became precarious. Conflict between the Indians and the settlers and soldiers worsened. In 1871, the U.S. army began a bloody campaign to force the remaining, half-starved Yavapai onto a reservation; resisters were massacred. By 1874, the surviving Yavapai (along with unrelated Apaches) had been forced onto a military reservation at Camp Verde. Promised a permanent home there, they worked hard and successfully to irrigate (by digging miles of ditches with sharpened sticks) and make productive their diminutive patch of land. But the following year they were forced off this land and driven by soldiers, on a brutal 200-mile march across snow-covered mountains in the dead of winter, to an Apache reservation at San Carlos. Many died on this Trail of Tears; more died soon after arriving. Over the next twenty-five years other Indian groups were dumped on this reservation, speaking unintelligible languages. Eventually the Yavapai were allowed to return to their homelands. There they found that the best land had been taken by white settlers. Starving, they petitioned the president, Theodore Roosevelt, for land sufficient for subsistence. Over much local opposition, the Fort McDowell Reservation was established by Roosevelt's order in 1903; illegal settlers were removed and legal claims bought out.

particular why they are environmentally and socially destructive, I especially recommend Marc Reisner, *Cadillac Desert: The American West and Its Disappearing Water* (New York: Viking, 1986) and Patrick McCully, *Silenced Rivers: The Ecology and Politics of Large Dams* (London: Zed Books, 1996).

[15] Espeland, *The Struggle*, p. 200.

This is the land that, a few decades later, the Bureau of Reclamation wanted to flood.

But in the intervening years the Yavapai were not left alone. They had good land, on the banks of a river and close to a growing city, and they quickly set about making the land productive. White farmers, irrigation companies, and the city of Phoenix were soon covetous of the Indians' land and especially their water rights, and before long, with the support of local politicians and government agencies, they demanded that the Indians once again be relocated. And then came the most serious threat of all: the proposal by the hitherto unstoppable Bureau of Reclamation, backed by the whole array of powerful political forces and business interests that pushed the Central Arizona Project, to build the Orme Dam.

> Sometimes when I think at night, tears come into my eyes when I look back on history, how my people were treated, how my land was taken. Today that land is worth billions. But to the Indian it is worth more than that. It was their home, where they were told to live by the Great Spirit. Our ancestors were slaughtered in the cave; they look down on us with tears in their eyes, and they say 'Stay with it; Stay with it.' We *will* stay with it.[16]

In the face of the threat from the Bureau of Reclamation, the Yavapai said – to those who were sent to interview them for the Bureau, to Wendy Espeland when she interviewed them for her dissertation, and to anyone else who would listen: the land cannot be sold, its value cannot be measured in money; in fact we cannot be compensated for its loss in any way at all, for it is unique; this is the unique place where all these things happened to us; this is where our ancestors lived and are buried and it is deeply insulting – a sacrilege – to disturb them; we do not own the land, we belong to it; our relation to it is a part – an absolutely central part – of what we are; the land holds us together, and through it we are connected to the past and the future; without it we are nothing.

---

[16] Bureau of Reclamation, *Final Report*, 2–14; quoted by Espeland, *The Struggle*, p. 200.

They said:[17]

> A lot of things have happened here... We remember the land.
>
> [The land] is my life. It's just part of me.
>
> The land is part of nature and everything around it... The Indian knows that his land and life is intertwined, that they are one unit.
>
> You can offer me all the money in the world and I wouldn't trade it for this land. This land to me has so many memories, and inheritance too. And it means so much... Like I said, it's more valuable than anything else... it is part of us.

But the Yavapai were not the only ones with identities, with values and ideals that they did not wish to compromise. In Wendy Espeland's fine study of the Orme Dam controversy (on which I rely here), there is an account of the interests and identities of the two groups within the Bureau of Reclamation at the height of the controversy – the Old Guard and the New Guard. The Bureau was a product of Progressivism and came fully into its own during the Great Depression and the New Deal. The conservationists of the New Deal had a productionist attitude to Nature: Nature was not to be laid waste for the short-run gain of the few; it was to be used, but for the common good of present and future generations, and to that end it was to be exploited efficiently, or *remade* to produce desired commodities more efficiently – as the U.S. Forest Service (USFS), born in the same era and of the same urge, tried to remake the national forests as an efficient production machine.[18] And just as the USFS wanted to make forests less "wasteful," so too the Bureau of Reclamation dedicated

---

[17] The first two quotes are from interviews with Espeland (*The Struggle*, pp. 200, 201); the last two are from the Bureau of Reclamation, *Final Report*, 2–40 and 2–41, quoted by Espeland at pp. 201, 202.

[18] For a brilliant account of this approach – and the ecological disaster it eventually produced – as it was played out in the forests of the Blue Mountains of Northeastern Oregon and Southeastern Washington, see Nancy Langston's *Forest Dreams, Forest Nightmares: The Paradox of Old Growth in the Inland West* (Seattle: University of Washington Press, 1995). James Scott's *Seeing Like a State: How Certain Schemes to Improve the Human Condition Have Failed* (New Haven, CT: Yale University Press, 1998), which begins with a discussion of "scientific forestry" and other "State Projects of Legibility and Simplification," pursues related themes on a larger canvas as it ranges over efforts to engineer human societies as well as ecosystems.

itself to taming Nature so as to make use of all the "wasted" wild water flowing to the sea down America's rivers. To this "problem," technology was assumed to be the solution, and the Bureau quickly gave itself over to the perceptions, values, and ambitions of engineers. The value of big dams and of large-scale water diversions was taken for granted. They were unquestionably a good thing. And when cost-benefit analyses of their projects were required, they always came out the right way – not necessarily because of dishonesty but because of their blindness to or devaluation of a range of costs and their enthusiastic invention or exaggeration of benefits, or, in a word, their (ideological) framing of the world.

These were the values of what Espeland calls the Old Guard of the Bureau, which by the time of the Orme Dam controversy had long been a complacent, insular, and confident organization. The big dams they built, especially those that they thought were beautiful engineering solutions, and their ability to control Nature, were a source of pride to the Old Guard. They identified wholly with them. These projects, these great structures, had been the life's work of men who typically made lifelong careers in the Bureau, to which they were intensely loyal. The big projects were what their lives had been about; they gave these men a sense that their lives had not been without significance, without meaning. Their values and ideals could be said to *frame* the world for them. Their commitment to those values and ideals, their identification with the Bureau, and the story of the lives they had led giving expression to those ideals, could be said to constitute their *identities*.

The Old Guard, then, like the Yavapai, had their values and ideals, their blinkers, their way of looking at the world.

Before the National Environmental Policy Act (NEPA) of 1969, the Old Guard *was* the Bureau. NEPA required federal agencies to take account of the environmental effects of their projects – to prepare environmental impact statements (EISs), as we now call them, including the tabulation of a project's costs and benefits to the whole society. The Bureau of Reclamation's first planning report on the Central Arizona Project, including the Orme Dam, in 1947, had made no mention of ecological or social costs. It made no mention of the inundation of the Yavapai's land and the relocation of the Indians. It found only benefits – including economic benefits that the

Yavapai could reap from the recreational opportunities the dam and reservoir would afford![19] But after NEPA, the Bureau had to write an EIS on the Central Arizona Project. Hoping that the courts were not going to take NEPA's requirements seriously, its first EIS (published in 1972) still ignored most of the social and ecological costs and inflated the benefits. (An example: the project would stimulate some frantic archeological investigation of sites to be inundated or buried in concrete, so without the project "archeological knowledge would suffer"![20])

In 1971, the Bureau issued an EIS on Orme Dam alone. The Bureau, hitherto dominated by engineers, had by this time been obliged to hire ecologists and other environmental specialists from a variety of disciplinary backgrounds and even sociologists, as well as lawyers and economists, to help write the EISs required by NEPA. These made up what Espeland calls the New Guard. They were diverse, generally younger, and politically more liberal than the Old Guard. Some were women; some were environmentalists. Understandably, they were seen by the Old Guard almost as a fifth column working for the environmental movement. They had not devoted (and most were not going to devote) their careers to the Bureau; they did not identify with it; they were not technophiles; they were not committed to dams and big water projects. If they were committed to anything it was to a style of rational decision analysis that aspired to be as objective and rigorous as possible, obliged everyone to be explicit about valuations, and was to be carried out in full view of members of the public, who would be kept fully informed and whose contributions would be welcomed. Their own diversity of training and expertise and their commitment to taking account of a much wider range of considerations than ever interested the Old Guard forced them to try to make trade-offs between different values and disvalues promoted by the project, to try to find ways to make these different values commensurable.

At the end of the day, the Old Guard did not get the dam it wanted – an unprecedented defeat for a Bureau that for fifty years had had little

---

[19] Espeland, *The Struggle*, p. 113.
[20] Bureau of Reclamation, *Central Arizona Project Final Environmental Statement* (Washington, DC: Government Printing Office, 1972), pp.197–198; cited by Espeland, *The Struggle*, at p. 114.

trouble in persuading Congress to approve and fund any project it wanted to build. The U.S. government decided in favor of an alternative to Orme Dam that did not require taking land from the Yavapai. The New Guard and the Yavapai had won. It is hard to say how much this was the result of the Yavapai's impact on public opinion and (directly or indirectly) on the way the New Guard did its work. In any case, the New Guard and the Yavapai did not see things in the same way. They did not have the same values and ideals. For the Yavapai there was no way in which they could be compensated for the loss of their land. In this respect, they had something in common with the Old Guard, whose members were not interested in the monetary costs of their dams and were blind to other kinds of costs; for them big dams were a nonnegotiable good. But for the New Guard, everything has its price, however difficult and for some of them perhaps painful it may be to determine it; all things must be made commensurable if "rational" decisions are to be made.

Stories like the ones I have told for the James Bay project and the Orme Dam – though usually with unhappier endings – could be told for many other dams and for countless other "development" projects all over the world. It has been estimated that the number of people displaced by dams worldwide is at least 30 million and probably closer to 60 million.[21]

1.5. "You do not sell the land the people walk on"

We come now to another case, also involving land and money, but one in which the motivations and dispositions are difficult to discern

---

[21] Here is a very small sample of the literature dealing with dams and displacement. Michael Lawson, *Dammed Indians: The Pick-Sloan Plan and the Missouri River Sioux, 1944–1980* (Norman: University of Oklahoma Press, 1994); Barbara J. Cummings, *Dam the River, Damn the People: Development and Resistance in Amazonian Brazil* (London: Earthscan, 1990); Arundhati Roy, "The Greater Common Good," in her *The Cost of Living* (New York: The Modern Library, 1999); Jean Drèze, Meera Samson, and Satyajit Singh, eds., *The Dam and the Nation: Displacement and Resettlement in the Narmada Valley* (Delhi: Oxford University Press, 1997); Enakshi Ganguly Thukral, ed., *Big Dams, Displaced People: Rivers of Sorrow, Rivers of Change* (New Delhi: Sage, 1992); and McCully, *Silenced Rivers*, cited earlier. The estimate for the number of oustees comes from McCully's indispensable book.

and disentangle. This is an astonishing case in which a group of economically poverty-stricken people declined a huge sum of money in compensation for an illegal government "taking" of their land, even though accepting the money would in no way prejudice recovery of the land. I was especially drawn to this refusal because it was made on the grounds that the land in question was sacred to those people and that no amount of money could compensate them for the loss of it.

In 1980, the Supreme Court upheld a historic decision by the U.S. Court of Claims, in *Sioux Nation v. The United States*, to award $106 million to the Sioux Indians as compensation for the illegal taking of the Black Hills from them in 1877. The decision ended 57 years of litigation. The award, of which $17.5 million was the estimated market value of the land in the 1820s, before it was known what the gold deposits in the Hills were worth, the remainder being interest at 5% since 1887, was by far the largest judgment ever made in an Indian land claim and at that time perhaps the largest in any claim against the U.S. government.[22] Congress promptly appropriated the amount. Then an extraordinary thing happened. The Sioux declined to accept the money. "The Black Hills," they said, "are not for sale." They wanted the land itself back. The money still sits in the U.S. Treasury accumulating interest. Soon it will be worth a billion dollars.

In 1868, a treaty with the Sioux had established the "Great Sioux Reservation": all of what is now South Dakota west of the Missouri River (roughly half the state) was forever to be "for the absolute and undisturbed use and occupancy of the Sioux." This reservation, though only a part of the vast territory the Sioux had laid claim to before the coming of the whites, included the Black Hills. A further large area was recognized as "unceded Indian territory" where white entry needed Indian consent, and in another area the Sioux retained hunting rights while the buffalo were plentiful. In 1874,

---

[22] Edward Lazarus, *Black Hills, White Justice: The Sioux Nation versus the United States, 1775 to the Present* (New York: Harper Collins, 1991), p. 375. This book is the best available treatment of the Black Hills claim and I have relied on it.

Custer led an illegal expedition into the Black Hills on behalf of
the U.S. government and gold was discovered. Thousands of miners flooded into the Hills. The government, which under the 1868
treaty should have kept the miners out, now decided it must acquire
the land, and after negotiations to buy the Hills failed, sent in the
army. Custer and his 7th Cavalry were destroyed at Little Bighorn. In
response, the government took its revenge on the Sioux. The reservation was further reduced and broken up into six separate reservations.
The final end came, in 1890, with the massacre of 300 largely dis-
armed Indians, two thirds of them women and children, at Wounded
Knee.

Now, a century after the Black Hills were taken from them and
after more than half a century of litigation, despite the desperate
poverty of the reservations, the Sioux were rejecting the monetary
compensation which, through their white lawyers, they had sought
through all the years.

The reasons for this refusal are complex, and any interpretation
must be somewhat speculative. In the first place, many Sioux now
seemed to believe that to accept the monetary award would be to
relinquish forever the right to win back the Black Hills themselves or
some part of them. But as their lawyers had advised them, and again
advised them when they had won their case, this was not so; indeed
the lawyers had recommended that, after winning compensation, they
should work for a congressional bill that would restore places in the
Hills of special religious or cultural significance to them. Perhaps
some Sioux believed that accepting money would weaken their *moral*
claim to the land. In any case, their lawyers *could not* sue for a return of
land; no court in the land would hear them, for Congress had never
authorized the courts to return land; it had instead authorized the
Indian Claims Commission to make monetary compensation. And
indeed, when the Sioux, having rejected the $106 million award,
filed suit against the United States for return of the Black Hills (and
$11 *billion* in damages), it was promptly dismissed for lack of jurisdic-
tion. Only Congress could return land, and when, in 1985 and again
in 1987, Bill Bradley introduced to the Senate a bill for the return of
Black Hills land – only federally owned land and with conditions as
to its use – it never got out of committee.

Most Sioux, it seems, had long resigned themselves to losing the Hills and were concerned only for monetary compensation.[23] Their first lawyer had made it clear to them from the beginning, in 1923, that only money could now be had from the courts and the Sioux had apparently accepted that. And the lawyers who had represented them continuously from 1956 until the Supreme Court's decision in 1980 had always worked on this clear understanding.

But in the mid-1970s, with the rise of Indian radicalism (inspired and driven by the American Indian Movement) and after the occupation of Wounded Knee on the Pine Ridge reservation and the shootout at the Jumping Bull compound that left an Indian and two FBI agents dead,[24] some Sioux elders joined angry young radicals in declaring that the Black Hills were not for sale. They said that *land and money are not interchangeable*, that to accept money for the Black Hills is a kind of *betrayal of Indian identity and of the Sioux past*, and finally that *the Black Hills are sacred to the Sioux* and (some Sioux were now saying) had been so for thousands of years.[25]

If the Hills were sacred to the Sioux, they had become so, it appears, only very recently. That the Hills were especially important to the Sioux, that they regarded them with great affection, that they were the jewel at the heart of their empire, is not to be doubted. Rising 4,000 feet above the dry plains, they offered shelter and refuge, provided game and herbiage, and were a source of mountain water, lodgepole pines for their tipis, and other good things. But according to Donald Worster, who makes this claim the center of his analysis of the Indians' refusal of monetary compensation, there is nothing in the record to suggest that the Sioux had earlier regarded the Hills as *sacred* – "set apart from the profane world in myth and ritual, to be approached only in a reverential mood."[26]

---

[23] Lazarus, *Black Hills, White Justice*, pp. 121–122, 350; Donald Worster, "The Black Hills: Sacred or Profane?," in his *Under Western Skies: Nature and History in the American West* (New York: Oxford University Press, 1992), at pp. 123–124.

[24] On the shootout at the Jumping Bull compound, see Peter Matthiessen's controversial book, *In the Spirit of Crazy Horse* (New York: Viking, 1991).

[25] Lazarus, *Black Hills, White Justice*, pp. 350, 354, 355, 405.

[26] Worster, "The Black Hills: Sacred or Profane?," p. 143.

To begin with, it seems that the Sioux did not migrate to the high plains until the eighteenth century. Forced out of their land much further east, around the Mississippi headwaters, by the Chippewa (who had obtained guns from the whites before the Sioux), they fought their way westward, pushing aside Crow, Cheyenne, Arapaho, Kiowa, and Mandan, and only secured complete control of the Black Hills in the early nineteenth century.

But something can *become* sacred, and quite quickly so, and one might have expected the Black Hills to have become sacred to the Sioux not long after they took possession of them. Yet none of the Indian leaders described them this way in any of their negotiations with government representatives. Nor did James Walker, who as the physician on the Pine Ridge reservation from 1886 to 1914 made an intensive study of traditional Lakota religion (published as *Lakota Belief and Ritual*), ever record that the Black Hills were sacred to the Indians. Nor, apparently, did Black Elk (1863–1950), ever explicitly refer to the Hills as sacred in the famous interviews with John G. Neihardt from which came *Black Elk Speaks*.

None of this is to deny that the Black Hills have much more recently become or are in the process of becoming sacred to the Sioux as they invest new meaning and significance in them and make them a focus for the renewal of Sioux culture. Perhaps, as Worster says, "Indians are trying to invest every acre, every valley and slab of rock, with high numinosity, not only the scattered sites like Harney Peak, the Wind Cave, and Deer Butte, where the evidence is strongest for religious significance, not only the handful of identifiable burial sites, but the whole mountainous landscape."[27] (They may in fact be doing precisely what certain environmental activists/philosophers are now urging us to do.)

If the Black Hills had been sacred to the Sioux, then the idea of selling them (though of course that was not, in 1980, something they were in a position to do), or even of accepting belated monetary compensation for the government's taking of the land, would have been abhorrent to them; their relation to land, to the Hills, would have been such as to nullify or exclude their desire for money as

[27] Worster, p. 150.

a motivating reason for them in this context. Crazy Horse had said, "You do not sell the land the people walk on," and his words were to be repeated in the 1970s and after the Court of Claims had finally made its award. But in the intervening hundred years, the Sioux, having apparently accepted that the Hills would never again be theirs, and though initially they must have found the idea of selling land most strange, had talked a great deal about monetary compensation for the Hills and had eagerly looked forward to it.[28] Given their desperate circumstances during most of this time, this is hardly surprising.

If the Black Hills were not, or were only then becoming sacred to the Sioux, and money was not entirely unthinkable as compensation for land, then what else could have been behind the refusal of the 1979 award? In part, perhaps, it was the simple fear, based in earlier experience, of what would happen if the money were simply disbursed to them individually. Vine Deloria himself worried that, if this happened, the money would all be blown away in short order, with no lasting effect. But the Sioux could have agreed to use the money to buy land, in the Black Hills or on the reservations, as Deloria and others suggested, or to trade for federal land in the Hills. Lazarus comments that the Sioux could have bought every piece of land that came on the market, indefinitely, with the income earned on the settlement.[29] Even these proposals have not found favor.

If the Black Hills were not truly sacred to the Sioux, if this connection to the Hills was not, or was only just in the process of becoming, a central constitutive part of Sioux identity, their identity may nevertheless have been at stake in another way.

The Black Hills, writes Edward Lazarus, and the claim arising from their theft "had come to symbolize all things Sioux, especially the tribe's sustaining myth that they had never given in to the white man's deceits. Whether described as "selling the Hills" or merely agreeing to "settle" the claim for their taking, to accept the Court of Claims verdict would be to end forever their century-old grievance

[28] Again, see Lazarus, pp.121–122, 147–149, and especially 327, 350; also Worster, pp. 123–124.
[29] Lazarus, *Black Hills, White Justice*, in the afterword added in the paperback edition (Lincoln: University of Nebraska Press, 1999).

against the United States and diminish their status as still defiant victims of its expansion. The Sioux had defined themselves in no small part by that status....”[30] To accept the money was to “sell out” to white values and white ways of doing things and hence to diminish their sense of themselves as a people with a distinct and superior culture. Accepting the award was portrayed as a repudiation of their *heritage*.[31]

On this interpretation, then, it was not, or not only, the concrete consequences of the acceptance of the money for the future – for Indian welfare if the money was disbursed, for the prospects of getting land returned, for some tribal leaders’ or activists’ potential prospects in their factional struggles. It was what it would do for their *past*, or rather (to put Lazarus’s point a little more optimistically) for their awakening sense of themselves, or for their new self-respect, where “self” is in part defined by their relation to the past – or to a partly imagined past, to the story they told themselves about their past. We can only understand this in terms of the new *self-understanding* that the Sioux (or those of them whose view of the money prevailed) had come to have of themselves.

In 1855, Isaac Stevens, governor of the Territory of Washington, persuaded what he assumed (over the Indians’ protests) were the representative leaders of the Yakama and other tribes and bands to “sign” a treaty in which the Indians ceded a vast area of their homelands (including about a third of what is now the state of Washington). In return for the ceded land they were promised a reservation, together with schools, mills, and blacksmith and carpenter shops, to be built for them by the federal government, and annuities of clothing, blankets, and so on in the years ahead. *After* the treaty was signed and the loss of most of their homelands was a fait accompli, the Yakama “chief” Kamiakin *refused* all this compensation. Similar refusals are still being made by Native Americans.

---

[30] Lazarus, *Black Hills, White Justice*, pp. 376, 428.
[31] Lazarus, p. 405. See also Frank Pommersheim, “The Reservation as Place: A South Dakota Essay,” *South Dakota Law Review*, 34 (1989), 246–270, and in William L. Lang, ed., *Centennial West: Essays on the Northern Tier States* (Seattle: University of Washington Press, 1991).

I do not believe we can understand refusals like this in Rational Choice terms. I think it massively distorts and trivializes the attitudes behind such choices to suppose that they amount to a weighing of material consequences, or of future benefits and costs, material or otherwise, or to say that these people act *as if* this is how they are thinking. We cannot understand their behavior – or any of the behavior I have been describing in this chapter – without first thinking about the *self-conceptions* or *self-understandings* that are *normative* for them. Let me now explain these ideas.

2 Narratives, identities, rationality

2.1. Narratives

I chose to tell the stories in the first chapter – about Marcel in John
Berger's novel, Eloi and Eulalia at Alto, the James Bay Cree and Inuit,
the Yavapai Indians and the Bureau of Reclamation, and the Sioux –
because they bring out, in various ways and more forcefully than
would a general theoretical analysis, some important truths about
how humans value and choose. In some, but not all of these stories,
the protagonists are unusual; in their choices they were in a minority.
But in the *form* of their valuing and choosing I believe they are not
atypical.

It might be thought that the attitude that informed the choices of
Marcel and Eloi and Eulalia was a remnant or holdover of an attitude
to money and commerce that was once common among the European peasantry. John Berger himself mentions the French peasant's
"in-built resistance to consumerism." Juliet Du Boulay talks of the
Greek villager's "basic reluctance to buy and sell at all." Two different
studies of rural Spain describe "a deeply rooted feeling against commercial trading" (Susan Tax Freeman) and "a kind of shame in the
pure market transaction" (William Christian). All these studies were
done in the 1960s and 1970s. Ruth Behar writes that she too found
that "something of [this] old European peasant ethic has remained
intact" into the 1980s in the village she studied in Spain, at least
among the older people.[1] So it may be that this was what, at least in

---

[1] Ruth Behar, *The Presence of the Past in a Spanish Village: Santa Maria
del Monte* (Princeton, NJ: Princeton University Press, 1991 [originally

part, lay behind the choices of Marcel and Eloi. It might also be true that something else was at work in the attitudes of the Cree and the Yavapai as well as those of Marcel and Eloi – something that also has less influence for many people in the modern world than it once did – and that is a sense of intergenerational continuity, amounting perhaps to a sense of identification with past and future generations.[2] But in its form, or structure, I believe the way in which these people saw and made their choices exemplifies something universal, or nearly universal, in the way humans see and make many of their choices. It is exemplified not only in all the choices I discussed in Chapter 1, but also, as we'll see later, in more mundane choice situations facing people of all kinds in the "developed" world; and in Part Three I'll argue that it helps to explain the willingness of many people to do their part in cooperative endeavors from which they benefit regardless of whether they cooperate.

We do not need special theories, explanations, or understandings for the behavior of Marcel, Eloi, and the rest, and quite different ones for everyone else's. In particular, they are not freakish exceptions to a general pattern of instrumentally rational behavior. On the contrary, I believe that they exemplify, in a particularly luminous and transparent way, the general pattern; and the exceptions, most of them only partial exceptions or deviations, are of *impaired* individuals – impaired in a sense I hope will become clear. (And if *their* behavior seems to be explicable by a Rational Choice theory in an obvious way – if they apparently are moved solely by material costs and benefits to

published as *Santa Maria del Monte* in 1986]). These quotations can all be found (with their sources) at pp. 31 and 302 of this excellent book.

[2] Alexander Zinoviev, in his monumental satire of the Soviet system, has "Visitor" say (in some "Thoughts about death"): "What is a normal human life? Your well-being? No. A normal human life is the continuation of the life and work of others, when they regard your life and your affairs as theirs, and when someone continues your life and your affairs. And taken together you form a whole . . . People say that life expectancy has increased by twenty years. No, it's been shortened by forty. A normal man is a unity of at last three generations. Add it up. And we – we are just truncated people, people without a past or future . . . The fear of death is just a recognition of this breaking of the thread of time." *The Yawning Heights*, trans. Gordon Clough (London: The Bodley Head, 1979), pp. 255–256 (Russian original, first published, Lausanne, 1976). Compare the thoughts of a Yakama Indian on being "alone in the present" discussed in Chapter 4, section 1, below.

themselves – then *this* is in need of explanation. Why, we would have to ask, did they pay attention only to such considerations, or reduce every consideration to commensurable benefits and costs?) Nevertheless, readers will not find here an alternative *theory*, comparable to the tidy, occasionally rigorous, and essentially quite simple theories of "rational choice." The idea of a single general theory of rational action now strikes me as preposterous.

Any adequate understanding of the behavior of the people I have described must pay attention to their *stories*: both the ("external") stories of their lives so far and the contexts in which they acted and were acted upon, and the stories they tell themselves about their lives – their understandings of their own past, an understanding that invariably takes a narrative form. We cannot, first, understand an event or an action – we cannot even define or characterize or bound an event or action – without placing it in a narrative, or at the intersection of a number of narratives. (Thus, neither an event nor an action can be a fundamental unit: histories are composed of events and actions but these can be characterized, made intelligible, only in the light of their narrative contexts.) We cannot fully understand any action without understanding its significance or meaning to the actor, and that meaning depends importantly, though not exclusively, on its location in a narrative.

A person's understanding of her own life, the story she tells (constructs and reconstructs) about herself, which itself of course becomes a part of her life, endows events with meaning, with significance for her. For most of us want to see things we have done and events in our lives as having some meaning. And we want to see some coherence in our lives as a whole.[3] So if some part of our past

---

[3] The historian William Cronon writes: "Our very habit of partitioning the flow of time into "events," with their implied beginnings, middles, and ends, suggests how deeply the narrative structure inheres in our experience of the world." "A Place for Stories: Nature, History and Narrative," *The Journal of American History*, 78 (1992), 1347–1376. My discussion of narrative is indebted also to Alasdair MacIntyre, *After Virtue: A Study in Moral Theory* (London: Duckworth, 1981), Chapter 15 – though I cannot follow MacIntyre everywhere he goes – and to the work of Jerome Bruner referred to below. There is also a very interesting discussion in Margaret A. Somers, "Narrativity, Narrative Identity, and Social Action: Rethinking English Working-Class Formation," *Social Science History*, 16 (1992),

seems meaningless or wasted, we try to redeem it, perhaps by construing it as in some way a necessary preparation or prelude to what came later, as contributing despite appearances to a larger purpose or pattern.

And we humans clearly have a powerful urge to tell stories. It seems to be a universal characteristic with us. Jerome Bruner talks of our "addiction to narrative."[4] That this should be so is hardly surprising, for telling stories is how we try to make sense of our lives (the parts, the whole) and our selves and our present situation. If we cannot *connect* ourselves to, or *place* ourselves in a coherent narrative, it is difficult (but not entirely impossible) for us to be sure who (or what) we are, where we are going, or what we should do. (But we should not forget that influence can run in the other direction as well, at least in the modern world, where our social roles are not all given to us and unchangeable: in late modernity, at least, a person works out a part of what she is and what her story is in part by working out what she should do, especially in novel or difficult choice situations.)[5]

Our yearning for meaning and our urge to tell stories, especially about our own lives, are thus intimately related.

Of course, our narratives can be changed; we can retell the story of our lives, and in doing so attach new meaning and significance to certain events; and this will have an effect on the way we see ourselves now, on how we define ourselves, and hence on how we think we should act. This seems to be what happened to the Sioux (or at any rate their leaders and activists), as a result in part of the emergence of the American Indian Movement and the growth of a new

---

591–630. The substantive historical part of Somers's argument is relevant also to the argument in Part Three below.

[4] Jerome Bruner, *Making Stories: Law, Literature, Life* (New York: Farrar, Straus, and Giroux, 2002), p. 30. This and the same author's *Acts of Meaning* (Cambridge, MA: Harvard University Press, 1990) contain much of interest on the nature of narrative and why we find narratives irresistible.

[5] MacIntyre, who says in *After Virtue* (at p. 201), "I can only answer the question 'What am I to do?' if I can answer the prior question 'Of what story or stories do I find myself a part?,'" does not add the qualification I have made in the parenthesis. While I have learned from MacIntyre, I do not accept his idea – and apparently his ideal – of the highly determinative and mechanical relation between roles and statuses (given, well defined, and fixed) and identity and action.

Indian consciousness and the radicalization of the Pine Ridge reservation in particular. As their long struggle to gain compensation for the loss of the Black Hills drew to an apparently successful conclusion, they began to see the struggle they had been engaged in, their past, perhaps their relation to the land and the whole idea of compensation, and hence their own selves, in a changed light: not a defeated and demoralized tribe dependent on their conquerors for alms, but a proud, defiant, and still distinctive nation of people who did not want what the white man and his civilization had to offer – whose cultural values were still radically different from (and superior to) those of the white man's civilization.

The importance for us of the pattern of our lives, of the structure we impose on our lives in our narratives, explains why it is also the case that isolated events or experiences, or states of affairs at any given time, cannot generally be *valued* in themselves, separate from their narrative context.[6] This is one important reason why the theory of value underpinning economics – and normative economics in particular – makes no sense.

2.2. Ideals, identities, and self-understanding

Constructing narratives of our lives is one way, a seemingly very natural and perhaps inescapable way, in which we humans, in order to understand ourselves, think about ourselves and form *self-conceptions*. We form ideas about, and reflect upon, what our lives are about and what we *are*. Owen Flanagan calls this our *self-represented identity*. It is one element in what he calls our *actual full identity*, our identity from the objective, descriptive point of view, constituted by "the dynamic integrated system of past and present identifications, desires, commitments, aspirations, beliefs, dispositions, temperaments, roles, acts, and actional patterns, as well as by whatever self-understandings (even incorrect ones) each person brings to his or her life."[7] We think

---

[6] See on this J. David Velleman, "Well-Being and Time," *Pacific Philosophical Quarterly*, 72 (1991), 48–77.

[7] Owen Flanagan, *Varieties of Moral Personality: Ethics and Psychological Realism* (Cambridge, MA: Harvard University Press, 1991), pp. 135–137.

not only about what we are but also about what we *ought* to be: about the kind of person we should be, and how we should live our lives, with what pursuits, attachments, commitments, and so forth. We have, in other words, *ideals*, though we may not articulate them, even to ourselves, or be particularly conscious of them. It is *these* self-conceptions – or those of them with a certain property I'll come to in a moment – that I shall take as constituting a person's *identity*.[8] Think of it, if you prefer, and to distinguish it from "actual full identity" (and from many other accounts of identity), as a person's *ideal* identity, the self-conception or self-understanding that is *normative* for her. Many people take a person's identity to be defined, or partly defined, by her social roles and group memberships. But these bear on a person's identity only if they are embraced or affirmed, and this is a way of saying that the *ideals* defining the roles and distinctive of the groups are endorsed by her.

And then, of course, we also think (some of us more than others) about the *discrepancies* between the ways our lives have gone and the ways we would like them to have gone and to go, and in particular about whether we have lived up to our ideals; we *assess* ourselves. These thoughts about our own actions and our selves can trigger *emotions* of self-assessment, like guilt and shame, remorse and regret, and they of course sustain or demolish our feelings of self-respect, which are so important to us. I take *shame* to be the emotion a person experiences when he sees that he has failed to live up to his ideals. (So it is truly an emotion of *self*-assessment, whereas guilt, which I take to be the emotion a person experiences when he recognizes that he has done something wrong or forbidden, is an emotion triggered by judgment of an *act*, not of the very self.[9]) Shame can be a very potent emotion – sometimes devastatingly and lastingly so – and this is precisely because of the great importance to most of us of living up to our ideals (obscure and unarticulated though they may be in our

---

[8] Elizabeth Anderson, *Value in Ethics and Economics* (Cambridge, MA: Harvard University Press, 1993), p. 6.

[9] I am favoring here, not any of the more usual accounts, which either run shame and guilt together or distinguish between them according to whether the emotion is triggered by public exposure (shame) or not (guilt), but the analysis in Gabriele Taylor, *Pride, Shame and Guilt* (Oxford: Clarendon Press, 1985). I'll have more to say about shame in Chapter 6.

minds), or if you like of the enormous normative power our (ideal) identities have in our lives.

The normative power of our ideal identities – this, I believe, is what is behind, and is indispensable to understanding, the choices made in the stories I told in my first chapter, the choices made by Marcel in John Berger's novel and Eloi and Eulalia at Alto, by the Cree, the Sioux, the Yavapai, and by the Old Guard of the Bureau of Reclamation. We simply cannot begin to understand what these people were doing without first recognizing that their choice situation was *structured* or *framed* by their ideals, by the self-understandings that were normative for them. We cannot, in particular, understand what effect a monetary incentive has on someone without first knowing how she frames the choice. Let us say now that a person's *identity* is constituted just by those ideals that function in this way. (I follow here the particular formulation of Elizabeth Anderson; but the idea of identity as providing us with a practical orientation or frame, or a set of parameters for deliberation and choice, is common to a range of discussions of identity.[10]) How does a person's identity, thus defined, frame her choice situation?

[10] Anderson, *Value in Ethics and Economics*, pp. 5–8. Another account of this general kind is David B. Wong, "On Flourishing and Finding One's Identity in Community," in *Midwest Studies in Philosophy, XIII: Ethical Theory: Character and Virtue*, eds., Peter A. French et al. (Notre Dame, IN: University of Notre Dame Press, 1988), pp. 324–341. Wong defines "practical identity" as "the set of attributes of the self that provides an individual with a practical orientation. This orientation is a kind of constant frame that fixes the parameters of practical deliberation." The account I favor has some relation to the one in David Copp, "Social Unity and the Identity of Persons," *Journal of Political Philosophy*, 4 (2002), 365–391, where a person's "(self-esteem) identity" is defined as "the set of propositions about her [her properties or relations to others], each of which she believes, where her belief grounds an emotion of esteem." Charles Taylor, of course, has long espoused an account of identity in which, among other things, a kind of framing plays a role. See especially his *Sources of the Self: The Making of the Modern Identity* (Cambridge, MA: Harvard University Press, 1989). Taylor's earlier work on the self (see the papers collected in his *Human Agency and Language: Philosophical Papers*, vol. 2. Cambridge: Cambridge University Press, 1985) helped me on the way to the views expressed in this book, but in the end I find his account of identity too moralistic and also too cognitivistic, if I can put it that way. (And his sentimental ideas about "ordinary life" – about labor and production and marriage and family life – as well as his views about the necessity of theism, preferably Christian, I find hard to take.)

Generally speaking we frame unconsciously; we are unaware, at least at the time of choice, that we are doing it. Considerations affecting the choice (or consequences of the possible actions) that would matter to us in other circumstances might simply drop out, or be *silenced*.[11] Money (for example) is something you would normally want, other things being equal, but if offered money for your child, it would count for nothing; this is a trade-off you would not even begin to consider, a trade-off that would be unthinkable. (But this would not be true for every parent in every culture.) In thinking about or simply making a choice like this, your relation to your child would function as an *exclusionary reason*, an idea introduced by Joseph Raz.[12] An exclusionary reason is a (second-order) reason to act or refrain from acting for some particular (first-order) reason or reasons. So an exclusionary reason is not one that dominates or overrides the other reasons because it is of greater weight than they are, but rather one that vitiates or invalidates them. A promise, explicit or implicit, or a commitment would normally function in this way. And a person's relation to his ancestral home and land might function in this way, as we have seen. An exclusionary reason does not necessarily exclude all first-order reasons and it may have exclusionary force only in particular circumstances.

Choosing and valuing of the kind exemplified in the cases I related earlier have been discussed by a few writers in terms of *constitutive incommensurabilities*, an idea also introduced by Joseph Raz;[13] and some of the Native Americans whose refusals of money for land we have discussed have themselves spoken of their land in terms strongly suggestive of its incommensurability with (at least) money. The general idea here is that to value a person or thing in terms of certain

[11] John McDowell uses the idea of silencing in his account of what it is to be a virtuous person: "Are Moral Requirements Hypothetical Imperatives?," *Proceedings of the Aristotelian Society* Supplementary Volume, 52 (1978), 13–29; and "Virtue and Reason," *The Monist*, 62 (1979), 331–350.

[12] Joseph Raz, *Practical Reason and Norms* (London: Hutchinson, 1975), sec. 1.2.

[13] Raz, *The Morality of Freedom* (Oxford: Clarendon Press, 1986), Chapter 13. Wendy Espeland, whose work (*The Struggle for Water*) I discussed in the first chapter, talks of the choices made by the Yavapai and the Old Guard of the Bureau of Reclamation in terms of incommensurability.

other goods, especially money – to be prepared to exchange, or even mentally to trade off that person or thing with such goods, to see the person or thing as *commensurable* with money – is incompatible with being in certain sorts of relationship with him or her or it. There are, in other words, incommensurables that are *constitutive* of such relationships. It is, for example, constitutive of friendship – it is part of what we mean by that relationship – that friends would not think of each other's value, or the value of the relationship, in terms of money; that they would not be willing, for example, to betray their friends for money. Such incommensurabilities can in principle be constitutive of the sort of relationship that the Native Americans in our examples claimed to have with their land, and that Marcel and Eloi apparently had to their places and to the old practices on the land that gave their lives meaning.

Raz, however, takes incommensurability to be incomparability – the impossibility of *comparing* the choice alternatives.[14] Yet the choice alternatives he discusses (children or money, for example) are *not* incomparable – far from it. So a little clarification is in order. Two options are said to be *incommensurable* if they cannot both be measured on a single scale of value, and they are said to be *incomparable* if they cannot be compared at all with respect to value. These are distinct conditions. Commensurability is a much more demanding requirement than comparability. But incommensurability does not imply incomparability – which is fortunate because without comparability there could not even be the trade-offs on which *all* of economic theory depends, and there could be no maximization of value at all.

Ruth Chang has argued, however, that comparability is not a serious practical problem – once it is accepted that it makes no sense to speak of the comparability or incomparability of things without specifying a *covering value* – some consideration with respect to which the evaluative comparison is to be made.[15] Cement *can* be compared with

---

[14] Raz is followed in this by James Griffin in "Incommensurability: What's the Problem?," Chapter 2 in Ruth Chang, ed., *Incommensurability, Incomparability, and Practical Reason* (Cambridge, MA: Harvard University Press, 1997).

[15] Chang, Introduction to *Incommensurability, Incomparability, and Practical Reason.*

strawberries (to borrow an example of Martin Hollis's) provided that the comparison is *relativized* to a covering value, such as edibility or gustatory pleasure, or brick-bonding ability. And we should add that if there are *no* covering values in terms of which two things can be compared, then comparison is pointless, and in real life choices between such radically different *kinds* of things never have to be made. For the rest, comparisons can always be made if they are relativized to some covering value.

Return now to Raz's argument that there are incommensurabilities that are constitutive of certain relationships and pursuits. If, like Raz, we equate incommensurability with incomparability, then this argument is wrong. Judging that one's child (Raz's own example) or a friendship is *incomparable* with money is surely not a requirement of these relationships. We might say that one is "incomparably" more valuable than the other, but this is in fact a colloquial way of saying that we can and do compare the two values and find one very much greater than the other. What is rejected here is not comparison (which makes choice possible) but commensuration.

Consider again the example I discussed earlier, in which people declined to give up or exchange their homes or land for money or for other pieces of land. For those who declined such offers, the loss of a particular piece of land cannot be compensated by another piece of land – even if the offered land has the same useful properties (is equally suitable for the same sort of farming, and so on) and the same market value – or by an amount of money representing its market value, or indeed by *any* amount of money, or by anything else at all. It is unique, and therefore irreplaceable, for the reasons I discussed earlier.

It is not that any of the things offered in compensation cannot be compared with the land or home in question. Those who refuse the "compensation" have no trouble making these comparisons. One could say (for what it's worth) that for them the options are comparable with respect to a certain covering value, such as preserving the integrity or continuity or meaning of their lives. Retaining their ancestral land is good for this, is valuable in this way, while giving it up for money or for another piece of land is no good at all, with respect to this covering value. This does not mean, however, that the land in question is *commensurable* with other land or with money.

But comparability, never mind commensurability, is a problem that someone in these situations would not have to wrestle with, because relations of this sort (to ancestral land, in my examples, to friends in Raz's) function in an *exclusionary* way, in the manner I have explained, to vitiate, suppress, or silence certain considerations – money, for example – or, in some cases, *any* other things offered in compensation. Such silencing is likely not to be the product of conscious deliberation and reflective judgment but to occur automatically, so that there appears to the choosers to be no comparison and no real choice to be made: there is only one thing they can do in the circumstances.

To have an exclusionary reason, or for certain (first-order) considerations to be (by whatever mechanism) excluded, silenced, or suppressed in certain contexts, is, I would say, the hallmark of having a *commitment* (which is not necessarily to have consciously *made* a commitment). This would be a stricter use of the term than is usual, so let me call it *strong commitment*. We can have commitments in this sense to a range of things: to particular persons or to our relationships with them, to social groups, communities and associations, to organizations and institutions, to our crafts and professions and to all sorts of other social roles and practices, to places, to private and public projects and pursuits, to religious ideals, moral principles, and norms. If we use the word "project" in the encompassing way Bernard Williams does and "practice" in the (less well known) sense of W. G. Runciman[16] according to whom practices are "units of reciprocal action informed by the mutually recognized intentions and beliefs of designated persons about their respective capacity to influence each other's behavior by virtue of their roles," then this great range of things to which we can be committed can be covered, I think, by saying that we can have strong commitments to persons, principles, projects, practices, and places.

---

[16] W. G. Runciman, *A Treatise on Social Theory*, vol. II (Cambridge: Cambridge University Press, 1989), p. 41.

2.3.   Desire and the structure of reasons

Now let us go back the stories I told in the first chapter. Recall, for example, Marcel's incredulity at the thought of selling his antique cider press, or Eloi's refusal to sell his mountain land. I speculated earlier that this had to do with the significance or meaning these things had for them. They were not ordinary goods whose value to them derived solely from their economic uses to the two men and that were therefore interchangeable with other devices or other land serving the same economic ends. To sell them, and especially for the purposes the buyers had in mind, would have been incompatible with the relations the men had with the land, with the old cultural practices on the land; it would be to rupture the continuities that gave their lives some meaning and dignity. So money and what could have been bought with it were considerations that were silenced for these two men in these particular choice situations.

Eloi's connection to his land and Marcel's connection to his cider press – the significance and meaning these things had for them – derived from their places in (doubtless not consciously formulated) self-narratives connecting them to the past and future. Eloi's connection to his land (or Marcel's connection to his cider press) was a nondetachable element of a way of life guided by a set of ideals or understandings, however inarticulate and unconsciously held, of how he should live, what mattered, how he was or should be related to past and future generations, and so on. For Eloi to see his land as saleable to a corporation and to be used for the production of marketable pulp (or for Marcel to consider selling his cider press to an antique dealer), given the story of his life as he saw it, and given the ideals and commitments that anchored and framed that life, would have been, as I have said, to undermine or rupture its coherence. It would have been to de-mean his life as he saw it. (This is not to say, of course, that he could not have seen it in a different light, could not have constructed his story differently – as did others at Alto who sold their mountain land to the corporation).

These two men and the other people whose choices we discussed in the first chapter were expected – Marcel was expected by his son Edouard, Eloi and Eulalia were expected by the corporation trying to buy their land, the Cree were expected by the government of Quebec, the Yavapai and the Sioux were expected by the U.S. government – to make "rational" choices in the sense of Rational Choice theory. (I am going to capitalize the initials of Rational Choice throughout this book whenever I am referring to this theory, because, as the whole book will make plain, I believe that this theory has got little to do with rationality, but on the contrary denies rationality to its subjects.) Marcel, Eloi, and all the rest were expected to balance competing self-interested desires. But they failed to do so. None of these people saw the choices facing them as a matter of weighing or balancing desires, of trading off different things they wanted ("goods") against each other, of maximizing a utility or preference function.

Nor does it make sense, or do justice to their behavior, to say that they acted *as if* they were doing any of these things. Nor can the attitudes of these people be represented by lexicographic preferences, as some economists have suggested to me. (A person has lexicographic preferences among some set of alternatives if she prefers any alternative to another just as long as it is preferred according to the criterion or attribute that she ranks first – deems most important, for example – in a ranked list of criteria, regardless of its desirability on all other criteria, or, if the two alternatives are equally preferred on this first criterion, is preferred according to the second-ranked criterion, and so on.) Lexicographic ranking fails to capture, among other things, the exclusion or silencing of some reasons by others that is a hallmark of the choices I am trying to understand here.

Let us look a little more closely at the general model of valuing and choosing from which the behavior of these people so strikingly deviates, and that forms the foundation of neoclassical microeconomic theory and of Rational Choice theory. Economists and other Rational Choice theorists are wont to say, especially when told that their theories and explanations are founded on a radical misunderstanding of how people choose, that all such criticism is irrelevant because their arguments don't depend on *any* assumptions about motivation, indeed on any psychology at all. As Kenneth Arrow (Nobel laureate in economics) says: "The theory of economic choice (or, more generally, rational choice) imposes rather weak conditions: transitivity and completeness [of preferences] . . . In quantitative choices, where there are questions of 'more or less' rather than 'all or none,' it is frequent, though not universal, to add a convexity condition, i.e., diminishing marginal rates of substitution." And he adds: "These conditions are very much those imposed by common sense..."[17]

But this statement (which expresses a view I've repeatedly encountered when criticizing Rational Choice theory) omits to say that, before you can make *these* assumptions, you must first tacitly make the very radical assumptions that human choices are correctly or even usefully seen solely in terms of preference satisfaction (or, equivalently, of utility maximization) and, where the convexity condition is required, that there *is* substitutability, that substitution of one good for another can take place to the satisfaction of the agent. I'll be saying more about both of these presuppositions later.

In any case, the statement that the theory of Rational Choice is committed only to these "weak" conditions on individual preferences, though it is a true statement about purely formal theories (models) of choice, is quite false as a statement about economists' and other Rational Choice theorists' explanations of behavior in the real world. The *formal* theory of Rational Choice is really a branch of mathematics and *as such* has nothing to say about the real world. (I do not

---

[17] Kenneth J. Arrow, "Contingent Valuation of Nonuse Values: Observations and Questions," Chapter XIV in Jerry A. Hausman, ed., *Contingent Valuation: A Critical Assessment* (Amsterdam: North-Holland, 1993). Actually I don't think transitivity (consistency) of individual preferences *is* a weak condition, but once you found your theories on preferences – on utility maximization – you're stuck with it, or something like it. One interesting reason why individual preferences are likely not to be consistent is an application of Arrow's General Impossibility Theorem to the aggregation, by a single individual, of the set of his transitive preference orderings each of which is a ranking according to one attribute or criterion or dimension of the alternatives. Think of choosing between different partners or candidates for a job: When you fix on any one attribute – brains or beauty or clubability – you can come up with a stable transitive ranking, but as you try to form overall preferences, trying (but probably failing) to keep *all* the relevant criteria in mind in a stable consistent way, you may find that your pairwise preferences among the alternatives do not add up to a transitive ranking, especially if there are a lot of alternatives. See Kenneth O. May, "Intransitivity, Utility, and the Aggregation of Preference Patterns," *Econometrica*, 22 (1954), 1–13.

intend this remark to be at all critical of mathematics and its uses in helping us understand the real world.)

In their applied, normative work ("welfare economics"), which I'll be discussing in Part Two, where economists are telling us what we collectively *should* do in deciding concrete issues of public policy, they must (and do) commit themselves to assumptions about *what* people value (and *how* they value) and what the sources of their well-being are. In their *explanations* of, for example, cooperation in the provision and use of public goods and other commons (the subject of Part Three), economists and other Rational Choice theorists have to (and do) commit themselves, not merely to formal or structural assumptions, but also to substantive assumptions about *what* people desire or prefer, as, for example, that they want only money and leisure, or material benefits and the approval of others, or that they want to maximize a weighted sum of their own payoff and the difference between their own payoff and others' payoffs, where "payoff" must in turn be specified if this is to be an explanation of (and be tested against) behavior in the real world.

At the most general level, and despite their disavowals and denials, Rational Choice theorists are in fact committed, in the first place, to some version of what philosophers call the Humean or (since it's not clear at best that Hume should be saddled with this theory) the neo-Humean theory of motivation.[18] It is this commitment that prevents them from understanding how – or *that* – the connections that the Cree and Yavapai and Marcel and Eloi had to places, practices, projects, and principles, and to the ideals that in part define these relations and to which they give expression, could have provided them directly with motivating reasons for action, and that their recognition of these ideals (however inarticulate they may have been about them) could moreover have had the effect of excluding or silencing or shaping or modulating other considerations, which in other contexts of choice would have provided them with motivating reasons for

---

[18] There is a voluminous literature arguing for and against neo-Humean theory. I'll be referring to the work of a number of authors who are critical of the neo-Humean line (Nagel, McDowell, Raz, Schueler, Searle, Dancy, Scanlon). The best *defense* of the theory I've encountered is Chapter 4 of Michael Smith's *The Moral Problem* (Oxford: Blackwell, 1994).

action. It is this commitment of Rational Choice theorists also – as we shall see in Part Three when we look at what economists have had to say about the role of the norm of fair reciprocity in bringing about cooperation – that prevents them from understanding among other things how – or *that* – endorsing a norm itself (and not any sanctions backing it up, or any benefits garnered by complying with it) can motivate a person directly.

The central idea of the neo-Humean theory is that both desires and beliefs are a necessary part of the explanation of any intentional action, with desire doing the motivational work. Beliefs, on this account, are a necessary adjunct to desire, but cannot alone move a person; they merely guide and subserve desire, telling the agent how to satisfy it. Thus, in noncooperative game theory, players' beliefs about the other players – that they subscribe to a norm of fair reciprocity, for example, or that they are highly risk averse – might help them to coordinate their strategies to bring about one and the same equilibrium out of the infinitely many, or several, that coexist in a repeated Prisoners' Dilemma game or in a one-shot game of Chicken, and in general help each of the players to satisfy her preferences as best as she is able; but no belief, even a belief that one *ought* to cooperate, has in itself any motivational power. Beliefs, it will be seen, are of different kinds (more on that in a moment), but on the neo-Humean account their motivational powers are all the same. So, of moral or other normative beliefs the economist has still to ask, "Does it pay you to do what you believe you ought to do?"

Desires, too, would seem to be of different kinds. Some desires – the kind we call cravings, urges, or impulses – seem to assail us; they are in a sense not *ours*, they come to us unbidden and are not always welcome. But we are, as I have said, reflective animals, and so, sometimes, we reflect on them, and we may decide that such desires – or what, if satisfied, they'll bring – do not provide (good) reasons for action, and in the light of this we may try to resist them. *These* kinds of promptings, whether we yield to them unreflectively or reflect on them and try to resist them, would seem to deserve to be called desires. But there are other desires, or preferences, that seem not to assail us but to *result from* reflection, from deliberation, and they seem to be *caused*, at least in part, by our beliefs, as when, *because* I believe and only *as a result of* believing (perhaps after some reflection) that it would be wrong or inappropriate for me to do a certain thing, I prefer or desire not to do it.

In these cases, the *beliefs* seem to be doing the motivational work, and the desires, if that is the right word for what the deliberating yields, are parasitic on the beliefs.[19] If these are indeed taken to be desires, along with cravings and urges and the rest, then it seems to me that the neo-Humean position is analogous to the revealed preference "theory" invented by economists to excuse themselves from worrying about psychology, or (as they thought, or claimed) from having to commit themselves to any views about motivation. According to this "theory," preferences are revealed by choices: if you choose A when B is available, you must prefer A to B. But choices quite obviously do not reveal preferences: if I am indifferent between two alternatives and toss a coin to decide, my choice does not reveal my preference; or again, my choice of the smaller of two pieces of cake, far from revealing a simple preference for less cake than more, could have resulted from any one of a large number of combinations of desires (for others' pleasure, to impress my host) and beliefs (about the going norms, about what others want, and so on).

But we do not *have* to say that the "motivated desires" that result from deliberation are desires – the same kind of beast as urges and cravings. If we do, then we should admit that the most we can say is that, when we are motivated, a desire (of some sort) is present but may not be a cause of or explain the motivation. What, then, is the relation between desire and motivation? The best answer, the one that best accommodates the facts about "desires" of all kinds, is the one given by Jonathan Dancy: that a desire just is the state of being

---

[19] Thomas Nagel calls desires of this kind "motivated desires" and he calls urges and other desires that simply assail us "motivating desires." But, as G. F. Schueler and Jonathan Dancy have argued, an unmotivated desire (one that is *not* a result of reflection or deliberation) does not have to be one that simply assails us. See Nagel, *The Possibility of Altruism* (Oxford: Clarendon Press, 1970), Chapter 5 (and the related discussion in McDowell, "Are Moral Requirements Hypothetical Imperatives?"), Schueler, *Desire: Its Role in Practical Reason and the Explanation of Action* (Cambridge, MA: The MIT Press, 1995), pp. 20–21, and Dancy, *Practical Reality* (Oxford: Oxford University Press, 2000), p. 80.

motivated (and some desires are caused by our beliefs, and when that is the case, it's therefore the beliefs that bring about the motivation).[20] Desires, then, do not cause or explain motivation.

I will return in a moment to desires (or preferences) and what should displace them at the foundation of our thinking about choice. But first I must comment on a further, crucially important assumption that economists make, and on which "welfare economics" particularly depends (as we'll see in Part Two), namely that everyone is compensable for any loss. Let me spell this out. If someone prefers B to A, where she has, let us say, more of some good x at A than she does at B but less of another good y, then there is always some additional amount of y that can be given to her so that her preference will be reversed or she will be indifferent between A and B. This has been called the *Axiom of Archimedes.* In other words, her having less of the one good (x) can be *compensated* for by an amount of the other good (y) – compensated, that is to say, to her satisfaction. This is an extraordinarily strong assumption. It implies that if you *take* anything from someone they can always be fully compensated (i.e., restored, at least, to their original level of "welfare," where "welfare" means preference satisfaction) by being given an (additional) amount of some other good. If it is further assumed, as economists usually do, that the values of all things are commensurable and money is their common measure, then it follows that, although not every *thing* (or person) is literally replaceable, the *value* of any thing (or person!) is replaceable: it can be replaced by an appropriate amount of money or by something (that money can buy) that is of equivalent monetary value. So: *anyone is compensable for any loss.*

Let us recapitulate a little. The general model of valuing and choosing that forms the foundation of Rational Choice theory (including microeconomics) takes the idea of *desire* or *preference* as primitive and foundational (without ever being clear about what a desire or preference is, and lumping together as "desires" all manner of disparate sorts of things). The choices or actions of individuals are to be explained by desires, with beliefs providing a sort of map to help us satisfy our wants but having no motivational power of their own. And

---

[20] Dancy, *Practical Reality*, Chapter 4.

moreover, these wants have the property that they can be balanced or traded off against one another: they are, as it were, all on the same level and can all be put into a single utility function to be maximized.

Thus, according to this general model that I wish to reject, the choice made by Eloi and Eulalia at Alto is to be explained in terms of their desire for the goods (including ease and comfort and maybe security) that the money they were offered would buy being *outweighed* by their *desire* (or *preference*) for continuing to live in the old way (a desire derived perhaps from their desire for continuity or for meaning, or their desire to do the right thing combined with their belief that giving up the old way or abandoning the land to commercial forestry is wrong). Or again, according to this model, in the cases of the Cree, the Yavapai, and the Sioux, their resistance to accepting monetary compensation for land was a matter of the value they placed on other things *outweighing* the value to them of the money they were offered. All these people, as I said earlier, were expected to conform to this general model by the various individuals (or corporations or government agencies) who made them offers. But in fact none of them saw the choices facing them in the way they were expected to, as a matter of weighing goods or balancing desires, making trade-offs between the different things they wanted (all of them with values commensurable *via* money), and then choosing as if they were maximizing a preference or utility function.

This general model is wrong not only for (what will seem to most of us) exotic choice situations like those described in my first chapter. It is wrong not only for precapitalist or premodern people or for people who had relations of the kind that ecosystem people had to the land, relations that we no longer have. It is wrong, I believe, as a general model of how human beings deliberate and choose. I will show in a later part of the book how badly wrong this model goes in understanding why many people are motivated to do their part in cooperative ventures – and why, therefore, this model fails as a general explanation of collective action. But, for now, and to illustrate some of the points I have been making, consider the following mundane, simple choice situations.

You have been married for some time, have lost sexual interest in your husband, and are now seduced by a most attractive man. You have (let us suppose) a pretty straightforward *desire* to have sex with this person (to ϕ, for short). You are also aware (though you may try to suppress this) that doing so risks hurting your husband. You also believe that to cause such hurt, or to be disloyal or dishonest to this person to whom you have made a commitment and who has come to rely on you, is wrong. How does your decision making go? One way it could go is like this. On the one hand, you have a desire to ϕ; on the other hand, you don't *want* to hurt (or be disloyal or dishonest to) your husband and, since you believe that ϕ-ing would hurt him (and so on), you don't want to ϕ. Your choice is determined by the *strongest* of these two desires, one for and the other against ϕ-ing. (*How* is it determined? Do the two desires directly go to work on you without "you" – some locus of free will? – being involved? Or do "you" somehow weigh them and *choose* the strongest? I'll come back to this in a moment.) In any case, the alternative you choose (the economist would say) is the one you *prefer*.

But is this really how it is with you, with us? Do we really weigh (in this example) two competing desires? In the case of the supposed desire to do the right thing, is it really a *desire* (in this case, a derived desire, one derived from a standing desire and a belief) that moves you? (Is such a "desire" really the same sort of beast as, for example, your beastly desire to ϕ?) Or are you not rather moved directly by the consideration that the action will hurt your husband, or the consideration that it is disloyal, or that it is wrong? And might not this consideration – the recognition of this as a compelling reason not to ϕ – rather than being weighed (consciously or not) against the competing desire to ϕ, tell you that the desire to ϕ, though it may not be extinguished, should not be heeded, should not count as a good reason, or in some way silence that desire as a reason or diminish its force as a reason? This, I am persuaded, is a truer understanding of how such a choice might in at least some cases be made.

And who is the *rational* chooser in a case like this – the person whose choice is determined by the balance of desires or the person influenced by reasons in the way I have described?

Consider a second mundane example. You are a member of a group of people, a university department say, choosing between two short-listed candidates for a job. You have spent some time with both of them during their visits. You find yourself strongly drawn to one of them on personal, in fact selfish grounds: he is more congenial, he shares your interests; if he is appointed you expect to have a colleague whose company you will enjoy. But, you recognize, the other candidate, who will be a perfectly acceptable but for you a less congenial colleague, is better qualified for the job. The right thing to do, you judge, is to vote for her, and you do. (You therefore *prefer* her to him, says the economist). Is your decision the result of a contest between two competing desires? Perhaps. But we do not have to see it in this way; and to see it in this way may be to mistake what is going on. There is, first of all, no need to suppose that there was a *desire* to act for the good of the department, a desire to do what you took to be the right thing. (It certainly didn't *feel* like a desire in the sense in which you had a desire to have the other candidate as a colleague, a prospect that gave you a warm feeling, gave you pleasure in anticipation.) If you judge that the fact that the second candidate is the best for the department is a good reason for supporting her, then no further motivation is needed for you to support her.[21]

Second, this judgment may lead you to see your desire to have the first candidate as a colleague in a different light, so that, although the desire may not disappear, it is recognized as not providing a good reason or a compelling reason to support this candidate. The judgment may not operate as a strictly *exclusionary* reason; the desire you have for the first candidate may not be totally *silenced* (you are not that virtuous!); but the judgment may diminish for you the force of the desire as a reason. This is a very general feature of practical reason. We often act for reasons, and when we do, we "decide" (though not necessarily at all deliberately or consciously) which considerations are

[21] See T. M. Scanlon, *What We Owe to Each Other* (Cambridge, MA: Harvard University Press, 1998), Chapter 1. Scanlon makes this argument in Section 7. As he says, this general argument to the effect that we can be motivated by the recognition of reasons without an intervening desire has been made by various writers, including Thomas Nagel, John McDowell, and Christine Korsgaard. My discussion here is especially indebted to Scanlon's book, but I was softened up for Scanlon by Nagel's argument in *The Possibility of Altruism*, Chapter V, and by McDowell's article, "Are Moral Reasons Hypothetical Imperatives?," which I referred to earlier.

to count as reasons, and sometimes among those that count there will be reasons that modify, in various ways, the reason-giving and hence motivational force of other considerations. Our reasons for action are in this way *structured*.

John Searle puts the general point a little differently (and perhaps a little too strongly). There are, he agrees, desire-independent reasons that can motivate a person directly. But before a reason can motivate you to act, you must *recognize* it as a valid reason for acting, and of several reasons operating on you, you (in acting freely) in effect *select* which one will be effective. If (in my example) the desire-independent reason that ϕ-ing would hurt your husband (or would be an act of disloyalty, or would be wrong) is the one that moves you, it is because you *made* it so.[22]

It should be clear now (and I think will become clearer still in the remaining parts of the book) why I said earlier that Rational Choice theory has little to do with rationality, indeed denies rationality to its subjects. We act rationally not when we let our choices be determined by the play of *desires*, but when we assess *reasons* (perhaps rejecting some and endorsing others as ones that should count) and are moved by *reasons*.[23] In assessing and acting on reasons, we exercise distinctively human capacities. To treat people as always "rational" in the sense of Rational Choice theory – to treat them as, in effect, members of another species, *Homo economicus* (as economists do, not only in their theories but also in their practice, as when they conduct and endorse the cost-benefit analyses that are now widely used by governments in the making of public policy and that in some cases are used by governments and corporations to determine the fates of entire communities and ways of life), is to deny them their humanity. Of course, people *sometimes* do something simply because they want to; they *sometimes* decide what to do simply on the basis of what they want most. But in general they do *that* – they allow themselves to do something just because they want (on balance) to do it – for reasons,

---

[22] John R. Searle, *Rationality in Action* (Cambridge, MA: The MIT Press, 2001), pp. 65–66.

[23] Scanlon, *What We Owe to Each Other*, especially pp. 23–25; Searle, *Rationality in Action*, Chapters 4 and 6.

though they may not be able to articulate the reasons and may not deploy them deliberately or consciously.[24]

Let us recapitulate the central ideas of this chapter by returning one last time to the stories I recounted in the first chapter. In all these cases I offered interpretations that I believe make unforced sense of the choices that were made – by Marcel (in John Berger's story), Eloi and Eulalia at Alto, the Cree and Inuit of James Bay, the Yavapai, and the Sioux. What all these interpretations have in common is the idea that a person's connections to other people, places, practices, projects and principles, and the narratives and the normative self-understandings of which they are a part, and the ideals that in part define them and to which they give expression, can directly provide compelling reasons for action, and a person's recognition of them (however inarticulate he or she may be about them) can moreover have the effect of excluding, silencing, shaping, or modulating other considerations – considerations that in other contexts of choice would provide this same person with motivating reasons for action.

I believe, as I have said, that this provides a better framework – it most certainly does not amount to a theory – for understanding human behavior than the approach of Rational Choice theory. Rational Choice theory sees – *must* see – only one sort of reason for action. Everything is to be explained in terms of fundamental, unstructured, competing desires. Desire-independent reasons have no role – so there can be nothing that structures desires, nothing that excludes, suppresses, diminishes, or qualifies them in any way. Hence, there is in this approach no place for ideals of any sort, including moral ideals. Hence, norms, even moral norms, by themselves have no power to move us. The motivational terrain is, so to speak, uniform or flat. There is only preference or desire, and although in these models there can be a desire for fairness (for example), or a desire not to be shamed, it is on the same footing with other desires, with which it must compete.

---

[24] Scanlon, *What We Owe to Each Other*, pp. 52–54. The same general point is made very forcefully (though in a different way) by Elizabeth Anderson in her *Value in Ethics and Economics*.

In Part Three of this book I want to bring these general ideas, to which we have, I hope, been led by the stories I told in the first chapter, to bear on the large and obviously fundamental topic of cooperation, and on the central role played in cooperation by what I'll call the norm of fair reciprocity. Rational Choice theory has a well-known set of arguments about this, which build (as they must, in a Rational Choice theory) on the idea that an individual will do his or her part in a cooperative enterprise when and only when it pays to. Recently, however, economists have come to see that people cooperate – do their part in mutually advantageous cooperative ventures – much more often than is predicted or explained by the selfishness axiom that is the central pillar of neoclassical economic theory. They have come to accept that people seem often to be disposed to act fairly – to conform to a norm of fair reciprocity. But in trying to explain why this is so, economists and other Rational Choice theorists have once again resorted to variations on the standard model, in which choice is seen always as, in effect, the outcome of a competition of unstructured, comparable desires. Any explanation of cooperation has to deal with the fact that people with common interests often fail to cooperate but also often succeed. Rational Choice accounts have of course to explain both outcomes in terms of the same selfishness axiom, so that they must show that the benefits and costs fall out differently in the two cases. I shall instead explore the idea that normative motivation – itself (when properly understood) not explicable in any Rational Choice scheme – plays a part in explaining cooperation, but that it may fail and be displaced by Rational Choosing in certain conditions, conditions having to do with the would-be cooperator's sense of being accepted and respected, or (as I will say) recognized.

The economists don't just use the standard model of Rational Choice to explain social behavior; they *idealize* a world in which it holds, a world in which there is no normativity and no moral motivation, a world in which there are no desire-independent reasons, no framing or structuring ideals, and whose inhabitants therefore lack identities and lead lives without meaning. This is the subject of the next part.

So this book is an attack on Rational Choice theory and on the economic way of thinking about the world, a way of thinking that is radically (and, as it is brought to bear on public policy by "welfare" economists, dangerously) reductive and dehumanizing. It is a way of thinking, an ideology, that denies to its subjects capacities and dispositions that are part of what makes us human. Because it denies their capacity to assess and be moved by desire-independent reasons, it denies them even their rationality. But before proceeding, let me make two things quite plain. First, I do not try in this book to give a comprehensive account of the failings of economic theory or its Rational Choice foundations. I don't even mention most of them, including, for example, the well-established failure of Rational Choice theory to account for choice in the face of uncertainty. Nor do I, on the other hand, try to draw an even remotely full and rounded picture of "human nature," of what it is to be human. (Nothing like that *can* be done, because so much remains to be discovered.) I only draw attention to, and draw out some implications of, certain characteristically human capacities and dispositions that are crucial to understanding what is most fundamentally wrong with Rational Choice theory.

Second – and if this is not already clear from what I have said in this chapter it will become abundantly clear in Part Three – I do not deny that people sometimes act "rationally" in the special sense of Rational Choice theory, or even, more particularly, that their behavior is sometimes greatly influenced by economic incentives. But an explanation of human behavior couched only in terms of desires or preferences, though it may be locally useful, is always *at best* radically incomplete. If someone does indeed appear to be acting "rationally," we must always ask why she would behave that way – would choose or allow herself to behave that way – in the context in question. We must ask *why* she thought it was alright to do what she wanted or preferred to do; why she saw her choice as one that was to be determined solely by the balance of her desires; and especially why (if this were the case) only material benefits and costs should determine her choice.

I have said that Eloi and Eulalia at Alto did not do what was expected of them: they did not respond in the expected way, "rationally," to a massive economic incentive. (Nor did the Cree, the Yavapai, or the Sioux). Others at Alto did respond in the expected way. In many, perhaps all, contexts, different people possessed of very similar resources may respond differently to identical incentives, large or small. So their behavior cannot be understood solely in terms of the incentives, as a matter of weighing costs and benefits, or more generally of balancing desires. We have first to know how they understand themselves: how, in particular, they see the economic – and all other – considerations, whether they even count as incentives for them at all. And in general, as I have argued, we have always first to know what considerations are taken by an individual to be reasons for action, and then to understand how those reasons are structured for him. Many people respond "rationally" – in the way the economists say we all do – to a change in the relative price of some commodity; but in many contexts there is no guarantee whatsoever that the introduction of an economic incentive or disincentive will have the expected effect. The introduction of an economic (dis)incentive, even a very small one (such as a library fine), can have on some people the *opposite* of the desired effect – of the effect standardly assumed by the economists – because it demobilizes or deactivates the moral motivation that is the product of the normative self-understandings of these people (who take themselves to be citizens, say, or to be part of a community of users of a commons – a public library, for example – with an obligation to do their part in maintaining it) and causes them to think about the choice before them in a cost-benefit or Rational Choice way, and having knocked out moral motivation, is itself simply outweighed by the perceived benefits of doing whatever it was meant to discourage. (We shall see how this works in Part Three.) But then also, as we have seen, we cannot assume that even a massive economic incentive will simply outweigh other considerations and determine a person's choice, or even that massive material benefits or costs will count in the circumstances as reasons for action at all. This is what we are being told by some of the actors in the (true) stories I recounted in Chapter 1.

Part two

Strokes of havoc

The market ideal and the disintegration of lives,
places, and ecosystems

3   The market utopia

Only economists still put the cart before the horse by claiming that the growing turmoil of mankind can be eliminated if prices are right. The truth is that only if our values are right will prices also be right.
Nicholas Georgescu-Roegen *Energy and Economic Myths*[1]

3.1.   The market ideal

The model of valuing and choosing that has been my target in Part One is used not only to explain but to justify: it plays an important normative role. It plays a crucial (though not always acknowledged) role in the justifications offered by economists (and those influenced by them) for political and legal institutions, and public policies, programs and projects, and in the solutions they advocate for a variety of social and environmental problems. Not only is there no place, in the *explanations* offered by neoclassical economists and other Rational Choice theorists, for those capacities and dispositions (described in Part One and put to work in Part Three) that make us truly social and (therefore) moral; the economists actually *idealize* and want us to inhabit a world from which they are banished. In the present part, I explore this ideal world and what it means for the lives of humans and their communities and for biological communities. I am going to pay special attention to biological communities, or ecosystems. Economists (and others influenced by them) have a distinctive way of thinking about our relations with the natural world, and about

---

[1] Nicholas Georgescu-Roegen, *Energy and Economic Myths* (San Fransisco, CA: Pergamon Press, 1976), p. xix.

the nature of environmental problems and what we should do about them, and it tells us a lot about the model of choice that forms the foundation of Rational Choice theory.

Behind their views about these things is a *model*, representing an ideal world. In this world, in which everything of value is privately owned, has a price, and is allocated in a perfectly competitive market to whomever is willing to pay the most for it, there would be no environmental problems. This is so *by definition*. According to economists, environmental problems just *are* the inefficient use of natural resources and this results from the failure or absence of markets. In order to solve or mitigate an environmental problem we must establish an appropriate market or correct for the failure of an existing one. Only then will resources be allocated efficiently. The failure to produce efficiency is what economists mean by market failure. They do not by this expression refer to the failure of markets to distribute resources fairly, or to guarantee everyone a minimally decent, dignified life, or to halt the degradation of the natural environment.

Efficiency – the efficient allocation of resources – is the economists' central guiding value, and markets, they say, if allowed or enabled to do their work properly, bring about such efficiency. They ensure that resources, including human and natural resources, will be put to what economists call their "most productive" uses. If government and law and morality have any justified part to play, it is solely to enable markets to work properly, to correct market failures, to mimic the market and make up for missing markets. In other worlds, they too exist, or should exist, for the same purposes as markets serve.

Among the requirements for markets to be efficient is that everything that is valued is privately owned and is commodified. Natural resources, in particular, are overexploited because they are not owned – property rights in them are not fully assigned – and they are not bought and sold. According to the economists, what happens in efficient markets tells us how we *should* treat resources, and it tells us what the *value* of everything is.

Thus, economist David Pearce and his coauthors, writing in the influential *Blueprint for a Green Economy* (prepared for the U.K. Department of the Environment): "One of the central themes of environmental economics . . . is the need to place proper values on the services provided by natural environments. The central problem is that many of these services are provided "free." They have a zero price simply because no market exists in which their true values can be revealed by the acts of buying and selling."[2]

This passage, which is perfectly representative of the thinking of economists, encapsulates a characteristic double feature of neoclassical economics: its assumption that every problem is reducible to or identifiable with the failure or absence of markets and that the "proper" or "true" value of anything is given by its market price. *These are extraordinary assumptions.* Economists are not here arguing that environmental problems, identified independently of market behavior (as they routinely are, in a range of scientific disciplines), could be solved or obviated by markets. Their idea of a right relation between people and the natural world *is* just a question of whether the consumers are getting satisfied efficiently. If natural resources are privately owned and traded in a competitive market yet still are exploited unsustainably, there is nothing more the economist, *qua* economist, can say, or would want done. But efficiency does not guarantee conservation, sustainable use, biological diversity, ecosystem resilience, or any other independently desired outcome. And all the different ways in which we *value* the natural world – as home and unique place and nexus of meaning, and with respect, love, awe, and wonder, as well as with more material and utilitarian attitudes – are every one of them reduced by the economists to one: what we are willing to pay. So that all the ways in which we might *express* those values are reduced to the acts of buying and selling (or some simulation of these).

This is how mainstream economists see the world. But it is not the way most people think about and value the natural (or the rest of the) world; nor should it be.

In the real world the conditions under which markets allocate resources efficiently often fail. This failure is what economists take to be *the* problem, to be solved ideally by more markets and only when that is not possible by government and law. But the ideal itself is in my view unattractive. A world in which the conditions for an economy to produce efficient outcomes are met would be a most horrible world. It would be a world in which the integrity or coherence of

---

[2] David Pearce, Anil Markandya, and Edward B. Barbier, *Blueprint for a Green Economy* (London: Earthscan, 1989), at p. 5.

people's lives, communities, and ecosystems would be lost or gravely weakened. Thus, neoclassical economic theory is an *ideology of dis-connection, of dis-integration.* Or so I shall argue.

Behind the economists' approach to environmental problems and their views about how we should use natural resources – behind all their particular arguments for the privatization and commodification of land, water, and genetic and other natural resources, and their proposals for "market solutions" to pollution problems, and their advocacy of cost-benefit analyses to assess the merits of public programs and projects with environmental impacts – behind all these lies a famous analysis by microeconomic theorists of how markets work under ideal conditions, and in particular a proposition known as the First Fundamental Theorem of "welfare economics," the normative branch of microeconomics. This Theorem says, roughly, that *when a competitive market economy is in equilibrium, the allocation of resources is efficient* – provided that certain conditions are met.[3]

Behind this Theorem is a simple idea: any exchange between two people, undertaken voluntarily, will make each of them better off (otherwise they would not have made the exchange); if *all* such possibilities for mutual gains are exploited and if none of these exchanges affects any third party, then the result must be a state of affairs in which nobody could be made better off without making someone worse off. This is all that is meant by saying that the outcome is allocatively *efficient.* This sort of efficiency, which is of course not what ordinary people – or engineers or business managers – mean by efficiency, is also called *Pareto optimality.*

In what follows we must keep in mind the *conditions* for the Theorem to hold:

1.   All agents must be perfectly rational and perfectly informed.
2.   Property rights must be well-defined and costlessly enforced.
3.   All transaction costs – the costs of making exchanges and making them stick – must be zero: the entire economy must be frictionless.

---

[3] Readers with a little mathematics can find a good discussion of this theorem in David M. Kreps, *A Course in Microeconomic Theory* (Princeton, NJ: Princeton University Press, 1990).

4. All commodities must be infinitely divisible, undifferentiated (a widget is a widget no matter where it comes from or who produced it or how), and substitutable for each other as a means to the generic goal of want-satisfaction, of "utility."

5. There are no externalities, including those associated with public goods. *Externalities* are present when an exchange, though it makes the parties to it better off, benefits or harms one or more third parties who do not consent to it. This condition implies that everything of value is consumed as a private good.

6. No agent – household or firm – is "large" enough to be able to affect prices.

When all these conditions are met, says the First Fundamental Theorem, the allocation of resources is Pareto efficient. Then, as economists (and lawyer-economists) say, *wealth is maximized* and resources will be put to their *most highly valued uses*. (The meaning and significance of these last two phrases will be examined later.) It should be obvious that these conditions are never met – or come anywhere near to being met – and therefore Pareto optimality is not achieved by actual markets. But should we care about this?

There are really two questions. First, should we care about efficiency? In particular, do we want it to guide the way we use natural resources and to determine who should own them? Second, would we want to live in a world where the conditions of the Theorem are satisfied? This would, after all, be a world in which everything that people care about is a commodity in a market, with a price.

3.2.   Efficiency in practice

They [my children] must know that there's a range of life that cannot be reduced to merchandize . . . and they must know that I will guard that for them.

Ilse Asplund at the trial of herself and others for monkeywrenching
Prescott, Arizona, 1991[4]

---

[4] As quoted by Susan Zakin, *Coyotes and Town Dogs* (New York: Viking, 1993), at p. 441.

Say that one state of affairs is *Pareto superior* to another if there is at least one person better off in the former and no one is worse off. Then a state of affairs is Pareto optimal if no other state of affairs is Pareto superior to it. But of course a move *toward* Pareto efficiency may not be a Pareto superior move, and in practice government policies, programs, and projects, including those intended to remedy market failures as well as many others that are claimed to be in the public interest, rarely if ever make Pareto superior changes. The economist would like to be able to point out Pareto superior moves, but these are hard to come by. So the efficiency criterion used in practice by economists and government agencies to evaluate changes is not Pareto efficiency but what is called the *Kaldor-Hicks* principle. This requires that the change, although it may make some worse off, is such that those who are made better off *could* compensate the losers so that, if the compensation were to be paid, nobody would be worse off and at least one person would be better off. Thus, the Kaldor-Hicks test is also known as the *potential* Pareto superiority principle or as the *hypothetical* compensation test. The compensation need not actually be paid, and in practice often is not paid or not fully paid. Sometimes, indeed, compensation is not even possible, as we'll see.

So in practice the principle of efficiency, though it starts out from and trades on the ideal of making everyone better off, can be used to justify making some people worse off.

To assess a policy or project in terms of its benefits and costs, both measured in terms of money and aggregated over all affected individuals, is to subject it to what is known as a *cost-benefit analysis*. CBA is a form of applied Utilitarianism – a form that very few philosophers or social theorists, other than economists, would now endorse. The Kaldor-Hicks principle provides a justificatory rationale for CBA, even though the principle is never verified in any actual CBA but is rather *assumed* to be satisfied on the basis of limited observations of markets or from surveys.

In some of the five stories I told in Part One, I discussed the reactions to government proposals to build certain giant dams of some of the people whose land would be inundated by the dams' reservoirs. My interest there was in the nature of their attachment to their land or to their way of life as they understood it and what this meant for how they thought they should live and for certain choices they were obliged to make. In the United States the era of giant dam building began in the 1930s. Those that were begun after World War II had first to pass a cost-benefit test before they could go forward: the total benefits of the dam had to exceed, by a certain ratio, the total costs. The CBAs carried out by the U.S. Army Corps of Engineers and the U.S. Bureau of Reclamation and the Tennessee Valley Authority were invariably fraudulent or, at best, the products of radically blinkered perceptions: on the one side of the ledger they were extraordinarily comprehensive and indeed creative in finding benefits and, on the other, often blind or at least absent-minded in searching out costs. (When the Corps of Engineers proposed to inundate the beautiful Round Valley of Northern California, for example, they counted the relocation of the Indians whose reservation would have gone under-water on the *benefit* side of the account, because they deemed the Indians' new site and the new dwellings they would have there to be superior to the old! The Indians disagreed.) Large dams are no longer being built in the United States – all the "suitable" sites, and many unsuitable ones, have in any case been used – but huge, destructive dams have since been built or are in the process of being built else-where, mainly in South America and Asia, often with the backing of the World Bank, and fraudulent or blinkered CBAs are used to jus-tify them. Sometimes the analysis neglects to attach a cost to the fact that large numbers of (invariably poor) people will have to be removed from land that they and their ancestors have lived on for centuries and resettled, or else it takes as the measure of this cost the amount of money needed to buy "equivalent" land for them elsewhere and to move them to it, having assumed that they can indeed be adequately compensated in this way. (In the "Less Developed Countries" this compensation, even when promised, is generally not paid.)[5]

Dam building is not the only occasion for cost-benefit analysis. CBA now plays a significant role in American politics, especially in assessing environmental regulations and projects with environmental impacts, and its use is increasing in Europe; that is one good reason for paying attention to it. It also brings out, with striking clarity, cer-tain fundamental aspects of the worldview of nearly all economists,

---

[5] See Patrick McCully, *Silenced Rivers: The Ecology and Politics of Large Dams* (London: Zed Books, 1996).

the ideology of disconnection that is the object of my concern here. It therefore warrants the scrutiny I intend to give it in this and the following section. Despite the fact that those who care about community, place, and the natural environment can now sometimes derive support from CBA, they should not in my view embrace it.[6]

For benefits and costs to be aggregated and compared, as required for a cost-benefit analysis, they must of course be reduced to a common measure. In CBA that measure is money. To build a dam (for example) requires among other things materials and labor, which are already traded in markets and can therefore be costed (but not valued!) relatively uncontroversially. But a dam and its reservoir require also the purchase or expropriation of land, land on which people live and work and which is furthermore part of a landscape and of a larger ecosystem. And the people who must be removed from the site may be connected to one another in communities and bound to each other and to the land through locally adapted cultural and agricultural practices. So the effects of a new dam might – as in practice they often do – include the disruption of people's lives and communities and cultures, a severing of all their vital connections – to

---

[6] Some writings that I found useful in learning about cost-benefit analysis are: John V. Krutilla and Anthony C. Fisher, *The Economics of Natural Environments: Studies in the Valuation of Commodity and Amenity Resources*, revised ed. (Washington, DC: Resources for the Future, 1985); Robert D. Rowe and Lauraine G. Chestnut, *The Value of Visibility: Economic Theory and Applications for Air Pollution Control* (Cambridge, MA: Abt Books, 1982); Robin W. Boadway and Neil Bruce, *Welfare Economics* (Oxford: Blackwell, 1984); R. G. Cummings et al., *Valuing Environmental Goods: An Assessment of the Contingent Valuation Method* (Totowa, NJ: Rowman and Allanheld, 1986); James T. Campen, *Benefit, Cost, and Beyond: The Political Economy of Benefit-Cost Analysis* (Cambridge, MA: Ballinger, 1986); Robert Cameron Mitchell and Richard T. Carson, *Using Surveys to Value Public Goods: The Contingent Value Method* (Washington, DC: Resources for the Future, 1989); Thomas O. McGarity, *Reinventing Rationality: The Role of Regulatory Analysis in the Federal Bureaucracy* (Cambridge: Cambridge University Press, 1991); Jerry A. Hausman, ed., *Contingent Valuation: A Critical Assessment* (Amsterdam: North-Holland, 1993); Kenneth J. Arrow et al., *Benefit-Cost Analysis in Environmental, Health, and Safety Regulation: A Statement of Principles* (Washington, DC: American Enterprise Institute, The Annapolis Center, and Resources for the Future, 1996); and Ian J. Bateman and Kenneth G. Willis, eds., *Valuing Environmental Preferences* (Oxford: Oxford University Press, 1999).

people and place and their past – hence perhaps the destruction of all that grounds their identities. I'll have more to say about this in the next chapter; but here is an example from North America. When the Falcón Dam was built in the 1950s over the Rio Grande (South of Laredo/New Laredo) by agreement between the United States and Mexico, it promised flood control, irrigation, electrical power (and recreation and tourism!)...

> But what was also accomplished was the total destruction of the ancient city of Guerrero, a city of cultural and historical significance and of great architectural refinement, one that predates our own country. The citizens of Guerrero were uprooted and displaced, essentially robbed of their heritage; their land; their homes; their sense of community; their civic pride; their places of worship, study and play; their culture; and their graves.[7]

If a CBA takes effects like these into consideration at all, it does not just gather information about them and put it before the public for deliberation. It "values" them in monetary terms, so that they can be compared with the revenue expected from the sale of electricity generated by the dam, the fees paid by anglers on the reservoir, the money that water skiers and power boaters are projected to spend locally, and so on.

How do economists go about ascertaining these values? Ideally, economists would like to derive people's "values" from their behavior in actual markets. This is because they believe that choices *reveal* preferences and preferences track values. By voluntarily buying something, a person shows that its value to her, which economists take to be the most she is willing to pay for it, is at least as much as the price she actually pays for it; otherwise she would not have bought it. Now, there are markets in all manner of natural resources – in oil and gold and other minerals, in water and its edible denizens, in plants and animals and land, and much more. But there are no markets in Grand Canyons, ozone layers, or ecosystems, no markets in which people can express their attitudes toward the survival of grizzly bears

---

[7] From Richard Payne's preface to *Guerrero Viejo*, Essay by Elena Poniatowski, Photography by Richard Payne (Houston, TX: Anchorage Press, 1997).

or their desire to live in a world wild enough for such animals to flourish. In the absence of a market, and hence of market prices, for all the goods and services in question – if there were such a market there would be no need of a CBA! – the economist turns to choices made in *surrogate* markets (transport markets, using the "travel-cost" method, or property markets, using the "hedonic price" approach) or, if even suitable surrogate markets are unavailable, to the choices people say they would make in imagined, *hypothetical* markets (about which more in a moment). The goal is always to mimic the market, to ascertain people's valuations as they *would* be revealed by choices made in the appropriate market, if only that (perfectly competitive, frictionless, free) market existed.

Suppose, for example, that a river or forest or wetland is to be valued, perhaps because it is to be decided whether to "develop" it or leave it as it is. In a recent economic study of mangroves, discussing the use of "extended" CBA in which the external and environmental benefits and costs are taken into account, the authors write, correctly: "The [CBA] model assumes that individuals regard environmental attributes and services as *commodities* which can be traded. Because a market price for a complete mangrove ecosystem does not exist, it is assumed that the demand for the ecosystem is the derived demand for the goods and services that the ecosystem supports and provides."[8] Some of these goods might be traded in actually existing markets – timber, finfish, mollusks, and so on. In this case, their "values" can be read off from their market prices (though not without difficulty). But an ecosystem also provides benefits that are not traded in markets. Among these are what some now call "ecosystem services."[9] Food, fuel, medicines, materials for tools and shelter, and so on, may be derived from a wide range of plants and animals. There may be off-site benefits and costs: intact forests moderate runoff; forest removal causes stream scouring, warming, and silting that are bad for salmon

---

[8] John A. Dixon and Padma N. Lal, "The Management of Coastal Wetlands: Economic Analysis of Combined Ecologic-Economic Systems," in Partha Dasgupta and Karl-Göran Maler, eds., *The Environment and Emerging Development Issues*, vol. 2 (Oxford: Clarendon Press, 1997). Emphasis added.

[9] See for example, Gretchen Daily, *Nature's Services: Societal Dependence on Natural Ecosystems* (Washington, DC: Island Press, 1997).

spawning and smolt survival; and so on. There may also be people, perhaps far from the site in question, who value the mangrove or forest for the as yet undiscovered uses that might some day be found for its products (economists call these "option values"). Others might derive comfort and joy from its mere existence even if they expect never to use or see it (its "existence value"). And associated with a place where people have long lived and worked there are likely to be other goods, intangible but of central importance in people's lives. All these goods were in the past frequently ignored in CBAs. If they are noticed in more recent analyses, they are treated as if they are commodities, their values estimated in surrogate or (more often, of necessity) in hypothetical markets, using the method of "contingent valuation."

In the contingent valuation (CV) approach, a survey is conducted in which the individual is asked what is the most money she would be *willing to pay* (WTP) to secure some environmental benefit or to prevent a loss (the survival of an endangered species, the restoration of Prince William Sound). Or she is asked what is the minimum amount of money she is *willing to accept* (WTA) to forego some environmental improvement or in compensation for an environmental deterioration or loss. Maximum WTP is normally used as the measure of the value of an individual's *gains*, and minimum WTA as the measure of the value of her *losses*.

Before considering CV, which is particularly revealing of the economic mindset and of what is presupposed by the Market Ideal (and fostered by the market in practice), let me say a few words about the foundations of *all* CBA methods – of, in fact, neoclassical normative economics.

Recall that all forms of CBA are predicated on the Market Ideal. If the conditions of the First Fundamental Theorem were satisfied, there would be no need of CBA. If everything people valued were privatized and commodified and traded in perfectly competitive markets, then on this view we would know the true value of everything and no CBA would ever have to be carried out. These conditions are not satisfied: markets are invariably incomplete. But, in the absence of a competitive (or any) market in the thing of interest, we must (say the economists) still try to infer people's valuations (of an ecosystem, say) from their choices in such markets as do exist (markets in, for example, the usable products of the ecosystem) or in relevant surrogate markets, if there are any, or the choices they say they would make in hypothetical markets (using CV). These *choices* are said to reveal people's *preferences* (assumed to exist, and to be stable and consistent) and these preferences are supposed to represent their *values* – all of them. And all that matters, on this view, is satisfying individuals' wants (which is said to increase their *welfare*) as expressed in their choices as consumers.

This is an extraordinary set of assumptions and, to all but economists, a wholly unsatisfactory foundation for normative argument. This follows from the argument I made in Part One (to be reinforced by further argument and evidence in Part Three). People do not in general have stable, consistent preferences; indeed they often do not have preferences of any sort among alternatives of the kind CBAs deal with. Such preferences as they have cannot in general be inferred from their choices, for their choices reflect and are caused by much else besides preferences. Their preferences are context-dependent and adaptive: they may have been formed in part as a result of or in response to the going social norms, to what goods, technologies, and so forth are available, to present and past public policies and programs, and much more.[10] Furthermore, many people frequently wish they did not have some of the preferences or desires they have; and their welfare might better be advanced in some cases

[10] On adaptive preferences, see especially Jon Elster, *Sour Grapes: Studies in the Subversion of Rationality* (Cambridge: Cambridge University Press, 1983). If many people's preferences are significantly affected by the very policy or program or project whose desirability is supposed to be justified by those preferences (as happens with any justification appealing to allocative efficiency), then preference-satisfaction as the standard for making public choices is undermined. This problem, it seems to me, is a serious one for neoclassical normative economics and indeed for any theory that attempts to justify or prescribe an institution, policy, project, technology, or whatever, by reference to fixed, given preferences. See Herbert Gintis, "A Radical Analysis of Welfare Economics and Individual Development," *Quarterly Journal of Economics*, 86 (1972), 572–599; and Michael Taylor, *Community, Anarchy and Liberty* (Cambridge: Cambridge University Press, 1982), pp. 56–57. A similar point was made by Kenneth Arrow at the start of his *Social Choice and Individual Values* (2nd edition. New York: Wiley, 1963), but he nevertheless went on to base his work, as have all subsequent contributors to social choice theory, on the assumption that individual preferences are unaffected by the decision process itself.

not by satisfying such preferences as they have but by overcoming or changing them, perhaps in accordance with their *judgments* about their own desires and their beliefs about the way the world *should* be.[11] These points have been made before, but the general argument made in Part One about desires, ideals, identities, and desire-independent reasons shows that the problems with CBA are not remediable flaws and that as an approach to making public policies (to choosing how we are to live together) CBA is radically wrongheaded. Economists profess respect for what they call *consumer sovereignty*, but public policy should respect its subjects as *persons*, as human beings with the distinctively human capacities and dispositions that I described in Part One; that, as we shall see, is also, and unsurprisingly, how people wish to be recognized.

So an approach that founds normative judgment about projects and policies upon the ideal of satisfying preferences revealed by choices faces some very general difficulties. Consider now the specific ways in which CBA attempts to ascertain values by contingent valuation (CV). Economists who conduct and generally endorse CBAs have themselves admitted that CV suffers from certain snags, including "strategic bias," "hypothetical bias," "instrument bias," and "information bias," as well as the "population survey biases" with which all public opinion surveys are afflicted. These are viewed as technical flaws, yielding mere "biases" in the valuations. But some of them at least are serious problems. "Strategic bias," for example, results from responses given in the belief that they could influence the outcome or in the hope of minimizing the respondent's contribution or increasing the compensation she is awarded; and "hypothetical bias," conversely, may result from responses given in the belief that they will make no difference to the outcome.

The more general problem, of which most of these "biases" are instances, is that we have little or no idea of what is going on in the minds of people when they give answers to CV questions, so that we cannot be at all sure what the responses to CV questions *mean*. We

---

[11] There is a large literature on these points. For a recent survey see Cass R. Sunstein, *Free Markets and Social Justice* (New York: Oxford University Press, 1997).

should therefore not take them very seriously. We have good reason to believe that what is going on in people's minds when they choose their responses is not what economists assume it to be (which is what it *has* to be if CV responses are to be of use).

In the first place, as I have said, many people simply do not have stable preferences or considered beliefs about specific environmental problems (or about the environment generally). But this will not necessarily deter them from answering CV questions. Of course, they might form opinions about the problem they are being asked about in the course of being asked about it and formulating their responses. Indeed, some people do not hear about an environmental problem (visibility at the Grand Canyon, endangered spotted owls) until they are asked CV questions about it; but again this may not inhibit them from telling the interviewer exactly how many dollars they are willing to pay to do something about it.

Second, there is, as I also remarked, a well-known general problem about inferring preferences from choices. If I choose to take the smaller of two pieces of cake that are offered to me, then, it is true, I could be said to *prefer* the smaller piece *all things considered*, but this is a trivial and generally useless truth: we would have to know what things were considered, and how, before this choice could tell us anything of the sort that would be useful in a cost-benefit analysis or in any public choice procedure.[12] My choice of the smaller piece of cake could have resulted from my lust for cake being outweighed by my desire to impress my hosts, or from my thought that the other guest would enjoy the bigger piece, or from my desire for cake being subdued or even silenced as a reason by my acceptance of what I take to be the local norm governing such choices, or by any one of a very large number of other possibilities. Choices alone do not reveal preferences, even if the chooser *has* preferences. It is not clear what *is* revealed by or *can* be inferred from choices.[13]

---

[12] For discussion of this issue (using this example), see Amartya Sen, "Environmental Evaluation and Social Choice: Contingent Valuation and the Market Analogy," *The Japanese Economic Review*, 46 (1995), 23–37.

[13] See the discussion of this in Nick Baigent, "Behind the Veil of Preference," *The Japanese Economic Review*, 46 (1995), 88–101.

This general problem is especially acute for the interpretation of responses to CV questions – which give the respondent a (highly constrained) choice of what to say she would do in a hypothetical (and generally underspecified) context about a problem of which she may have little knowledge and in which she may have little interest. Even when respondents have definite preferences and beliefs about environmental matters, including the environmental problem they are being asked about, these may not be revealed by the answers given to CV questions (or by their refusal to answer such questions). So, for example, those who do cooperate in such surveys and state a WTP may be signaling not their WTP (they may consider such questions silly or underspecified or that policy ought not to be decided in that way) but rather their general support for, or opposition to, environmental protection, or their beliefs about the locus of responsibility for the environmental problem in question. In stating that they are willing to pay some nonzero amount to deal with an environmental problem, they may be signaling only a *belief* that something *ought* to be done about the problem.[14] Believing that something ought to be done does not, of course, imply that they really are willing to contribute to (the cost of) such an effort – that will depend on certain conditions, which I'll discuss in Part Three – but those holding such a

---

[14] Kahneman and Knetsch have inferred from experiments they conducted that responses to WTP questions reflect not preferences but the "moral satisfaction" that such payments would "purchase." They found an "embedding effect" in which respondents were WTP about as much for dealing with a *subset* of environmental issues as they were WTP for the whole set. Earlier Kahneman had found that people in Toronto were not willing to pay much more to prevent a decline in fish populations in all the lakes of Ontario than to prevent a decline in a small subset of those lakes, and this effect was confirmed in a very thorough study done by Desvousges et al., who found that people in Atlanta were not WTP more to save 200,000 migratory wildfowl (from dying in uncovered ponds containing contaminated wastewater from oil and gas drilling) than to save 20,000 or 2,000 of these birds! See Daniel Kahneman and Jack L. Knetsch, "Valuing Public Goods: The Purchase of Moral Satisfaction," *Journal of Environmental Economics and Management*, 22 (1992), 57–70; Kahneman, "Comments on the Contingent Valuation Method," in Cummings et al., *Valuing Environmental Goods;* and William H. Desvousges, et al., "Measuring Natural Resource Damages with Contingent Valuation: Tests of Validity and Reliability," Chapter III in Hausman, ed., *Contingent Valuation.*

belief are likely at least to *say* that they are willing to contribute. Saying that they are not willing to give anything at all, on the other hand, may mean that, although they care a great deal about the state of the environment and believe that something ought to be done about this particular problem (and may actually be prepared, if it comes to it, to contribute to the cost of remedial action), they believe that they themselves *should* not have to pay for it, since the problem was created by the Exxon Corporation or by those people upwind in Los Angeles.

Another large reason why it is difficult or impossible to infer preferences from the answers to CV questions is that such questions generally do not and, so far as I can see, cannot provide meaningful larger contexts for the choices they ask people to imagine themselves making: a respondent in a CV survey might reasonably be wondering whether her contribution is to be part of an enforceable fair scheme of contributions, or whether this is the only environmental program she is going to be asked to contribute to, or what trade-offs will be involved, or whether the government can be trusted to use her money in the way that's being suggested. Certainly it's clear from the stated WTPs found in many CV surveys that people cannot be thinking, or thinking clearly, about the larger context of overall spending on environmental problems (never mind spending of all kinds). One study computed that if people were willing to pay as much for every endangered species in the United States as they said they were WTP to save the endangered whooping crane, then it would cost the average person several times the average individual income of Americans![15] (Some responses to WTP questions are plausibly interpreted as signaling, not the respondent's genuine WTP to deal with the concrete problem in question, but her general willingness to *do her part* in an unspecified cooperative effort to deal with the problem in question or even to protect the environment generally).[16]

---

[15] See Walter J. Mead, "Review and Analysis of State-of-the-Art Contingent Valuation Studies," Chapter VII in Hausman, ed., *Contingent Valuation*.

[16] See David A. Schkade and John W. Payne, "Where Do the Numbers Come From? How People Respond to Contingent Valuation Questions," Chapter VI in Hausman, ed., *Contingent Valuation*. This would provide another (related) explanation for the findings of Kahneman and Knetsch and Desvouges et al. referred to in a previous note. The "moral satisfaction" suggested by Kahneman and Knetsch could be associated in the

Finally, there is the obvious fact that how much a person is willing to pay is likely to depend on his *ability* to pay. Hence, even his choices in actual markets, never mind statements about WTP or WTA, cannot be take to express or reflect *preferences*. Though obvious, this is an extremely important point. And it would seem to catch cost-benefit analysis in a cleft stick. For if WTP is not indexed to some measure of ability to pay, then it cannot be said to represent what it is supposed to represent, namely willingness to sustain the relevant costs. But if, on the other hand, the WTPs (of the members of the society or group in question) are indexed to ability to pay, then they cannot be aggregated to yield net social utility, so that CBA breaks down as an algorithm of social choice.[17]

3.3.   Consumers, citizens, human beings

Contingent valuation asks people to think like consumers, as separate individuals who value the natural world and places and their past and other people in monetary terms. It tries to impose market thinking where markets are absent and in some cases impossible. In taking this approach, indeed in doing CBA in any form, economists *assume* that market valuation, as expressed by the amounts of money people are willing to pay or willing to accept, is the *only* way in which people value Nature. That is because they take for granted a monistic and reductionist theory of value, which fails to recognize that we value things and persons in many, irreducibly different ways, and which rests on the assumption that all things are commensurable with one another and fungible with money.[18] I doubt if most economists or their emulators have thought through the consequences of this extreme, dessicated understanding of value. *There is nothing, on this view, that I would not give up in exchange for some amount of money; there*

---

respondents' minds with "doing one's part in a cooperative effort" (helping other people) *or* with "saving (helping) the environment," or with both.

[17] I owe this last point to Alan Carling (personal communication).

[18] See in particular Elizabeth Anderson, *Value in Ethics and Economics* (Cambridge, MA: Harvard University Press, 1993), and Michael Stocker, *Plural and Conflicting Values* (Oxford: Clarendon Press, 1990).

is absolutely nothing that cannot be replaced by something else of equivalent (monetary) value.

But values and attitudes cannot all be properly expressed through market (or market-mimicking) choices, and to ask people to value things in this way is often to ask them to value those things inappropriately, to devalue and demean them perhaps, in some cases even to betray commitments and to sever connections with their past, their communities and cultures.

So it is hardly surprising that many people respond to WTA questions by giving very large, sometimes infinitely large, figures for the amount they would require in compensation, or by refusing to name a sum at all, or even terminating the interview, sometimes violently. In some surveys, the proportion of people in these categories has been more than 50 percent.[19]

There are several possible reasons for such refusals. The choices available generally offer no scope for the expression of a range of values and attitudes. Some respondents might view WTA questions as invitations to accept bribes, and in stating a very large WTA they might be signaling their unwillingness to accept bribes. Above all, a person might want the matter decided not by adding up monetary valuations, or by aggregating individual *desires* in some other way, but by paying attention to people's *beliefs* or *judgments* about what is the *right* thing to do, perhaps through a process of public *deliberation* – and deliberation is a process in which she might expect her preferences and beliefs about the issue, and her view of what perspective she should adopt and what considerations should count as reasons in deciding the issue, to be formed and modified. Perhaps, in other words, the respondents who reject contingent valuation believe with Burke that (as he famously put it in his Speech to the Electors of Bristol) "government and legislation are matters of reason and

---

[19] See, for example, Robert D. Rowe, Ralph C. D'Arge, and David Brookshire, "An Experiment on the Economic Value of Visibility," *Journal of Environmental Economics and Management*, 7 (1980), 1–19; Rowe and Chestnut, *The Value of Visibility*, at p. 81; Kahneman and Knetsch, "Valuing Public Goods: The Purchase of Moral Satisfaction." See also the discussion in Mark Sagoff, *The Economy of the Earth* (Cambridge: Cambridge University Press, 1988), Chapter 4.

judgment, and not of inclination..." This, as Kelman, Sagoff, and others have said, is in effect a desire to be treated as *citizens*, not as mere consumers.[20] And citizens – participants in a conversation about the common good – might be willing to do their part in realizing it. (I take up this last thought in Part Three.)

There is evidence that many people simply do not – and in some cases believe they should not – think about and value the natural world in the way that the economists assume. Economists themselves have been singularly unenthusiastic about testing their assumptions about valuing. Apparently unperturbed by the many who refuse to cooperate with CV surveys or who declare very large WTAs (these responses are usually "truncated," i.e., ignored!), they have shown almost no interest in finding out why people respond in the way they do to CV questions or what they think about the whole approach. I can find only four such studies (though there have been more than 2,000 studies and papers on contingent valuation!).[21] The best of these was done by some geographers, who held in-depth discussions *about* a CV survey with its participants. In the group discussions, the participants – farmers and others who had been asked how much they'd be willing to pay for an environmental conservation scheme on the farmers' land on the Pevensey Levels, one of the few remaining wetlands in England – said they found this a very difficult question to answer (but they felt obliged to answer it anyway!). They thought the whole exercise was peculiar, that valuing nature as a private good, as a commodity, was not right. They said that this was not the way to decide the issue, that it was a matter of the common good – concerning something that belonged to everyone – and not of their individual benefits and the amount each would be willing to pay. In discussion they talked about their lives on the Levels, their memories, the

---

[20] Steven Kelman, "Cost-Benefit Analysis: A Critique," *Regulation* (Jan./Feb., 1981), 33–40; Sagoff, *The Economy of the Earth*, pp. 7–8 and Chapter 3. Daniel Farber is skeptical about the extent of this disjunction between private consumer and public citizen. See his *Eco-Pragmatism* (Chicago: The University of Chicago Press. 1999), at pp. 51–58.

[21] Richard T. Carson, et al., *A Bibliography of Contingent Valuation Studies and Papers* (San Diego, CA: Natural Resource Damage Assessment, Inc., 1995).

meanings this place had for them. Some thought the whole exercise was undemocratic.[22]

How (on earth) do economists defend CBA, as most of them do? The main defenses offered are, briefly, as follows. i. Since resources are scarce and choices have to be made, CBA is *necessary*. ii. Though it is flawed, there is no *better* way. In some accounts CBA is superior to all the alternatives because it is the only *objective* approach. (And in some accounts there is simply *no* other way). iii. CBA alone is *precise*. These are distinctly unimpressive arguments. Societies have not generally made choices using CBA, so they clearly do not *have* to (any more than individuals have to conduct a personal CBA whenever they have choices to make). There are obviously alternatives to CBA, notably democratic deliberation.[23] That economists are blind to this alternative is not surprising, given the normative neoclassical framework that provides their rationale for carrying out CBAs. There is no place in that framework for the characteristic human capacities and dispositions that we considered in Chapter 2 – above all to endorse and be moved by ideals that structure or modulate one's other reasons. Human beings, who do not always behave like cats,

---

[22] Judy Clark, Jacquelin Burgess, and Carolyn M. Harrison, "'I Struggled With This Money Business': Respondents' Perspectives on Contingent Valuation," *Ecological Economics*, 33 (2000), 45–62. The three other studies are: Dan Vadnjal and Martin O'Connor, "What is the Value of Rangitoo Island?," *Environmental Values*, 3 (1994), 369–380; D. A. Schkade and J. W. Payne, "How People Respond to Contingent Valuation Questions: A Verbal Protocol Analysis of Willingness to Pay for an Environmental Regulation," *Journal of Environmental Economics and Management*, 25 (1994), 88–109; and Roy Brouwer et al., "Public Attitudes to Contingent Valuation and Public Consultation," *Environmental Values*, 8 (1999), 325–347. The Rangitoo Island study found attitudes similar to those found in the Pevensey Levels study. In Schkade and Payne's study a majority of respondents clearly failed or declined to think in the way required by the CV surveyors: many of them seemed to be reacting to the project's "general symbolic meaning" (which gives rise to another of those biases – "symbolic bias") and many of them just made WTP numbers up. Brouwer et al. found more support for CV (or more precisely for a CV survey they themselves had conducted), but here too there were many skeptics and much support for a participatory deliberative approach.

[23] For a discussion of one way in which this might be done in the environmental context, see Hugh Ward, "Citizens' Juries and Valuing the Environment: A Proposal," *Environmental Politics*, 8 (1999), 75–96.

want those distinctively human abilities and dispositions recognized, or at least not set aside and considered irrelevant to how they should live their lives in common. That, of course, is what deliberation is at least capable of allowing. So it is not surprising that, in the few studies (that I referred to previously) of how participants in contingent valuation surveys themselves view such surveys, deliberation is the alternative to which many respondents point. (Of course, these people, should they decide that some project should go forward, would no doubt want their money spent wisely, or cost-effectively; but that is not at all the same thing as using a CBA to decide whether the project is good in the first place). And if people are allowed to deliberate together, especially if they do this in face-to-face discussion, then they are more likely to consider what ought to be done for the common good rather than argue for outcomes that satisfy their selfish preferences,[24] and they are also much more likely to do their part in any mutually advantageous cooperative endeavor (to cooperate, in fact, in situations where Rational Choice theory would predict non-cooperation) – there is strong evidence for this second intuitive idea, as we shall see in Part Three.

CBA, far from helping such deliberation, displaces it; it is anti-democratic in its insistence on forcing people into its preferred way of valuing and thinking about the world. It in effect denies its subjects the narratively grounded identities that real people actually have (the identities I described in Part One) and in doing so denies them

---

[24] On this see Jon Elster, "The Market and the Forum: Three Varieties of Political Theory," Chapter 4 in Jon Elster and Aanund Hylland, eds., *Foundations of Social Choice Theory* (Cambridge: Cambridge University Press, 1986). Elster's argument against "social choice theory" (the approach to social choice inaugurated by Kenneth Arrow's "general possibility theorem") parallels part of my argument against cost-benefit analysis. Social choice theory, he says, is "representative of the private instrumental view of politics" and "the objection to the political view underlying social choice theory . . . is, basically, that it embodies a confusion between the kind of behavior that is appropriate in the market place and that which is appropriate to the forum." For a superb, sustained, critical examination of this approach to social choice (as it has been put to work by Rational Choice political scientists to undermine the case for democracy and relied upon by economists hostile to government), see Gerry Mackie, *Democracy Defended* (Cambridge: Cambridge University Press, 2003).

the real and various bases on which they exercise their autonomy. Far from gathering and providing impartially the information that a genuinely democratic deliberation would require – an exercise that would, among other things, oblige the cost-benefit analyst to *listen* to people open-mindedly and at length, to discover *all* the ways they value or think about or connect with the proposed project and all that will be affected by it – CBA *imposes* (or tries to impose) on people a single way of thinking and valuing, namely that of consumers in a market.

Of course, democratic deliberation is also flawed. To economists, it seems, all alternatives to CBA are flawed because they involve – politics! Apparently, markets and market-mimicking methods like cost-benefit analysis – which depend on, among other things, well-defined and enforced property rights – are not tainted with politics and accordingly are impartial and objective.

The third defense of CBA, that it alone is precise, is quite simply specious. A CBA is in a sense precise but it is not accurate: it produces precise numbers like the figure of $34.84 that according to one CBA is the amount the average Washingtonian is willing to pay to save the northern spotted owl,[25] but the numbers do not accurately measure or track what they are supposed to. (It's not clear, as we've seen, what they do track.) In the context of making public policy at least, precision without accuracy is pointless and may be dangerous.[26]

It should be said that, though all economists appear to support CBA (how could they not, given their premises about preferences and choice, value and welfare?), not all of them endorse contingent valuation. But note the principal (and entirely predictable) reason for this. It is that answers to CV questions may not (in the opinion of these economists) express *preferences*, and "Because answers to

---

[25] Jonathan Rubin, et al., "A Benefit-Cost Analysis of the Northern Spotted Owl," *Journal of Forestry*, 89 (1991), 25–30.

[26] Perhaps CBA has found favor with the governments of formally democratic countries (especially the United States) because, with its *appearance* of objectivity and impersonality, it serves to deflect public pressure and disguise accountability. See Theodore M. Porter, "Objectivity as Standardization: The Rhetoric of Impersonality in Measurement, Statistics, and Cost-Benefit Analysis," in Allan Megill, ed., *Rethinking Objectivity* (Durham, NC: Duke University Press, 1994).

surveys do not measure preferences, they are not a suitable source of information on values in benefit-cost analysis."[27] And it is not just any kind of preferences that a CBA must be based on; they must be selfish economic preferences. So that another reason for an economist to be skeptical about CV questions is that the answers may be contaminated by unselfish motives or ends – for example, a stated WTP may reflect concern for others' welfare as well as the respondent's own, or (as we noted earlier) reflect moral beliefs of the respondent. As the economist Paul Milgrom explains: "The purpose of benefit-cost analysis is to identify potential Pareto improvements . . . Within the standard neoclassical model of the economy, it is a theorem that a public project is a potential Pareto improvement exactly when the sum of each citizen's willingness to pay for the project exceeds the cost of the project. . . ." And this model "incorporates very particular assumptions about people's values . . . Value is treated as a purely personal matter that is related to the personal benefits each individual receives from the project."[28] It follows that any parts of respondents' stated WTPs that result from nonselfish and noneconomic concerns – including concerns for or beliefs about their duties to future human generations, animals, landscapes, and so on – must be purged from the cost-benefit calculation; otherwise the CBA cannot be relied upon to tell us whether the project will yield a potential Pareto improvement. Cost-benefit analysis, in other words, serves the Market Ideal (which is where we began this chapter), and that ideal cannot be realized if people's values do not conform to those required by the premises of the First Fundamental Theorem. In other words, the economist's favored way of making social choices (if they cannot be left to the market) *cannot* recognize the very capacities and dispositions that make us human. But then, the economist might be relieved to know, when these capacities and dispositions are denied,

---

[27] Peter A. Diamond and Jerry A. Hausman, "On Contingent Valuation Measurement of Nonuse Values," Chapter I in Hausman, ed., *Contingent Valuation*, at p. 29. This volume is an excellent collection of criticisms by economists of the CV approach.

[28] Paul Milgrom, "Is Sympathy an Economic Value? Philosophy, Economics, and the Contigent Valuation Method," Chapter XI in Hausman, ed., *Contingent Valuation*.

when people are treated as though they are nothing other than specimens of *Homo economicus*, they are more likely to act as if they are in
fact such beasts – or so I shall argue in Part Three.

There are people in the environmental movement who believe that,
although CBA is fundamentally rotten, it should be accepted on the
pragmatic grounds that, when it is used honestly, as they believe it
usually now is,[29] without inflated or invented economic benefits and
with wide accounting of direct and indirect effects on the environment and on human lives and communities, most of the "development" projects to which they are opposed would not pass muster, or
(they say) it can be used to make polluters pay fully for *all* the harm
they do. But in accepting CBA for this reason, those who care about
the environment or about human communities will undermine their
defenses in cases where a CBA goes against them. They will in the
long run undermine their own and others' commitments to the ideals
they really do hold and make it harder to persuade others to share
them. (It might in the short run be a psychologically consistent attitude for environmentalists to say, "Well, if you're going to play the
CBA game, we can win it – if the CBA is done properly, but don't
expect us to accept a losing result, because we don't accept the rules
of the game." I doubt, however, that this is likely to be a persuasive
stance or a stable one). It is not implausible to suppose that cost-
benefit analysis, if it is used more widely and more publicly, would
tend to foster and help to legitimate and entrench the view that we
must think about Nature, about life, in terms of what we individually
want and, moreover, of what we (with our limited budgets) can *afford*,
what we are *willing to pay*. For to think in this way – to think about
the fate of whooping cranes or old-growth forests in the same way as
we think about a new car or TV (Can we *afford* to keep the cranes?
Does biodiversity *pay?*) and indeed to see their benefits as competitive with those of a new car or TV (what am I prepared to give up to
keep whooping cranes in the world?) – is to turn away from valuing
these things *in their own terms* and it is to turn away from thinking

---

[29] But see "Army Corps Falsified Data for a Project, Study Says" (*New York
Times*, December 7, 2000), which reports on the recent manipulation of
economic analyses by the Army Corps of Engineers.

about what we – individually and collectively – *ought* to do, and it is surely not a way of looking at the natural world that environmentalists should be encouraging.

Those environmentalists who embrace CBA only opportunistically should think hard about what CBA's implicit value theory could condone. Would they favor slavery if it passed the Kaldor-Hicks test? "Efficient rape"? The dumping of America's toxic wastes in poor countries, whose citizens would lose less by it than Americans would gain?[30] It is understandable that environmentalists should countenance cost-benefit thinking when they believe an honest CBA would help them stop a project that (like some actual dams) will devastate the lives of hundreds of thousands of people, destroying their communities and ancient cultures, and inundating their valley homeland and all its significant places. But why is CBA less grotesque in these cases than in the case of "ordinary" rape?

[30] The writer who is best known for his willingness to at least discuss almost anything in cost-benefit terms is Richard A. Posner. See for example his *Economic Analysis of Law*, 5th ed. (New Yark: Aspen Law and Business Books, 1998) – rape is discussed at pp. 238–239 – and *Sex and Reason* (Cambridge, MA: Harvard University Press, 1992). In the fourth and fifth editions of *Economic Analysis of Law*, he does, however, allow that "the fact that any sort of rape license is even thinkable within the framework of the wealth-maximization theory . . . is a limitation on the usefulness of that theory." See the discussion of this and other contestable uses of "market rhetoric" by Margaret Jane Radin, *Contested Commodities* (Cambridge, MA: Harvard University Press, 1996), Chapter 6. The idea of "encouraging *more* migration of the dirty industries to the LDCs" was entertained by Lawrence Summers (then chief economist of the World Bank, later secretary of the U.S. Treasury) in an internal Bank memorandum. After it was published in *The Economist* (February 8, 1992), Mr. Summers protested that it was meant only "to sharpen the debate on important issues by taking as narrow-minded an economic perspective as possible" (*The Economist*, February 15, 1992). The United States, I should add, already exports considerable quantities of toxic trash to poor parts of the world, and is the only developed country that is not a signatory to the 1989 Basel Convention aimed at limiting the export of hazardous waste.

4   Dis-integration

4.1.   The market dystopia and the loss of self and meaning

Karl Polanyi wrote in *The Great Transformation* that "To allow the market mechanism to be sole director of the fate of human beings and their natural environment...would result in the demolition of society....Nature would be reduced to its elements, neighborhoods and landscapes defiled, rivers polluted..."[1] Polanyi's account of the history of actual markets and what (he thought) preceded them has not found much support from subsequent historical (and prehistorical) research. But *this* statement, I believe, is broadly correct – as a claim about what would happen if the market mechanism were allowed to become "the sole director," a claim, that is, about what would happen in the world of the Market Ideal, where everything of value is privately owned, has a price, and is allocated in a perfectly competitive market. I briefly discuss the "demolition of society" in this section. I take up the disintegrative effects of markets on Nature in the following section. On this subject, Polanyi adds very little to the remark I've just quoted (see his Chapter 15). But at a time when almost no writer on economics, politics, or history so much as mentioned the "natural environment" (as one old guy, depicted in a recent *New Yorker* cartoon, said to another, as they smoked their cigars by the fireside, "I remember a time when there *was* no environment"), it was a remarkable claim to make; now, half a century later, we have some relevant empirical studies to draw on. My interest throughout

[1]   Karl Polanyi, *The Great Transformation* (Boston: Beacon Press, 1957 [orig. ed. 1944]), p. 73.

this chapter is limited to drawing out some consequences of the economic way of seeing the world both for our lives and our relations with each other and for biological communities and our relations with the natural world. For many people these two sets of effects are not wholly separable.

Markets in the real world, of course, have significant effects on *place-based community*. Two minimal requirements of community, I think, are direct, multistranded relations and more-or-less stable membership – so that we interact with the same people on many fronts and expect to continue to do so for some time to come. Both characteristics tend to be undermined by markets. First, two kinds of specialization grow as markets extend their reach (to more goods and services, to more people and places): the social division of labor, or specialization by individuals within societies and within local groups, and spatial specialization, or division of labor by geographic region. And as specialization grows, relations between people become less multistranded and less direct – they increasingly deal with each other as specialists or in separate social spheres, and to interact with fewer people in the places where they live. Second, markets increase social and geographical mobility, which diminishes the stability of place-based community and attachment to local places and place-based practices. These are important, direct effects of real markets on place-based community (and, especially insofar as the market fosters economic growth and development, there are of course others). But if the Market Ideal were ever to be fully realized in the real world, the consequences for our connections, and our sense of connection, to people, places, and our past would be more radical. Let me now comment briefly on some of these consequences.

To value things and people in the manner assumed by economists is incompatible with certain relationships and attachments – relationships and attachments we can have to other people, past and future generations, places, social practices, and projects. In some cases it is in part *constitutive* of these relationships that their object is not so valued;[2] in others it is contingently true that valuing them or thinking

---

[2] The idea of constitutive incommensurabilities was introduced in Chapter 2 of Part One.

about them in this commodified way would undermine the attachment. To commodify some things is to change them. Of course a person can decide (as Alberich did when he chose the Rhinegold) that money and what it can buy are worth more to him than (for example) friendship and love; but he cannot have friends if he puts a price on them.

If this is true, then it follows immediately that not all things can have a market value or be valued in monetary terms.

What is involved in cases like this is not so much incommensurability – the lack of a common measure, such as money – as it is a *refusal* to trade off the thing or person in question with money or even to think of doing so. It is a repudiation and sometimes an incomprehension of the very idea of monetary valuation or exchange for money.

It is not that the alternatives are incomparable. They can be compared, and a choice made between them. But, as I have said (in Chapter 2), comparability, never mind commensurability, is a problem that someone in these situations would not normally have to wrestle with, because relations of this kind function in an *exclusionary* way to vitiate or silence monetary considerations. The same could be true, in some cases, when what is at stake involves giving up one's land or home or one's way of life, where these things, or one's relation to them, have given one's life value and meaning and, perhaps, constituted in part one's very identity.

If a person thought and valued in the way that contingent valuation methods invite him to do and economists in general assume him to do, he simply *could* not have *commitments* to people, social practices, certain principles, and long-term projects. He would therefore lack strong connections of this kind to communities and their cultures, to places, and to past and future generations. And on almost any interesting account of identity, he would not have one. Let me elaborate a little on these strong claims.

The vanishing self

We cannot (I argued in Part One) understand action without recognizing the distinctive capacity of humans to think about themselves, to form and then be affected by self-conceptions, which include ideas about the sort of person they *ought* to be and how they *should* live their lives. Of these ideals – these self-conceptions or self-understandings that are normative for a person – some function to frame and structure her choices. The self-understandings that are normative for a person and that structure choice in this way are what I took to constitute a person's identity. On this view of identity (and on any of the related accounts of identity that give it a similar role of framing choice),[3] the self disappears in the world of the Market Ideal. We have seen how this is brought out explicitly by CBA, as it is practiced in the field and endorsed by economic theorists: public choices, according to economists, should be determined by what people want (more specifically by what they are willing to pay) and not by what they believe ought to be done or by any other desire-independent reasons (discovered or modified, perhaps, in the course of collective deliberation). And, more generally, it is an immediate implication of my argument about desires and the structure of reasons (in the final section of Part One) that the inhabitants of the world of the Market Ideal – a world in which the values of all things are commensurable and everyone is compensable for the loss of anything and all choices are based on desires or preferences – *cannot* have identities.

For this reason and others we'll come to immediately, neoclassical economic theory deserves to be called an ideology – perhaps *the* ideology – of disconnection, of disintegration. It is an ideology because its narrow axiomatic base, which leaves out of account most of what makes us human, structures the way the economist sees everything. It is an ideology of disconnection, of disintegration, because it assumes and idealizes a world in which a person's acts are disconnected from his or her life and people's lives are disconnected from cultural practices. It is a world without coherent lives and without coherent communities and cultures. And, as we shall explain in a moment, neoclassical theory is also an ideology of *ecological* disintegration. The world of the Market Ideal is a world in which everything of value is a privately owned and enjoyed, separable good or service whose value is fully fungible, a world of universal commodification,

[3] See footnote 10 in Chapter 2 of Part One.

of perfect mobility. It is the antithesis of relation, attachment, community, and coherence.

The loss of meaning

I have said that in the world of the Market Ideal, the sense that one's life has meaning would disappear along with the self. What is meaningfulness and where does it come from?

I think Susan Wolf is roughly right when she says that "meaningful lives are lives of active engagement in projects of worth," and like her I believe that meaningfulness (or perhaps we should say the meaning we impose on our lives) "is an important element of a good life."[4]

For a life to seem to its possessor to have meaning it must surely be at least strongly *connected* to something beyond itself, something that transcends its own limits. The connection must (ultimately) be to something having intrinsic, noninstrumental value. Something of purely instrumental value cannot itself give point to my life. I can value things I do not care about, things of no great importance to me; and I can value things that I believe I should not value or that I do not regard as in some sense valuable independently of my valuing them. So the connection must be to something independently valuable, and it should be, not an indifferent or passive or disengaged connection but a relation, as Wolf says, of active engagement, ideally perhaps a matter of *commitment*, which has the effect in some choice contexts of silencing or excluding certain competing considerations. For I can be engaged in a practice or project that has worth and value independently of my valuing it but which I am not engaged *by*, a practice or project that I pursue for purely instrumental reasons and would therefore be willing to abandon for equally instrumental reasons.

If this is what it takes to give us a sense that our lives have meaning, then clearly the denizens of the world of the Market Ideal must live

---

[4] Susan Wolf, "Happiness and Meaning: Two Aspects of the Good Life," *Social Philosophy and Policy*, 14 (1997), 207–225. See also Joseph Raz, "Attachment and Uniqueness," Chapter 1 in his *Value, Respect, and Attachment* (Cambridge: Cambridge University Press, 2001).

without one. And of course they cannot add meaning to their utility functions as just another good to be traded off against other things they desire; that would be incoherent.[5]

Disappearing places

Consider again the people who have resisted removal from their homes and land and have refused compensation whether paid in supposedly equivalent land elsewhere or in money sufficient to buy supposedly equivalent property elsewhere. They would appear to be strongly attached to these particular *places*, among other things. Of course they may strongly wish to stay in place because they are familiar with it, and have an intimate knowledge of it, knowledge that is not all portable; or they may be afraid of the unknown, and so on. But some at least of the refuseniks may have a stronger, irreplaceable bond. What they are attached to is not a place merely in the sense of a landscape or a geographical space with a particular set of physical features, or a site or stage or setting. It is a place with a history, a place made meaningful to them by events. It is the place in which their past is written, the place where their ancestors lived and worked. It is a source of continuity within their own lives and between the generations. It is an integral part of their (narrative) selves. It may be a site of or integrally a part of cultural practices and projects to which they are committed. For all these reasons a real *place* is unique; it is not interchangeable with any other 'place,' and its loss cannot be fully compensated with money or with anything else.

Place in this sense is not recognized by cost-benefit analysis and is not possible in the world of the Market Ideal. In that world everything has its price; every *person* has his or her price; everyone is compensable for the loss of anything; nothing is unique, so everything is replaceable; everyone is mobile (rationally so) and uncommitted. Places are assumed to be valued by people just for the income or the goods and services they can be made to yield.

---

[5] See Anderson on "hybrid consequentialism": *Value in Ethics and Economics,* pp. 79–86.

Place in the true sense disappears in the normative world of the economist – as it all too often does in the actual eyes of the planner, the bureaucrat, and the corporate executive. Places in their view are apt to be mere sites or locations, usable for larger, external purposes – to erect a factory or shopping mall, impound water, grow trees for lumber or pulp, explode bombs, or test missiles – and as such are interchangeable.

The world of the Market Ideal is to the economist a utopia, a no-place of ideal perfection. To me it is a dystopia, a bad place, because it is among other things a place without place.

"Alone in the present"

At Celilo Falls, before they were drowned, the Columbia River narrowed into a long gorge and passed over and around a number of ledges and rock islands. Huge numbers of mature salmon fought their way upriver through these obstacles on their way home to spawn, and the Falls (put there, of course, by Coyote) provided an ideal place to take them. It was the greatest fishery of the whole vast Columbia watershed. The archeological evidence suggests that Indians had fished there since at least 7,700 B.P. (And it has been said, on less firm ground, that the fishing community around the Falls was the oldest continuously inhabited human settlement in the Americas.) In 1957, the U.S. Army Corps of Engineers put it all under water. The Engineers built a dam at the Dalles, a few miles downstream, and the dam's backwater inundated the Indian villages of Celilo (on the Oregon side of the river) and Spearfish (on the Washington side), along with the Falls themselves.

After the dam had been planned and while construction was proceeding, the Corps negotiated with the Indians – who were opposed to the dam and sought to the last to stop or delay its construction. The Corps acknowledged that the Indians had fished there "since time immemorial," and that the dam would "inundate and completely destroy" the fishing places that had been expressly reserved to them in perpetuity by the treaties they had signed with the U.S. government in 1855 (treaties in which they ceded vast areas of Washington, Oregon, and Idaho in exchange for several reservations and these fishing rights). But, the Corps said, "normal progress and industrial development warrants the dam construction even though it will adversely affect the Indians." The "water resources" of the River basin were there, after all, to be developed for "the greatest benefit of all users." It did, however, believe (and this really was progress for the Corps) that it had to make "fair and proper compensation to the Indians for their losses."[6]

The Corps deemed that this place was of value to the Indians only as a place to catch fish, and this value could be cashed out. The Indians were to be given a sum of money that, if invested in government bonds at 3 percent, would yield – over a 100-year period – an annual amount equal to the market value of the fish caught at the Falls in a typical year (based on an average of recent years and the projected value of the catch in future years). The Corps eventually calculated that the amount of money needed to "replace" the Indian catch was close to $27 million. For at this time the river was providing the Indians at the Falls with about 2,500,000 pounds of salmon per annum (for their own consumption and for sale), despite all that it had already been subjected to, including the building of Bonneville Dam just downstream of the Dalles (which drowned Cascade Falls, another great fishing place) and Grand Coulee Dam upstream (which inundated Kettle Falls – another important salmon fishing place on the river – along with thousands of acres of Indian land, and blocked

---

[6] *Special Report on Indian Fishery Problem, The Dalles Dam, Columbia River, Washington-Oregon*, prepared by Portland District, [U.S. Army] Corps of Engineers (Portland, OR, March 10, 1952). There is a large literature on the Columbia River dams and the decline of the wild salmon runs. A fine general introduction is William Dietrich, *Northwest Passage: The Great Columbia River* (New York: Simon and Schuster, 1995). The best book on what has happened to the wild salmon runs of the Pacific Northwest is Jim Lichatowich, *Salmon Without Rivers: A History of the Pacific Salmon Crisis* (Washington, DC: Island Press, 1999). A very useful collection of documents is provided by Joseph Cone and Sandy Ridlington, eds., *The Northwest Salmon Crisis: A Documentary History* (Corvallis: Oregon State University Press, 1996). On the native peoples of the mid-Columbia (which includes the Celilo Falls area) there is nothing to match Eugene S. Hunn, *Nch'i-Wana, "the Big River": Mid-Columbia Indians and their Land* (Seattle: University of Washington Press, 1990).

the passage of salmon to more than a thousand miles of productive river).[7]

But Celilo Falls meant much more to the Indians than a source of (in principle, replaceable) food. The salmon themselves were of great cultural significance to them: their lives had been intertwined with the great salmon runs for thousands of years; they deified these animals, venerating them as supernatural beings. And the Falls were a great meeting place to which Indians came – from nearby and from as far away as the Great Plains – to fish (if they had the right connections) and to trade and to participate in social and ceremonial events. Above all, this was for the Indians truly a *place*.

So the Falls were of the utmost significance to those who lived there, and were still a significant place to those who had moved to the reservations after 1855 but continued to fish at their "usual and accustomed fishing places" at Celilo. This place was the center of their lives.

Looking back on what had been done to them, Indians of the Yakama Nation later said: "The intent of the federal government, of course, was to separate the Nch'i-Wana [Columbia] Plateau people from their ancestral lands and resources ... To the Yakama people this meant leaving religious, spiritual, cultural and traditional areas ... being torn from their ties to the past, a traumatic privation that would leave them alone in the present."[8]

---

[7] The Corps professed to believe that the dams, if provided with fish ladders, did not do significant harm to the salmon runs and even claimed that the Dalles Dam was a good conservation measure, because the fish would do better going up the fish ladders than running the combined gauntlet of Celilo Falls and the Indian fishery, which the dam would eliminate. (The Indians disagreed, of course.) The problem was that far more harm was done to the salmon runs by the passage of the young salmon through the dams as they migrated downstream than was done to the returning mature salmon as they passed through the ladders. By the end of the twentieth century, with the construction of many more dams on the Columbia and its largest tributary (the Snake), many of the salmon runs (each of which is considered to be a "species," or Evolutionarily Significant Unit, for the purposes of the federal Endangered Species Act) had been extirpated entirely and the rest were in danger of extinction.

[8] Yakama Nation comments, in the Army Corps of Engineers System Operation Review, 1994, quoted in Roberta Ulrich, *Empty Nets: Indians, Dams,*

Alone in the present: that is what it can mean to lose your significant *places*, in the sense I described earlier. To be removed from a place is to be disconnected from much more than a piece of real estate. It is, among other things, to be "torn from [one's] ties to the past." Hence, places, real places in this sense, are not, as I have said, interchangeable with other "places," and those attached to them cannot be compensated for their loss, with money or with anything else. But the Corps of Engineers did not see things that way – at Celilo or at any other place it "developed." It calculated that more money could be earned by using the river at this "place" to generate electricity, and by making a stretch of the river more easily navigable, than could be earned from salmon, even after the costs of building and operating the dam, buying the land, and "compensating" the Indians had been taken into account. (The benefit-to-cost ratio it came up with was 1.25:1.[9] Of course, this ratio always came out right for any dam the Corps wanted to build, and the Corps never did a CBA for a dam it didn't want to build.) So the river would be put to its "most productive" use, and that, say the economists, is how it should be.

4.2.   The "most productive" use of ecosystems

> After-comers cannot guess the beauty been.
> Ten or twelve, only ten or twelve
> Strokes of havoc ùnselve
> The sweet especial scene.
> Gerard Manley Hopkins, *Binsey Poplars, felled 1879*

The effect of a market on an ecosystem or a biological community (as on a human community), we saw earlier, is likely to be disintegrative and centrifugal. Although an ecosystem as a whole cannot be owned and *some* of its properties and services cannot be privatized, there will be pressure in a large-scale market toward private ownership and commodification of every potentially profitable part

---

and the Columbia River (Corvallis: Oregon State University Press, 1999), at p. 94.

[9] House Document No. 531, 81st Congress, 2d Session: *Letter from the Secretary of the Army, etc.*, in eight volumes (Washington, DC: U.S. Government Printing Office, 1952), vol.1, at p. 280.

or property of an ecosystem, and a tendency to simplify it to make it more productive of what is taken to be its currently most "valuable" (i.e., saleable) commodity, if not straightforwardly and directly to destroy it in the process of extracting something to sell. The ecosystem will be disassembled and stripped down, many of its parts much reduced or exterminated, in order to further the efficient production of the targeted commodities: trees (for lumber, or pulp) from forests, water (for irrigation, or hydropower) from rivers, forage (for cattle and hence beef) from grasslands, and so on.

The Market Ideal of normative economic theory approves of this. This is brought out especially clearly by the theory and practice of cost-benefit analysis. Earlier, I quoted two economists who write correctly that "The [CBA] model assumes that individuals regard environmental attributes and services as commodities which can be traded." To this we should add that the model first assumes that Nature, or an ecosystem, like everything else, just is a divisible or separable collection of usable objects.

In the world of the Market Ideal, when the conditions of the First Fundamental Theorem are satisfied, markets will allocate resources to what economists call their "most productive" or "highest-valued" or "highest and best" uses. Unimpeded exchange between "rational" actors will ensure that resources will wind up in the hands of those who will use them the most "productively," which is to say those who can best use them to provide the goods and services that consumers "value" most. This, say the economists, is good. And those who take the purpose and aim of government and law to be efficiency, or making up for missing markets, believe that governments and the courts should act to ensure this happy outcome. But this talk of "most productive" and "highest and best" uses should not be allowed to obscure the fact that all that is meant here is that resources will and should be allocated to those who are *willing to pay* the most for them, usually because they can use them to produce and sell whatever can make the most money in the market. Of course, if subsistence farmers or fly fishers or nature lovers just want to leave the resource intact in its place – the trees in the forest, the water in the river, the gold in the mountain – they can bid against the developers, corporations, and cities, who may be willing to pay large amounts of money in order to have the rights to take the trees out of their forest ecosystem and turn them into lumber and pulp, or to take the water out of its watershed and use it to irrigate a desert golf course or run a snow machine at a ski resort or develop a new suburb.

As the market becomes more extensive, as the whole world more nearly approaches the Market Ideal – as every corner and part of it become thoroughly integrated into a worldwide market, as every impediment to the mobility and saleability of every part and person is removed – so will resources in fact find their "most productive" uses.

Some economists and economic analysts of law seem to believe that it is good in itself that things (and people!) are in the hands of those who are willing to pay the most for them – these are, after all, the people who "value" them the most – and that therefore arrangements or mechanisms that facilitate the movement of goods into the hands of those who are willing to pay more for them are to that extent good. Now, voluntary exchanges result in such movement. When two people make a voluntary market exchange – voluntary, of course, *given* the parties' opportunities and preferences, which may have been brought about in such a way as to make the exchange seem anything but voluntary to one of the parties – one of them relinquishes something for an amount of money no less than the least he is, in the circumstances, willing to accept for it (his minimum WTA), while the other pays for it no more than the most he is willing to pay for it (his maximum WTP). According to the economist, these two figures, min WTA and max WTP, represent the *values* that the thing exchanged has for the seller and buyer respectively. The exchange, if it is voluntary, takes place only if the max WTP is no less than the min WTA. Because one party has got something for less than his max WTP and the other has sold it for more than his min WTA, the exchange is said to increase *social wealth*. (Richard Posner, who uses this expression in this strange way, has famously argued that the common law evolves so as to maximize social wealth and that common law judges *should* make judgments that maximize it).[10]

---

[10] See Posner, *Economic Analysis of Law.* For discussions, pro and contra, of efficiency as an ideal in the law, see the pieces by Posner, Ronald Dworkin, and Anthony Kronman in *The Journal of Legal Studies,* 9 (1980) and by Posner, Dworkin, and Jules Coleman in *Hofstra Law Review,* 8 (1980).

But notice that, since the buyer (call him R) "values" it more – is willing to pay more for it – than the seller (call him P), social wealth would be increased, on this account of the matter, if the thing were simply transferred from P to R without any money changing hands, in other words, without P being compensated for his loss. (R's willingness to pay more for it than P is prepared to accept for it may of course be a product of his greater *ability* to pay more – his being richer than poor old P.) Thus, if increasing social wealth, defined in this peculiar way, is a good thing, or if, equivalently, it is good that resources are in the hands of those willing to pay the most for them, then there is *something* to be said for simply taking things from those who "value" them less and giving them to those who "value" them more![11]

Needless to say (except to the economists and the economic analysts of law), increasing social wealth need not increase total well-being or welfare; indeed it will often decrease it.

All this is far from being a purely academic matter. Many millions of people (as I noted earlier) have been moved off their land, usually without full (or any) "compensation," to make way for dams and their reservoirs, and for countless other "development" projects. Their land was taken from them so that it could be put to "more productive" or "higher-valued" uses. In cases like these, economists who dismiss the claims of those who say they are unwilling to part with their land for *any* sum of money or to accept any other land in compensation are in effect countenancing forced transfers. In still other cases it may come to pass, no doubt through a series of entirely "voluntary" and legal exchanges, that poor owners of land find themselves in a position in which they are willing to accept, for land that not only provided them with a livelihood but had been in their families for generations, a sum of money less than the developers of suburbs or ski resorts are willing to pay. In all these cases, the belief that "social

---

[11] This argument is made by Ronald Dworkin in "Is Wealth a Value?," *The Journal of Legal Studies*, 9 (1980), 191–226, which appears also as Chapter 12 in his *A Matter of Principle* (Cambridge, MA: Harvard University Press, 1984). Here Dworkin also, I think, effectively demolishes the alternative, instrumental or "false-target" argument for social wealth maximization – that social wealth should be maximized because doing so is a means to some other independently valued end.

wealth" would be increased, that it is good for resources to be in the hands of those who would put them to their "most productive" uses, no doubt helped to justify the transfers in the minds of those who were responsible for bringing them about.

I am not laying all the blame – for all the dispossession and environmental destruction carried out in the name of "development" or to advance what the Corps of Engineers at Celilo Falls called "normal progress" – at the feet of neoclassical economists. Their chief contribution has been to have helped to legitimate all this furious activity. Before the advent of neoclassical (and for that matter of classical) economic theory, other ideas and ideologies were made use of to do the same job: racist ideologies, for example, and Christian ideology, and a line of thought, exemplified by John Locke's theory of property, that is a precursor to neoclassical economics (or all of these three in combination).

Locke, in his *Second Treatise of Government*, famously argued that, although land was given by God to mankind in common, individual people could come to have justified private property rights in land by mixing their labor with it.[12] Their labor would give them property not just in "the Fruits of the Earth, and the Beasts that subsist on it" – or the flow of products that their labors produced – but "*the Earth it self*," so that "*As much Land* as a Man Tills, Plants, Improves, Cultivates, and can use the Product of, so much is his *Property.* He by his Labour does, as it were, inclose it from the Common." The justification for this move is that "every Man has a *Property* in his own *Person* . . . The *Labour* of his Body, and the *Work* of his Hands . . . are properly his."

This argument justifies, says Locke, the appropriation only of what a man can produce by his own labor and only as much as he can use before it spoils, and only if "enough, and as good" is left in common for others. But this clearly would serve to justify very little private appropriation; so Locke, after suggesting that, what with all the remaining "vacant places of *America*," everyone in the world might

---

[12] John Locke, *Second Treatise*, Chapter V, in *Two Treatises of Government*, ed. Peter Laslett (Cambridge: Cambridge University Press, 1960). All the quotations in the text are from this chapter.

still have all the land they could work with their own hands (an observation he wisely would "lay no stress on"), goes on to argue that, once
money has been introduced (or gold or shells or any tokens that do
not spoil), a man may rightfully come to possess more land than he
can work himself and more than would leave "enough and as good"
for others. The crucial argument that supports this move is this: by
enclosing and cultivating a piece of land, a man makes it much more
(at least "ten times more") productive than it would be if left "lyeing
wast in common," and from this it follows, says Locke, that "he, that
incloses Land and has a greater plenty of conveniencys of life from
ten acres, than he could have from an hundred left to Nature, may
truly be said, to give ninety acres to Mankind." By this reasoning,
Locke concludes that a man would be justified in appropriating for
himself more than would leave "enough and as good" for everyone
else; for, putting his land to productive use (and exchanging its surplus products for money, to the introduction of which, says Locke,
everyone has tacitly consented), he makes others better off, even the
poorest, including those with no land or other wealth at all. (A "day
Labourer in *England*" is better off than "a King of a large and fruitful
Territory" in *America*.)

The reader will have no great difficulty seeing the affinity of this
argument with the argument of our twentieth century economists
who praise markets for their wondrous ability to produce efficient
allocations of resources – to allocate resources to their "most productive" or "highest-valued" uses, and hence, to increase "social wealth."
This argument, as we have seen, serves to legitimate transfers of land
(and of all other things), whether by force or coercion without compensation, or by the exercise of eminent domain, or by voluntary
market exchange, from poor and powerless people to government
agencies, developers, or private corporations, or to those who are
willing to pay more for it. So too was Locke's argument used to justify the theft of land from the native peoples of America.[13] Locke, who

---

[13] For more on the Lockean justification and for some interesting discussion of Indian notions of property, see William Cronon, *Changes in the
Land: Indians, Colonists, and the Ecology of New England* (New York: Hill
and Wang, 1983), especially Chapter 4. For other arguments, or ideologies, that served this same purpose, see for example: Francis Jennings,

had no understanding of the requirements of hunting and gathering or of the long history of Indian horticulture and agriculture or of native ideas of property, took it that there were many "vacant places" in America, and that the natives held their land in common and were not using it as "productively" as it could be used by European settlers.[14] The argument that it was justifiable to take land from such people because it could be put to more productive (i.e., more profitable) use did not originate with Locke: it is to be found in writings of the previous century – in Thomas More's *Utopia*, for example, and in Luther and Calvin.[15] So the argument, still alive and influential (though usually now separated from the racist and religious strands with which it was once interwoven), is an old one; but its antiquity does not make it a good one.

Water flowing uphill toward money

Let us look at an example of how this doctrine of "most productive uses" is being played out in practice. Consider the ancient Hispanic

The Invasion of America: Indians, Colonialism, and the Cant of Conquest (New York: Norton, 1976), Richard Drinnon, *Facing West: The Metaphysics of Indian-Hating and Empire-Building* (Minneapolis: University of Minnesota Press, 1980; reprinted New York: Schocken Books, 1990), and David E. Stannard, *American Holocaust: Columbus and the Conquest of the New World* (New York: Oxford University Press, 1992).

14 Part of this was, as William Appleman Williams puts it, "A Psychologically Justifying and Economically Profitable Fairy Tale: the Myth of Empty Continents Dotted Here and There with the Mud huts, the Lean-tos, and the Tepees of Unruly Children Playing at Culture." This is the title of Chapter 2 of Williams's *Empire as a Way of Life* (New York: Oxford University Press, 1980). If there were "vacant places" in the Americas at the time Locke was writing and at the later times at which Europeans and Euro-Americans first entered various parts of the continent, it was only because the European invaders and their diseases – which often ran ahead of them and did their work before the newcomers arrived on the scene – had made them so. Roughly 95% of the precontact population of the Americas – now estimated to have numbered between 75 million and 145 million – would perish from the conquerors' violence and diseases.

15 See Richard Schlatter, *Private Property: The History of an Idea* (New Brunswick, NJ: Rutgers University Press, 1951); C.B. Macpherson, *The Political Theory of Possessive Individualism: Hobbes to Locke* (Oxford: Clarendon Press, 1962); and Stannard, *American Holocaust*, pp. 233–238.

irrigation communities of the upper Rio Grande basin in northern New Mexico. Each of these communities is organized around its irrigation ditch, or *acequia* (the word is also used for the association of irrigators). The water in the *acequia* is shared among the irrigators whose land is served by that ditch. No individual has a right to a fixed amount of water; what water there is in a stretch of river at any time is *shared*. Traditionally, and until very recently, none of the members could transfer or sell his right to a share of water: it was tied to the land and was not privately owned. But now, water rights are being "adjudicated"; i.e., legal rights are being established for individual members of the *acequia* to fixed amounts of the water in an entire regional stream system, and these rights can then be sold or leased to anyone, anywhere in the state of New Mexico. In other words, through this process rights to the water are divorced from ownership or use of the land and become private property that can be traded in a market.

But that is not all. The *acequias* have for hundreds of years sustained real *communities*, whose practices have been so well described by Stanley Crawford.[16] Each *acequia* is a little participatory democracy, a self-governing association whose members cooperate to maintain the ditch, tax themselves to pay for the *mayordomo* they elect, resolve all the conflicts that sharing irrigation water is bound to generate, and so on. The sale of any water right means the loss of another member and his participation in the affairs of the *acequia*, and is hence a blow to the community.

Crawford writes, "With its interminable court hearings, the adjudication process can sweep through a community and undermine traditional arrangements that have stood in place for hundreds of years, in order to convert what has been held in common to that which can be owned privately." This is a version of an old story. It is an important part of what the enclosure movement in England

[16] Stanley Crawford, *Mayordomo: Chronicle of an Acequia in Northern New Mexico* (Albuquerque: University of New Mexico Press, 1988). For a scholarly study, see the excellent article by Gregory A. Hicks and Devon Peña, "Community Acequias in Colorado's Rio Culebra Watershed: A Customary Commons in the Domain of Prior Appropriation," *Colorado Law Review*, 74 (2003), 387–486.

was all about. For what we have here is the creation of clearly specified, legally documented, private property rights as a necessary step
toward freeing the resource (in this case water) from its entangle-
ments with the land and the human community dependent on it and
the flexible imprecise informal traditional norms of sharing it – freeing it up so that it can be "voluntarily" transferred to those who can
put it to a "higher-valued" use. In other words, water in the old Hispanic communities of northern New Mexico is finally being "made
to flow uphill toward money,"[17] as it has been for some time all over
the American West, beginning with the transfer of water from Owens
Valley to Los Angeles.

For the right to an acre-foot of water a farmer might be paid by a
developer or a city many times the value it has, in strictly economic
terms, when it is used to irrigate a meadow of grass (this value being
the difference it makes to the market value of what the farmer produces on the land). To the developer, the right to an acre-foot of water
per annum can be worth as much as $50,000. "In some cases, water
brokers working for developers will come to small communities and
seek out *acequia* members who are in financial trouble" and offer to
buy their water rights.[18] And in this way the water rights on which
farming and farming communities depend are being transferred to
cities, the developers of ski resorts for snow-making machines, mining
corporations, and so on.[19]

---

[17] Stanley Crawford, "Dancing for Water," *Journal of the Southwest*, 32 (1990),
265–267.

[18] Bruce Selcraig, "A Home-Grown Water War," *High Country News*, 31
(October 11, 1999), 6–9.

[19] Needless to say, not all irrigation water in the U.S. West supports long-
established communities or sustainable farming practices. Far from it.
Much irrigation practice there is environmentally destructive and in some
places large-scale irrigation farming should never have been begun. The
transfer of water rights from some of these projects – with the result that
farmers would use less water and use it more carefully or fallow some land
entirely – would be a good thing. But of course these are generally projects
that themselves transferred water away from its ecosystem. I should add also
that some states now have laws that limit the right to transfer water – and
hence limit its full privatization and commodification – when there would
be large impacts on the ecosystem, economy, and human community from
which the water is to be withdrawn. See the report to the National Research

The sale of any one of these rights is a direct loss to the *acequia* community, but it contributes also to the gradual demoralization of those who remain, and eventually these communities, like others before them whose land has been enclosed and commodified, must find themselves inhabiting a place that is no longer psychologically theirs.

Here then are human communities and biological communities, which have coevolved in specific places over several centuries and are both especially dependent on one component of the ecosystem, being dismantled because this crucial component, the water delivered by the river, is being *separated* from the land, from the rest of the ecosystem, made into private property, and sold for uses far away. Efficiency requires this. It requires that everything be put to its "most productive" use.

Recall now, in this context, some of the cases I discussed in Part One: recall, for example, at Alto, how the spring water that irrigated the terraces, and was thereby crucial in sustaining a coherent local economy and culture, one that operated within the limits of the local ecosystem and was probably indefinitely sustainable, was expected to dry up as a result of converting the surrounding mountain land to plantations of eucalyptus trees for the production of pulp and paper for use in distant places; and how the James Bay project would destroy the wild rivers flowing into James Bay – rivers that were the lifeblood of a still viable hunting culture – for the purpose of producing hydro-electric power to be transmitted to consumers in cities far away.

Consider now a somewhat different example.

An island no more

This is the story of Nauru, a tiny coral island, situated midway between Hawaii and Australia.[20] Polynesians settled it more than 2,000 years ago, and lived there in isolation (its nearest neighbor is another small island some 250 kilometers away) until the arrival of

Council, *Water Transfers in the West: Efficiency, Equity, and the Environment* (Washington, DC: National Academy Press, 1992), esp. Chapter 3.

[20] I am indebted here to Christopher Weeramantry, *Nauru: Environmental Damage Under International Trusteeship* (Melbourne: Oxford University Press, 1992), and Carl N. McDaniel and John M Gowdy, *Paradise for Sale* (Berkeley: University of California Press, 2000).

Europeans in the late-eighteenth century. The island is only 20 kilometers in circumference. Most of it is a plateau ("Topside"), which is fringed by a narrow coastal belt. Until the coming of the Europeans, the Nauruans, of necessity, lived entirely from the island's limited natural resources. The coastal strip, though generally infertile, supported coconut palms, which gave them (storable) food, oil, and materials for utensils, skirts, mats, baskets, and cord for nets. Topside and the coast supported the pandanus tree, whose edible fruits yielded also a juice that was dried into storable sheets and whose leaves yielded mats and baskets, roof thatching, and other useful things. Topside trees supplied timber for houses and boats, and Noddy birds were caught there. Fish were reared in an inland lagoon and were caught at sea. The human population had of course to be held at a level these resources could sustain.

Beginning in the middle of the nineteenth century, passing ships paid visits to the island. Steel tools, firearms, alcohol, tobacco, and assorted baubles were traded for coconut and pigs. As a result of these visits it was eventually discovered – by the Pacific Islands Company operating out of Australia – that Topside's soil and vegetation covered a rich deposit of phosphate, a substance that is much in demand in countries, like Australia, whose soils are deficient in this essential requirement of productive agriculture.

That was in 1899. Nauru had recently been annexed by Germany, which had been interested in exporting *copra* (dried coconut meat) from the island. The Germans then sold to the British Phosphate Company (formerly the Pacific Islands Company) the right to mine the phosphate ore. Mining began immediately (in 1906), with the phosphate being shipped to Australia to improve farmers' soils. The owners of Topside – individual Nauruans – were not a party to the agreement, and were to be paid only a very small royalty (a halfpenny per ton of phosphate). With these monies, the islanders began to enter, in a small way, into a market economy.

At the end of World War I, Nauru was transferred under the Covenant of the League of Nations to the "trusteeship" of Great Britain, Australia, and New Zealand – and mining continued. By the time the island was granted independence, in 1968, these "trustees" had extracted about 34 million tons of phosphate worth more than $300 million (Australian) at world market prices. And by that time *a third of the island had essentially been destroyed*, for the removal of the phosphate ore leaves behind a badlands moonscape of bare jagged pinnacles of fossil coral, on which it would take many centuries for the natural forest to reestablish itself.

The newly independent Nauruans brought suit against Australia in the International Court of Justice and in 1993 settled for $107 million, payable over twenty years.

But the land was not all that was mined. The islanders' *culture* too had once sustained them, and now it too had been much altered. After a century of contact with Westerners, Japanese occupation, and Allied bombing in World War II, and the royalties earned from mining, they had now largely abandoned their old self-sufficient way of life and had become dependent upon imported food and other material resources and on the knowledge and understanding of outsiders.

At independence the Nauruans could have decided to scale back the phosphate mining (and eventually halt it) and to use the proceeds from the transitional mining to restore the degraded third of the island. They could also have restored some of their old culture, choosing to be somewhat less dependent on the outside world and gradually reducing the island's swollen population to a level that the island's own natural resources could sustain. But they chose instead to allow mining to continue at the same rate and, knowing that the phosphate would one day run out (it was estimated at independence that the remaining phosphate would last about forty years and yield annual profits of more than $9 million), to invest the profits with a view to ensuring an income stream to sustain future generations of islanders. The profits went into Air Nauru, their own shipping line, and properties and enterprises in several parts of the world. Some of these investments were unwise to begin with; some have soured or have been mismanaged. The phosphate has now been depleted. And in recent years the government, hugely in debt, has been reduced to making money from unregulated offshore banking and the laundering of dirty money (especially from Russia) and to offering use of the island as a holding station for refugees trying to enter Australia, funded by the Australian government.

Every family owns at least one car – though there are only 18 kilometers of paved road – and TVs, VCRs, washing machines, and motorboats are common. Almost the entire island apart from the narrow coastal strip (itself now much "developed" – and vulnerable to any rise in sea-level) is a largely lifeless moonscape; and the islanders now suffer many of the "developed" world's health problems – high rates of obesity, diabetes, heart disease, and cancer. And of course they are utterly dependent on trade with the outside world, for they could not now support their present population – or even the very much smaller precontact population – with the locally available or producible resources, even if they could retrieve the lost knowledge, skills, and practices that once helped to sustain them in their isolation.

What has happened on Nauru is an epitome of market integration, representing in a particularly stark and concentrated form something that is happening, or has already happened, all around the world. All over the world, *as market demand is focused on a single local natural resource*, mountains are taken apart, rivers poisoned, valleys flooded, watersheds devastated, habitats destroyed, and species extinguished, while, interwoven with these ecological consequences in many cases, millions of people are removed from their homes and land,[21] communities dismantled, local cultures destroyed, and in some cases, the people themselves physically destroyed. (To *dismantle*: originally, to destroy the defensive capability of.) Market demand has been brought to bear on American bison, beavers, fur seals, sea otters, and whales; on elephants (to use only their tusks for combs and piano keys) and rhinos (their horns for aphrodisiac); on tropical and other forests – to level and replace them by monocultures of sugar cane, banana trees, pineapples, coffee bushes, rubber trees, eucalyptus, and other trees to be pulped for paper, or grass pastures for the production of hamburger; on valleys and great rivers everywhere, for hydropower or irrigation water; or on mountains, to be taken apart and ground to dust for the extraction of gold by cyanide leaching.[22] The list is

---

[21] See, for example, Patrick McCully, *Silenced Rivers: The Ecology and Politics of Large Dams* (London: Zed Books, 1996) and Christopher McDowell, ed., *Understanding Impoverishment: The Consequences of Development-Induced Displacement* (Providence, RI and Oxford: Berghahn Books, 1996).

[22] The literature is large. See, for example, Michael Watts, *Silent Violence: Food, Famine and Peasantry in Northern Nigeria* (Berkeley: University of

endless. Almost anything, anywhere, can be grist to the mill of the world market. What is involved is the stripping down, dismantling, degradation, or utter destruction of a local ecosystem for the purpose of producing or extracting just one thing to be exported as a commodity for use or consumption elsewhere. The crucial point is that through the wider market, a far larger demand for the resource than could be generated locally is brought to bear on the local ecosystem. The extraction, serving external ends, rarely respects local integrities, the integrities of local communities, cultures, and ecosystems.[23] With respect to these things, the market's tendency is centrifugal.

Markets, then, make possible the focusing of large-scale demand on the resources of ecosystems. But the effects of market integration on local ecosystems and their interwoven human communities are further facilitated by the *separation* that markets bring about between people and both their local natural environments and those distant environments from which they draw their resources.

The more extensive a market is – the more people and localities are drawn into it – the more all of them can gain economically from specialization and trade, and to the economist this is good. Of course,

California Press, 1983); Stephen G. Bunker, *Underdeveloping the Amazon: Extraction, Unequal Exchange, and the Failure of the Modern State* (Chicago: The University of Chicago Press, 1988); William Cronon, *Nature's Metropolis: Chicago and the Great West* (New York: Norton, 1991); J. R. McNeill, *Mountains of the Mediterranean World: An Environmental History* (Cambridge: Cambridge University Press, 1992); J. R. McNeill, "Of Rats and Men: A Synoptic Environmental History of the Island Pacific," *Journal of World History*, 5 (1994), 299–349; Peter Dauvergne, *Shadows in the Forest: Japan and the Politics of Timber in Southeast Asia* (Cambridge, MA: MIT Press, 1997); Richard P. Tucker, *Insatiable Appetite: the United States and the Ecological Degradation of the Tropics* (Berkeley: University of California Press, 2000); Mike Davis, *Late Victorian Holocausts: El Niño Famines and the Making of the Third World* (London: Verso, 2001). McNeill believes that the effects of concentrated market demand are one of two general processes responsible for the "skeletal mountains and shell villages" found in mountain areas all around the Mediterranean, the other being demographic "overshoot." See *Mountains of the Mediterranean World*, pp. 8–11 and 237–240.

[23] A good discussion of an example of this is to be found in Narpat S. Jodha, "Reviving the social system-ecosystem links in the Himalayas," Chapter 11 in Fikret Berkes, Carl Folke, and Johan Colding, eds., *Linking Social and Ecological Systems* (Cambridge: Cambridge University Press, 1998).

as a group of people becomes more specialized, it moves away from autarky or local self-sufficiency, away from meeting all its needs out of its own local natural and human resources, so that (among other things) its knowledge of the local flora and fauna and the workings of the local ecosystems and what can be grown and produced in and from them, and in general all its accumulated knowledge of how to live in that place, will wither.

We can describe this transition, using terms coined (I think) by Raymond Dasmann, as one in which *ecosystem people,* who live almost wholly from and *within* their local ecosystems, become *biosphere people,* who draw their resources from far and wide.[24] From an ecological point of view, this transition is of enormous significance.

Ecosystem people – the Nauruans before contact with Europeans, to take an extreme example (there is of course a continuum here) – *have* to be knowledgeable about their local environments, and those are the only environments they affect. (I hasten to add that I am not saying here that ecosystem people are, as many have supposed, necessarily good conservationists with a correct understanding of their natural environments and their own impacts on them, still less that in their dealings with the natural world they are guided by a conservation ethic,[25] or that ecosystem living – even on a completely isolated, small island – guarantees sustainability).[26] But the biosphere people

---

[24] Raymond Dasmann, "Future Primitive," *CoEvolution Quarterly,* Fall (1976), 26–31, and "Toward a Dynamic Balance of Man and Nature," The Ecologist, 6 (1976), 2–5.

[25] See the careful analysis by Eric Alden Smith and Mark Wishnie, "Conservation and Subsistence in Small-Scale Societies," *Annual Review of Anthropology,* 29 (2000), 493–524. They say, correctly in my view, that "to count as conservation, any action or practice should satisfy two criteria: It should (a) prevent or mitigate resource depletion, species extirpation, or habitat degradation, and (b) be designed to do so." And they conclude that, although in small-scale societies there is often sustainable use of resources and habitats and even biodiversity enhancement, conservation in the sense defined is rare. For a fascinating study bearing on this, see Robert Brightman, *Grateful Prey: Rock Cree Human-Animal Relationships* (Berkeley: University of California Press, 1993), and for a survey of North American cultures, Shepard Krech III, *The Ecological Indian: Myth and History* (New York: Norton, 1999).

[26] That ecosystem living does not *guarantee* sustainability is shown by the well-known case of Rapa Nui (Easter Island) and the less well known but

of modern industrial societies, drawing materials and products from all over the world (though not yet quite at the extreme to which the economists would take us), are fairly comprehensively ignorant both about what remains of their own local nature and about those distant ecosystems from which they draw their resources (and the people directly dependent on them) and the impact that their consumption

remarkably similar case of Mangaia. Mangaia, one of the Cook Islands in Eastern Polynesia, is a mere 52 square kilometers, a third the size of Rapa Nui. Polynesians arrived there by about 2400 BP. Shifting cultivation on the volcanic cone, and an increasing population, stripped the mountain slopes of their indigenous forest cover. Most of the exposed soil was eventually washed down to the valley bottoms, and the resulting alluvium, which amounted to less than 2 percent of the island, was intensively used for irrigated cultivation of taro. By the time Europeans arrived, tribal groups were at war over these irrigated lands. Meanwhile, in the centuries after 1000 BP, with the human population growing exponentially before it collapsed precipitously in the eighteenth century, the bones of pigs and chickens (introduced by the Polynesians) disappeared from the archeological record, and fish and shellfish and birds declined steeply. (More than half the bird species were driven to extinction.) As all these sources of food declined, the Mangaians turned to rats and human cannibalism for their protein. Tikopia, another small island of the South Pacific, shows what *could* have happened on Rapa Nui and Mangaia. For about a thousand years after it was settled by Polynesians around 3000 BP, Tikopia developed much like Mangaia. But then something remarkable happened: the people moved gradually from a system of shifting cultivation to an arboriculture or orchard gardening that mimicked the multistory diversity of the rainforest, a practice that survives down to the present and is described ethnographically (in Raymond Firth's 1936 monograph, *We, the Tikopia*). At the same time the Tikopia introduced a range of strategies for the more careful use and conservation of resources, including strict regulation of fishing, and took measures (some of them rather draconian) to hold population growth in check. By these means the islanders avoided the "overshoot" and crash that were the fate of the other two islands. Patrick V. Kirch attributes the success of Tikopia, compared to Rapa Nui and Mangaia, to scale, both geographic and social: the Tikopia say "We, the Tikopia," seeing themselves as acting together. See Kirch, "Microcosmic Histories: Island Perspectives on 'Global' Change," *American Anthropologist*, 99 (1997), 30–42; Kirch and Douglas E. Yen, *Tikopia: The Prehistory and Ecology of a Polynesian Outlier*, Bernice T. Bishop Museum Bulletin, 238 (Honolulu, HI: Bernice T. Bishop Museum, 1982); Kirch and T. L. Hunt, eds., *Historical Ecology in the Pacific Islands: Environmental and Landscape Change* (New Haven, CT: Yale University Press, 1997). Paul Bahn and John R. Flenley, in their *Easter Island, Earth Island* (London: Thames and Hudson, 1992), take the fate of Rapa Nui to be what could be in store for the planet Earth.

has on them. Most of us have no idea of where our food comes from, in what conditions it is grown and with what effect on local ecosystems. We do not know that our computers and their monitors contain lead, copper, and gold, and that mining these elements is invariably a disaster for local environments. We do not know that our cell phones, as well as our laptops, depend on a super-heavy mud called coltan (from which is derived tantalum, used in the manufacture of capacitors for the circuit boards), and coltan is dug out of the ground – after the removal of large areas of the forest cover – in the rainforests of Eastern Congo, including the Okapi Faunal Reserve, a "protected" area, and helps to perpetuate the civil war in that region. Many of us do not even know where our water comes from.

And even when we know a little about these things, it is hard for us to *care:* these places and people are so remote, they are not around to engage our emotions or our sympathies.

And even if we can be made to care, it is hard for us to see that we bear individual responsibility for what we collectively cause, and harder still to act on this perception. For the world of biosphere people is a world in which many of our actions, taken separately, do a very small (perhaps even imperceptible) amount of harm to each of a very large number of people (or to an ecosystem, or to the healthy functioning of natural processes affecting life on Earth), but *jointly* cause many people to suffer, in some cases horribly, or destroy or degrade an ecosystem. Together, by our actions, we devastate entire watersheds, landscapes, and ecosystems, but each of us makes only a miniscule contribution to this havoc.

This is nicely brought out in Jonathan Glover's parable. A hundred hungry bandits descend on a village of 100 unarmed tribesmen just as they are sitting down to lunch. Each bandit takes at gunpoint the lunch of a single tribesman – who thus goes hungry for the day. By and by the bandits are troubled by the suffering each of them is obviously causing to an identifiable person. They therefore resolve that henceforth, when they raid the village, each of them will take only one bean from the plate of each tribesman. Since each plate contains just 100 beans, the net effect of this new policy is that the tribesmen are all left completely lunchless – as before. But now each bandit can console himself with the thought that, since taking one bean from a tribesman does him no noticeable harm, he has done nobody any harm and therefore has done nothing wrong.[27]

This, of course, is the way it is now for much of what we do. If what each of the fictional "reformed" bandits does is wrong, then so is much of what we in fact do, especially in the affluent parts of the world. But most of us still do not see things this way. Most of us have, or act as if we have, the self-deluding and self-serving beliefs of the "reformed" bandits.

Nauru is an example of the *market as centrifuge* – the market as disintegrator of ecosystems, human lives, and the place-based, inter-generational communities that are both fostered and required by living within the constraints of healthy local ecosystems. But what the Nauruans chose to do (how freely they chose, given what had been done to them and their island before independence, I'll not try to judge) is just what economists would have recommended. They were willing to sell their phosphate (and with it, most of their land, most of the ecosystem of which formerly they had been a part and on which they had depended) and others were willing to buy: so their land was put to a "more productive" use, as is the water of the old Hispanic irrigation communities of New Mexico and as were the lands of the original Americans. In choosing to complete the destruction of Topside, the Nauruans presumably hoped that the investments made from the proceeds of mining would generate a stream of income that would sustain future generations indefinitely (and perhaps also that they would be able to move away from the island when it was ruined). They had hoped for – banked on, as it were – what some call *weak sustainability*. What they aspired to was, in effect, to meet the only obligation that most economists think we have to future generations: we should not reduce their *income*. We cannot predict what *desires* or *preferences* future people will have, and we cannot tell them how they should live their lives. (They too are sovereign consumers, whose preferences will be revealed by their choices and whose welfare lies

---

[27] Jonathan Glover, "It Makes No Difference Whether Or Not I Do It," *Proceedings of the Aristotelian Society*, Suppl. Vol. 49 (1975), 171–190. See also Derek Parfit, *Reasons and Persons* (Oxford: Clarendon Press, 1984), Chapter 3.

in satisfying those preferences.) All we must leave them is the generalized wherewithal to satisfy their desires, and given that the values of everything are fungible and everyone is compensable for any loss, all this requires is that we leave them enough money. We have no obligation to leave them any particular thing – wild salmon, for example, or clean air, or any particular functioning ecosystem, such as Nauru's. (But how many Nauru's can we afford to lose, before even weak sustainability ceases to be achievable?) We need not worry about what will be in the world (apart from generic money capital). There are no *needs* in neoclassical economic theory, only preferences or desires. There is nothing in particular that anyone *must* do or have. There are no particular things that the world *must* contain. We can (continue to) act to transform the planetary climate and hence also all the world's ecosystems – if it pays. (Economists have been busy doing the cost-benefit analyses on global warming – helping governments, with this tool backed by the Market Ideal, to decide the fate of all the world's ecosystems as they have in the past helped to decide the fate of many particular ecosystems.) This absurd yet dangerously influential doctrine really is what is implied by the assumptions of normative neoclassical economic theory ("welfare economics") and, if there should be any doubt about it, economists have spelled it out explicitly.[28]

[28] A representative statement (and by a Nobel laureate in economics) is Robert M. Solow, "Sustainability: An Economist's Perspective," Chapter 11 in Robert Dorfman and Nancy S. Dorfman, eds., *Economics of the Environment: Selected Readings*, 3rd edition (New York: Norton, 1993). There is a good discussion of this issue in Bryan G. Norton and M.A. Toman, "Sustainability: Ecological and Economic Perspectives," *Land Economics*, 73 (1998), 553–568, and Bryan G. Norton, "What Do We Owe the Future? How Should We Decide?," Chapter 17 in Virginia A. Sharpe et al., eds., *Wolves and Human Communities: Biology, Politics, and Ethics* (Washington, DC: Island Press, 2001).

Postscript to part two: "Can selfishness save the environment?"

I borrow the title of this postscript from the title of an article in *The Atlantic Monthly*.[1] The gist of this (glib and sloppy) piece is that, yes, selfishness can save the environment, indeed it is our only hope, because moral suasion, "normative pressures," or "appealing to people's better natures" simply do not work, at least in this area of getting people to stop trashing the natural environment. But this view is not confined to journalists; it is standard among economists. For example, Geoffrey Heal, an economist of repute who has published widely over several decades on the economics of natural resources and the environment, says that there are three broad ways of "persuading people to conserve the natural environment": government regulation, using sanctions; appeals to "principle" or relying on people doing what they ought to do; and arranging things so that choosing conservation is in people's "economic self-interest." Most of us, he goes on to say, would find the first route unacceptable, so it wouldn't work. As for the second approach – "appeals to the best in human nature" – he says "historically this has not worked, and there are no reasons to expect a change in the near future." This leaves the use of economic incentives, which "stands out" and has generally worked and "must be our first line of defense."[2]

---

[1] Matt Ridley and Bobbi S. Low, "Can Selfishness Save the Environment?," *The Atlantic Monthly*, September (1993), 76–86.

[2] Geoffrey Heal, *Nature and the Marketplace: Capturing the Value of Ecosystem Services* (Washington, DC: Island Press, 2000), pp. 129–130. But it has to be said that Heal's statement is a small improvement over Milton Friedman's (in *Capitalism and Freedom*): "Fundamentally, there are only

Readers who have come this far will not be expecting me to assent to Heal's (and, explicitly or implicitly, most economists') dismissal of the second approach (and I hope they will be even less likely to after reading Part Three of this book). Heal offers no argument and no evidence whatever in support of his view. I will come back to this shortly. As for the dim view Heal takes of government regulation – also a standard reflex among many economists (and of course many politicians) – we should note, *first*, that government regulation, though sometimes badly designed and badly implemented, unquestionably has been successful in many areas – including some areas of consumer and environmental protection and of occupational safety and health, as well as in race and gender discrimination, and elsewhere; and *second*, that the "market solutions" actually proposed by economists for environmental problems (I'll describe them shortly) all involve government in some way – indeed markets presuppose and require governance and could themselves be said to be a form of regulation. (This is widely understood, though many economists still seem to suppose that markets arise spontaneously – that they are natural while governments are unnatural impositions on them). Further, like most economists, Heal shows no awareness that government regulation does not have to work in the way he seems to envisage. It does not have to be wholly coercive, but can make use of (and even foster) those capacities and dispositions that (I argue in Parts One and Three) lie behind moral motivation, and in doing so can be both more acceptable and more effective.

What economists usually refer to as "market solutions" to environmental problems are of three kinds.

The first remedy, often called *Pigovian* (after the economist A.C. Pigou),[3] consists simply of imposing taxes on undesirable economic activities and paying subsidies to the producers of desirable goods. In this way, (some of) the external cost imposed on society by an

---

two ways of coordinating the economic activities of millions. One is central direction involving the use of coercion – the technique of the army and the modern totalitarian state. The other is voluntary cooperation – the technique of the market place."

[3] A. C. Pigou, *The Economics of Welfare*, 4th edition (London: Macmillan, 1932).

economic activity can be, as the economists say, internalized – made a part of the producers' costs – so that the total private costs of production are more nearly in line with the social costs; and similarly for external benefits. This approach can of course be used to discourage *any* economic activity deemed undesirable and it was advocated and put into practice before "the environment" became an issue. We should note that, if social costs really are to be brought wholly into line with private costs in this way, we (or the government imposing the taxes and subsidies) would have to know *all* the external harms and benefits of the economic activity in question and we would have to value *all* of them in monetary terms.

The second approach proposes that externalities – those that are "Pareto-relevant," i.e., are such that they can be abated through Pareto-superior moves – can be dealt with through voluntary negotiation (i.e., without government or any third-party intervention) between those who cause the externality and those who suffer or benefit from it ("the victims" for short). The approach is often called *Coasean*, after the economist Ronald Coase.[4] (I'm not sure it should be, since the idea of negotiation, of voluntary agreement, as a way of dealing with external effects surely predates Coase's 1960 article, and the argument for which this article is famous – that if transaction costs are zero negotiation will lead to the same efficient outcome no matter what property rights the parties' start with – is, if true, a useless tautology: if transaction costs are zero, no externalities would ever emerge because they would be dealt with instantaneously as soon as they began to emerge; but transaction costs are never zero in the real world and this theorem tells us nothing about that world. In any case, the theorem holds only for two parties – two "rational" parties sharing knowledge of their preferences – and only when there are no wealth or endowment effects.) Perhaps what we owe to Coase is his insistence that, if externalities are to be abated through voluntary negotiation (and, of course, the enforcement of the resulting agreement), then property rights must first be established. Suppose a rancher's straying cattle eat or trample a farmer's crops. Then, if

---

[4] R. H. Coase, "The Problem of Social Cost," *Journal of Law and Economics*, 3 (1960), 1–44.

the rancher has the right to let his beasts do this (the farmer lacks the right to prevent it), the farmer could pay the rancher to desist, if they could successfully negotiate an agreement to this end. If on the other hand the right is with the farmer, then the externality could be dealt with by the rancher compensating the farmer – by in effect buying the right to damage her crops.

Consider a real-world example that is supposed, by those who favor "market solutions" to environmental problems, to demonstrate the power of the Coasean approach.[5] Much of New York City's water comes from the Catskills, some ninety miles northwest of the city. The natural filtration processes ("ecosystem services") of this 2,000 square-mile watershed, which was almost entirely forested in the early twentieth century, have been effective enough that New York City has not had to treat water from this source, even after much economic development and great increases in runoffs of herbicides, pesticides, fertilizers, oil, and so forth, and the discharge of treated and untreated sewage from often malfunctioning sewage treatment plants in the Catskills – though it is likely that this happy situation would not have lasted much longer. In any case, in 1989, the Environmental Protection Agency (the EPA) issued a new regulation, the Surface Water Treatment Rule, pursuant to the Safe Drinking Water Act, which would have required New York City to build a filtration plant, at a cost of $6–$8 billion, with annual running costs of $300 million. But the EPA could waive this requirement if the city would commit itself to a satisfactory program of restoring and protecting the watershed. This latter would involve, among other things, constructing or improving sewage and septic systems in the watershed, buying land to create buffers around reservoirs, paying farmers for conservation

---

[5] Two books (by authors who are enthusiastic advocates of "market solutions" for environmental problems) that discuss this case (inaccurately) are: Heal, *Nature and the Marketplace*, and Gretchen C. Daily and Katherine Ellison, *The New Economy of Nature: The Quest to Make Conservation Profitable* (Washington, DC: Island Press, 2002). For a more accurate account of what happened, see John Cronin and Robert F. Kennedy, Jr., *The Riverkeepers* (New York: Simon and Schuster, 1997), and for more on this case, see Henry J. Vaux, *Watershed Management for Potable Water Supply: Assessing the New York City Strategy* (Washington, DC: National Research Council, 2000).

easements, and compensating other residents. The price for the city was estimated to be $1.5 billion and, though it was something of a gamble and though there was, needless to say, strenuous opposition, especially from the development lobby, the city and the state eventually agreed on this path. Other cities, in various countries, have taken a similar approach.

The negotiations between New York City and the Catskills property holders and local authorities were complex. They nevertheless had a simplifying feature that would not be shared by negotiations around many environmental externalities: the sources of the externalities in the Catskills were numerous, while the "victim" was really the (relatively unitary and organized) government of New York City, which had an obligation to provide clean water to the city's residents. In most cases of environmental externality, the victims are numerous and unorganized (and usually nearly powerless) while the perpetrator is a powerful corporation. In situations of the latter sort, the prospects for an "efficient" negotiated outcome – or for that matter *any* negotiated agreement – are slender. (This is in the real world, where transaction costs are never zero.) And where the corporation has the right to produce the externality, even if the victims can agree among themselves (perhaps with the help of lawyers or some other go-between) about their approach to the corporation, the most they may be willing to pay (influenced no doubt by what they are *able* to pay) for an abatement of the externality may be less than the least the corporation is willing to accept. (There may be no Pareto-superior moves.) Moreover, it may not be the case – as I hope is clear from Part One and from my earlier discussion of cost-benefit analysis – that the victims *can* be compensated – a crucial (and unremarked) presupposition of the Coasean approach, as it is of all "market" approaches to environmental problems.

It was not a concern for the environment – for the integrity or resilience of ecosystems or for sustainable use of natural resources – that informed Coase's analysis of "the problem of social cost." His concern was market failure resulting from (Pareto-relevant) externalities. Whether the outcome of Coasean negotiation will be good for the environment will depend of course on the preferences of the parties. There is no guarantee that, even if negotiation produces agreement (with "compensation"), the externality will cease: the degree of abatement will depend on the costs and benefits of the parties and (in the real world) on where they start from – their property rights – and it will depend also on their "willingness to accept" or, if the boot is on the other party's foot, their "willingness to pay" for abatement of the externality or for putting up with it. An outcome dependent on these willingnesses does not necessarily have anything to commend it from a noneconomic – a moral, for example, or an ecological – point of view, apart from its having been reached through voluntary exchanges (which seems to be the whole of morality for some economists). The goal of Coasean negotiation is just the same as the goal of a cost-benefit analysis (Coase's analysis is, after all, an extension of the First Fundamental Theorem with which we began this part)[6] and the presuppositions are the same also: it is alright to wreck anyone's environment (or their life) providing you compensate him or her – and everyone can be compensated, with money.

The third approach, sometimes referred to as "cap and trade," involves the creation of what (following Carol Rose) I'll call *tradable environmental allowances*.[7] An important example is the market in rights to emit sulfur dioxide created by the 1990 amendments to the Clean Air Act. These amendments displaced (or to be more precise extended a process that had already partially displaced) a much criticized approach to regulating sulfur dioxide emissions from power stations – an inflexible, top-down, command-and-control system in which a federal agency determined exactly how and by how much every power station must reduce its emissions. Under the new Clean Air Act the EPA issues each utility with a number of allowances, each one permitting it to emit a ton of sulfur dioxide without penalty.

---

[6] See on this Richard D. McKelvey and Talbot Page, "Taking the Coase Theorem Seriously," *Economics and Philosophy*, 15 (1999), 235–247.

[7] See Carol Rose, "Common Property, Regulatory Property, and Environmental Protection: Comparing Community-Based Management to Tradable Environmental Allowances," Chapter 7 in National Research Council, *The Drama of the Commons* (Washington, DC: National Academy Press, 2002). A good survey is Tom Tietenberg's chapter in the same volume: "The Tradable Permits Approach to Protecting the Commons: What Have We Learned?"

If the company wishes to exceed its limit, it has to buy additional allowances, and if it overcomplies with its limit it can sell the unused allowances. The trading is administered by the Chicago Board of Trade. It is left to each company to decide whether and how to comply with its allowed limit. For various reasons (age of plant, proximity to lower-sulfur coal, and so on), some companies will find it cheaper to overcomply and sell allowances, others to undercomply and buy them. The result is that this approach is more efficient than the old command-and-control approach, in the sense that the total cost of meeting any given aggregate level of sulfur dioxide emissions (the "cap") is lower.

The same idea, applied to emissions of carbon dioxide, the principal gas implicated in global warming, is a part of the Kyoto Protocol. (But it's not clear to me whether this application of the idea is workable.)

A similar approach has also been adopted in several fisheries in a new attempt to deal with the overfishing that has brought about the collapse of almost all of the world's commercial fisheries.[8] Here the tradable environment allowances are usually called ITQs – individual transferable quotas. First, a total allowable catch has to be determined (in theory, one that is compatible with a sustainable fishery, but determining what is sustainable is not an easy or uncontroversial matter). Then, consistent with this, quotas are allocated to vessel owners (perhaps according to their average catch in recent years), each quota giving its owner the right to catch so many tons of the target species. The quotas can then be bought and sold, with the consequence that any given aggregate level of fishing (yielding the total allowable catch) will be carried out more "efficiently"

---

[8] A good introduction is Chapter 8 of Michael Berrill, *The Plundered Seas: Can the World's Fish Be Saved?* (San Francisco, CA: Sierra Club Books, 1997). This book gives a good general view of the state of the world's fisheries and how they got that way. On ITQs in U.S. fisheries, see especially the National Research Council report, *Sharing the Fish: Toward a National Policy on Fishing Quotas* (Washington, DC: National Academy Press, 1999). The chapter by Tietenberg mentioned in the last footnote has a good discussion of fisheries ITQs. See also Alison Rieser, "Prescriptions for the Commons: Environmental Scholarship and the Fishing Quotas Debate," *Harvard Environmental Law Review*, 23 (1999), 393–421.

than it would if the same target were achieved through such command-and-control methods as sharply limited fishing seasons (as short as a single day in some actual fisheries).

But the "price" of this efficiency, especially in the case of markets in fishing rights, may be greater inequality or indeed the pauperization or destruction of communities where fishing has been a way of life for centuries.

All three approaches – Pigovian taxes and subsidies, Coasean negotiation, and especially tradable environmental allowances – are promoted by economists simply as "market solutions" to environmental problems. But it is grossly misleading to speak of them in this way. They are *political* solutions that make *use* of economic incentives. Pigovian taxes and subsidies must of course first be set by political decision and must then be levied and collected by a government. And they presuppose a market to intervene in, a set of property rights and trading rules that must be adjudicated and enforced by central government. Coasean bargaining, likewise, requires state-enforced property rights. And markets in tradable environmental allowances have to be put in place and then regulated by government: government allocates the allowances (which are property rights) and monitors and enforces compliance (verifying, for example, that a utility company emits in the course of a year only as much sulfur dioxide as it has a right to, through allocation and purchase), and, before that, the new property rights and the trading rules had to be legislated and the target or cap (the total emissions or the total allowable catch), which is revisable, had first to be politically decided.

It is not, in other words, the free market that produces a solution; central government is involved, is indeed absolutely necessary to these schemes, but in a different way than it is in command-and-control regulation. In both cases, the "solution" is coercive, in the broad sense: both make use of government sanctions. But the "market" approaches make greater use, and in a more decentralized way, of purely economic incentives – they take full advantage of the desire of most people to pay less for a product (all else being equal), and the desires of producers to lower their costs, hence, to make a larger profit (all else being equal), and, if they must satisfy government regulations, to have some freedom in choosing how they do so.

In the case of Pigovian taxes and markets in tradable environmental allowances, then, we are talking about *means* – the implementation of ends that have been deemed socially desirable or at any rate have been politically decided. *The grounds on which the ends are chosen do not have to be economic ones.* The case for these "solutions" made by economists should be thought of as a case for their *cost-effectiveness* as *means*. To the economist, the *end* is Pareto optimality. But it does not have to be. Geoffrey Heal, for example, an enthusiast for "market" approaches to environmental problems, tells us explicitly that the basis for his advocacy is the First Fundamental Theorem (which we discussed earlier) and the goal is to try to meet the conditions for that theorem to hold.[9] But, as I argued earlier, efficiency does not guarantee conservation or sustainable use of natural resources or ecosystem resilience or any other independently desirable outcome, and it should not be our guide and standard. The failure of markets to achieve efficiency should not be the starting point and organizing principle for our approach to Nature (or to anything else): a world in which the conditions of the First Fundamental Theorem are satisfied would be a most horrible world, as I have argued. The role of markets in solving environmental problems should be a restricted, subordinate role. It should be subservient to social ends set independently of the Market Ideal. Thus, for example, constrained markets in water might be allowed to allocate only the water that the people first decide is not necessary to conserve and protect local ecosystems and human communities.[10] And markets in fishing quotas might be constrained in order to preserve fishing communities and individual livelihoods. The Market Ideal and its criterion of allocative efficiency should not be permitted to set or mold our environmental ends, because market failure is *not* the defining characteristic of an environmental problem. Economists, qua economists, have no substantive competence to tell us (for example) what our relations with each other and with the

---

[9] Heal, *Nature and the Marketplace*, pp. 23–25.

[10] See, for example, Sarah F. Bates, et al., *Searching Out the Headwaters: Change and Discovery in Western Water Policy* (Washington, D.C.: Island Press, 1993), and Brent M. Haddad, *Rivers of Gold: Designing Markets to Allocate Water in California* (Washington, DC: Island Press, 2000).

natural world should be. Their role should be confined to helping us achieve our goals, goals set independently of the Market Ideal. And this is emphatically not what they do when they use cost-benefit analysis to decide whether, for example, a valley should be flooded and its inhabitants forced to live their lives differently.

But many economists go much further than advocating these "market solutions." They make the much more sweeping claim that only economic incentives can be relied on to deal with environmental problems. I said earlier that economists generally believe that, if you want to get people to refrain from poisoning and trashing the environment, then you will not get far with "appeals to the best in human nature" (as Heal puts it) or with any sort of moral exhortation. (Or, as Al Capone is said to have remarked, "You can get so much further with a kind word and a gun than you can get with a kind word alone.") Given the assumptions about "human nature" that economists and other Rational Choice theorists make, they are bound to take this line. But they have (understandably) provided little in the way of argument and evidence to support their view. The arguments I make throughout this book would, at the least, strongly suggest caution in embracing the economists' view of this matter. Let me add here a final comment on this, to conclude this Postscript and introduce the next part of the book.

We learned, I hope, in Part One (if we did not already know), of the importance in human lives of ideals and commitments (including moral ideals and commitments to principles) and of living by them, and we shall see further in Part Three how these can, in the right conditions, provide motivating reasons to act, reasons that, moreover, structure and modulate other reasons we have (reasons that may include a desire for money) – and it is reasons, not desires, that explain our actions. All this is ignored or dismissed by economists, who, in proposing or designing "solutions" to environmental problems, thus throw away a sometimes powerful source of motivation. Worse yet, people may in some circumstances (as we began to see in discussing contingent valuation) *resent* being treated as if they valued things (and people) and were motivated and made choices in the way that economists assume, and we shall see in Part Three that if they are so treated, or if they are invited or encouraged to think and act in this way, their inclination to do what they believe they ought to do may be undermined or demobilized. These points apply even to the owners and managers of business firms, and taking account of them leads to a different view of environmental regulation than the one Heal (like most economists) apparently takes for granted when he dismisses (without argument) government regulation as an approach to solving environmental problems. I will take up this alternative view in the book's final chapter.

We should also recall from our earlier discussion of contingent valuation that many people believe that some things are not properly valued in monetary terms and that some public choices should not be made by aggregating individual monetary evaluations (intended as a surrogate for the "choices" that would be produced by a competitive market) but should rather be made by deliberation with a view to arriving at what the people, collectively, believe *should* be done, or should at least pay attention to their judgments. Even when, in response to questions in contingent valuation surveys asking them to put a dollar figure on the value to them of saving Northern spotted owls from extinction, or preserving wild rivers, or repairing ruined landscapes, people say they are willing to pay some nonzero amount, this should not be taken to mean that the number they pick really is the value to them, in dollars, of saving the owls, or whatever. Their response might rather indicate a *belief* that something *should* be done and perhaps also that, if something were to be done, they themselves ought to contribute to the effort, to do their fair share in it. And to say that you are willing, because you believe you ought, to contribute your fair share to a cooperative effort is not at all the same thing as saying that you will personally benefit from this effort.

In any case, for the economist and the Rational Choice theorist, knowing that a person believes that she ought to do her fair share in a cooperative effort still leaves us with the question – the question that the Rational Choice theorist always has to ask – whether it is rational, whether it *pays* to do what she believes she ought to do. On the individualistic (asocial and amoral) conception of rationality assumed by neoclassical economics and Rational Choice theory, it is not rational, in many circumstances, to do your part in a cooperative venture, especially one from which you will benefit even if you do not contribute to it. But, as I shall argue in the next part of the book, normal self-reflective human beings whose choices are framed by their normative self-understandings are *not* rationally required to think or act in this way, but are instead generally disposed to refrain from doing what they take to be wrong, which includes failing to do their individual parts in cooperative efforts from which they will benefit even if they do not contribute, and normative motivation of this kind – motivation to obey a norm of fair reciprocity – is likely to be undermined if they are treated as nothing more than specimens of *Homo economicus*: radically unsocial and therefore amoral, their behavior manipulable by the use of incentives and threats.

I am speaking here of the motivations of people who share a concern for the state of the environment. But many people – whatever they tell the surveyors of public opinion – do not care much about the natural environment or do not understand the effects their own actions have on it. It would certainly be a good thing, if moral appeals are to save the environment, if far *more* people came to see that a great deal of what they are doing is, cumulatively and in the aggregate, environmentally destructive, and to believe that much of it is morally wrong.

Part three

Living in unity, doing your part

Rationality, recognition, and reciprocity

5 Introduction: doing your part

Why do people cooperate? Why do they act in the common interest, for the public good? Why do they do their part in cooperative ventures, in promoting outcomes that will benefit everyone, or everyone in their society or group? For people do sometimes play their part, even when doing so is not without cost to themselves. They vote in elections – going well out of their way, in rain and snow, waiting in line, even (in some places) braving intimidation – though they surely know (most of them) that it is extremely unlikely that their individual votes will make any difference to the outcome. They devote unpaid hours to political campaigns. They mail checks to causes and organizations they support. They join protests, sometimes at considerable risk.

But not everyone does his or her part in mutually beneficial cooperative ventures. Many, for example, do *not* vote, though they have a preference for one candidate over the others and believe that competitive elections are a good thing. And of those who do vote, most do nothing more in the political sphere. Most people do not participate in protests, or join and support political and other organizations from whose efforts they will benefit. Most Americans claim (in surveys) that they want a healthier environment but continue to be wasteful and extravagant consumers and to use any number of products that harm the environment. They do not want fisheries to be destroyed but continue to kill or eat fish from rapidly dwindling stocks. They want to breathe cleaner air and to live in uncongested cities but continue to drive (usually alone) their oversized cars and trucks.

There is a highly influential argument, according to which a person will do his part in mutually beneficial cooperative ventures only if it "pays" – only if the benefits that accrue to him from his participation or contribution outweigh the costs to him. This is the Rational Choice theory of cooperation.[1] Its advocates believe it explains the behavior of those who do not cooperate *and* the behavior of those who do cooperate. Cooperators and noncooperators alike are seen as the same sorts of people, motivated in the same way (assessing the balance of benefits and costs); it's just that the costs and benefits fall out differently for the two groups.

Rational Choice theorists tend to see noncooperation as the default state-of-affairs, and cooperation as problematic. The problem is seen as especially acute in the case of cooperation to produce a *public good*, the technical term introduced by economists for a good that is both *non-excludable* (it's hard to prevent anyone from benefiting from it, once it's around) and *non-rival* or, as I prefer to say, *non-subtractible* (which means that when someone uses or benefits from the good, it does not diminish the amount available for others). Gravity is as pure an example of a public good as one can find – but we don't have to worry about whether people will cooperate enough to keep gravity going. Other examples (perhaps not perfectly non-subtractible in every case) are the protection afforded by the stratospheric ozone layer, broadcast radio waves, biodiversity, the outcomes of elections and certain public policies (these last two being public goods for those who favor them, public bads for those who don't). If a public good is provided (in any amount), an individual will benefit from it whether or not she contributes to its provision; moreover, no matter how many others "consume" it or benefit from it, there'll be just as much of it "left" for her. Why, then, would she contribute to its provision (send money to her public radio station, refrain from using her car) if this is costly to her – assuming that she is "rational"?

[1] The literature on this is very large, and very uneven. There is no decent, reasonably comprehensive treatment of the subject. A good, nontechnical introduction is Chapter 11 of Avinash Dixit and Susan Skeath, *Games of Strategy* (New York: Norton, 1999). It is conventional, especially among nonspecialists, to cite Mancur Olson, *The Logic of Collective Action* (Cambridge, MA: Harvard University Press, 1965) at the origin of the recent wave of writing, but this book is deeply flawed (even granted its Rational Choice premises) and now badly out of date. The basic ideas of the theory can be found in Hobbes, Hume, and Rousseau.

But if people are indeed "rational," there is a problem about cooperation for certain *subtractible* goods as well. Many subtractible goods are used exclusively by one person. Others are *jointly used* or used *in common* by a number of people (just as public goods are – necessarily). There is usually a good reason – often, though not necessarily or exclusively, an economic reason – for this. Grazing land is often used jointly; so are many fisheries. Most forests were jointly used by local groups until recently. Coastal waters, rivers and lakes, aquifers and irrigation systems, streets and parks – all subtractible – may be used in common in this way. It has become conventional to label goods of this kind as *common pool resources* (CPRs), defined as goods that are subtractible and nonexcludable; but the writers who use this definition then proceed to apply it to resources from which potential users are in fact excluded, and quite easily so![2] The point about joint use combined with subtractibility is that the resource can be *over*used – and hence become congested, or degraded, or even destroyed entirely – unless there are effective controls on the use of

---

[2] A very large literature has been produced on resources of this kind in the last twenty years or so. Although it has been produced not just by economists but by people from every social science and by natural scientists interested in natural resources of every kind, this literature, if it is not explicitly Rational Choice theoretic, has been hugely influenced by Rational Choice theory. Much of it is conceptually confused, historically illiterate (about, for example, the nature of the common rights of English villagers before enclosure), and, concerned as it largely is with the efficient production of consumables, unecological. In my view a fresh approach is needed, one that takes on board, among other things, the arguments I make in this book. Fine early work was done by Margaret McKean – see, for example, her article, "The Japanese Experience with Scarcity: Management of Traditional Common Lands," *Environmental Review,* 6 (1982), 63–88 – and by Robert McC. Netting, *Balancing on an Alp: Ecological Change and Continuity in a Swiss Mountain Community* (Cambridge: Cambridge University Press, 1981). A good short review is provided by McKean in "Success on the Commons: A Comparative Examination of Institutions for Common Property Resource Management," *Journal of Theoretical Politics,* 4 (1992), 247–281, and a longer one by Jean-Marie Baland and Jean-Philippe Platteau, *Halting Degradation of Natural Resources* (Oxford: Clarendon Press, 1996), Part II. (Part I of Baland and Platteau's book is a lengthy review of the parts of economic theory – including game theory – that are supposed to be relevant to understanding these "common pool resources," but almost none of it is made use of in the empirical Part II).

the resource. Obviously it can help if those who share the resource can control *who* is allowed to use it, but excludability is in general neither necessary nor sufficient for preventing overuse.

I prefer to use the word *commons* for all those goods or resources that are used in common, whether they are subtractible (and *perhaps* non-excludable, but perhaps with a mechanism of exclusion in place) or non-subtractible and non-excludable (as in the case of public goods, which are *necessarily* used jointly).

All the beneficiaries of such a good – a public radio station's audience, the joint users of a fishery – have a common interest in the continued existence or health of the resource. But according to Rational Choice theory this in itself is not enough to motivate any individual to contribute or to refrain from excessive use, because the benefit to himself of the (typically tiny) difference his contribution makes directly to the provision or maintenance of the good would be outweighed by the cost to him of making it – in a word, it pays to take a free ride on the efforts of the other beneficiaries – *unless* there are further benefits that arise from his contribution or penalties that result from his free riding. For an individual's contribution can have consequences other than a direct increase in the amount of the shared good. First, it can have an indirect effect on the provision of the good by causing other individuals to contribute or to refrain from contributing – as would happen when others' choices are *conditional* on his. Strategic interaction of this kind is the subject of what is called noncooperative game theory. In public goods and other commons problems, the players' preferences are often taken to be those of the repeated Prisoners' Dilemma game (with exponential discounting of future payoffs); and many students of the commons are comforted by the theorems that game theorists have proven, to the effect that, in repeated Prisoners' Dilemmas conditional cooperation (or "tit-for-tat," with the result that all players cooperate in every constituent game) can be an equilibrium if no player discounts future payoffs too steeply.[3] Unfortunately, there is another finding of the

---

[3] Public goods provision as a repeated n-person Prisoners' Dilemma game was first explored in detail in my *Anarchy and Cooperation* (London: Wiley, 1976). The preferences at each point in time of players involved in public goods provision or other commons problems are not necessarily those

theory of repeated games, the so-called Folk Theorem, which implies that when (for example) simple "tit-for-tat" is an equilibrium, there are also very many other equilibria;[4] and agreement is lacking on how "rational" players should act in order to select one of these equilibria, and whether players in practice are likely to succeed in doing this. So the theory of repeated games has turned out to be a lot less helpful than was once thought – even if one accepts the (deeply asocial) conception of rationality (and hence the centrality of Nash equilibrium) on which it is built.

In addition to the direct and indirect effect that an individual's contribution has on the provision of the shared good, there may be selective benefits contingent on his cooperation or penalties if he fails to cooperate. But if we are to explain cooperation by appeal to such "selective incentives" (or "sanctions," if we use this term broadly to cover the promise of benefits as well as the threat of penalties), what can count as a selective incentive? Economists would like to restrict these to material or economic incentives. Thus, a "rational" worker would not join his trade union just because it promised goods he would get whether or not he joined, such as better pay, but mainly because of a variety of selective incentives, such as the sanction of the closed shop; and a "rational" environmentalist would not send money to the Nature Conservancy if they did not send him a nice magazine every quarter. But there are no selective material or economic incentives available to explain turning out to vote, participating in a range of protests and social movements, doing unpaid volunteer work for political campaigns and for some organizations, or doing one's part

of a Prisoner Dilemma. This was argued in Michael Taylor and Hugh Ward, "Chickens, Whales and Lumpy Goods: Alternative Models of Public Goods Provision," *Political Studies,* 30 (1982), 350–370, and again in my book, *The Possibility of Cooperation* (Cambridge: Cambridge University Press, 1987), Chapter 2. I should add that I agree with Ken Binmore that "much of what has been said about the tit-for-tat paradigm is overblown or mistaken." See Binmore's *Game Theory and the Social Contract,* vol. II (Cambridge, MA: MIT Press, 1998), sec. 3.3. (The quote is from p. 313.)

[4] Drew Fudenberg and Eric Maskin, "The Folk Theorem in Repeated Games with Discounting or with Incomplete Information," *Econometrica,* 54 (1986), 532–554. For more on folk theorems, see Drew Fudenberg and Jean Tirole, *Game Theory* (Cambridge, MA: MIT Press, 1991), sec. 5.1.

in many other cooperative ventures and practices. So the Rational Choice theorist may widen the range of admissible selective incentives to include what are sometimes called "social" sanctions, most notably social approval and disapproval. If even these do not suffice to explain some particular cooperative behavior, the Rational Choice theorist can add – as sanctions, as benefits and costs – the pleasant and unpleasant feelings that result from his approval or disapproval *of himself*. Both of these classes of "incentives" have been hauled in to "explain," for example, the fact that quite a lot of people turn out to vote (about 100 million of them in recent U.S. presidential elections, for example) – because without these "social" and "psychological" "incentives" voting would not be "rational." (We will take a closer look at the case of voting in Chapter 8.)

Rational Choice theory is in this way often guilty of "*post hoc* embellishment"[5] – adding incentives (desires) until the behavior at issue is "explained." It is at the same time guilty of "explaining" behavior by redescribing it – finding an incentive behind every action, turning every sort of consideration that affects human behavior into a desire, in effect into a benefit or cost that can be incorporated into individuals' utility functions.

A great deal of evidence – from several decades of experiments with public goods and other games as well as from more naturalistic settings – has strongly suggested that the selfishness axiom is very often violated in situations where people can choose to do their part in mutually beneficial cooperative ventures or alternatively free ride on the contributions of others. Recently, even the economists (who are now taking experimental work more seriously) have concluded that pure selfishness is often moderated by a concern that outcomes be *fair*, or that a *norm of reciprocity* – a norm telling the individual to do his part in a cooperative enterprise if others do theirs – has some influence over people's behavior. But – I shall argue in the rest of this part – they have failed utterly to understand how normative considerations affect behavior and in particular how and when people

---

[5] The phrase is from Donald P. Green and Ian Shapiro, *Pathologies of Rational Choice Theory* (New Haven, CT: Yale University Press, 1994), which discusses examples of this tactic.

are motivated to abide by norms they endorse, such as the norm of fair reciprocity. They have understood these things in terms that can be assimilated to the model of unstructured, competing, foundational desires that I began to criticize in Part One, a model that assumes that acceptance of a norm – believing that one ought to act in certain way – is in itself motivationally inert; or, at best, they have treated norms as shared beliefs that have merely the role of enabling people to coordinate their choices so as to bring about one of the many Nash equilibria that usually coexist in a noncooperative game, with unstructured desires still doing all the motivational work.

In the next chapter I first provide a brief sketch of some principal findings of several decades of experiments with public goods and other games, then comment on the ways in which economists and other Rational Choice theorists have responded to these findings. In the following chapter I make my own argument about how, why, and under what conditions people are motivated by norms of fair reciprocity to do their part in mutually beneficial cooperative ventures. (To repeat a point I made earlier in the book, this argument most certainly does not amount to a general theory of human cooperation. Indeed I find the whole idea of such a theory – never mind one that purports to cover other organisms as well as humans – quite preposterous). In the final chapter I show how this argument appears to account for the behavior of people in a variety of real-life (nonexperimental) settings.

6 The rationality of reciprocity

6.1. Some experimental games

The ultimatum game

Suppose that you are given $100 but on the condition that you must agree with a total stranger on how it should be divided between the two of you. The stranger is in another place, and you must make him an offer – any amount between zero and $100. If he accepts the offer, he gets the amount you offered and you keep the remainder of the $100. But if he rejects the offer, the $100 will be withdrawn and neither of you will get anything. No further offers can be made; there is no communication between the two of you (apart from the communication of the offer); and there will be no further contact of any sort between you and no other consequences of your choices (of the size of the offer, of the decision to accept or reject it). Both of you – the proposer and the responder – know the total sum to be divided. In fact, both of you know all of these things and each knows that the other knows this to be the case.

If the responder is "rational" in the sense standardly assumed by economists and Rational Choice theorists, and is therefore interested solely in maximizing his monetary gain, he will accept any offer, however small. He cannot, after all, do anything else to increase his monetary gain from this situation and he will have no further contact with this stranger. If the proposer believes this to be the case and is also "rational," she will therefore offer the smallest possible amount.

But when people are asked to play the roles of proposer and responder in experiments, proposers rarely make minimal offers and responders nearly always reject very small offers.

This little exercise is known as the *Ultimatum Game*. It was introduced by Werner Güth, Rolf Schmittberger, and Bend Schwarze.[1] In their 1982 article, they reported on experiments they conducted at the University of Cologne, using graduate students. The experiment was subsequently conducted with many other groups in various European countries, the United States, and Japan. The results were always roughly the same. For example, in experiments conducted by Alvin Roth and his collaborators in Pittsburgh, Ljubljana (Slovenia), Jerusalem, and Tokyo, and by Robert Slonim and Roth in the Slovak Republic, the mean offer varied from 40 to 50 percent of the pie, with the modal offer generally at 50 percent. These average offers were nearly always accepted, but offers below 20 percent were usually rejected.[2]

One obvious doubt about the relevance these experiments might have for the real world beyond the university laboratory is that the amounts of money involved are very small, of the order of US$10 for the total pie. The suspicion naturally arises that if, say, $100,000 was the size of the pie, a responder would probably not reject an offer of say 10 percent of this – $10,000 – and that therefore proposers would not be afraid to offer such stingy portions. Universities and research foundations were obviously not going to provide the millions needed to test this suspicion.

---

[1] Werner Güth, Rolf Schmittberger, and Bend Schwarze, "An Experimental Analysis of Ultimatum Bargaining," *Journal of Economic Behavior and Organization*, 3 (1982), 367–388. A useful commentary on the early work on this game is Richard H. Thaler, "The Ultimatum Game," *Journal of Economic Perspectives*, 2 (1988), 195–206, reprinted in his *The Winner's Curse: Paradoxes and Anomalies of Economic Life* (New York: Free Press, 1992).

[2] Alvin E. Roth, Vesna Prasnikar, Masahiro Okuno-Fujiwara, and Shmuel Zamir, "Bargaining and Market Behavior in Jerusalem, Ljubljana, Pittsburgh, and Tokyo: An Experimental Study," *American Economic Review*, 81 (1991), 1068–1095; Robert Slonim and Alvin E. Roth, "Financial Incentives and Learning in Ultimatum and Market Games: An Experiment in the Slovak Republic," *Econometrica*, 66 (1997), 569–596.

But then an anthropologist, Joseph Henrich, had the game played by the Machiguenga, a seminomadic society of horticulturists of the Peruvian Amazon tropical forest, with whom he had previously done field work. He also ran a nearly identical game with a control group consisting of graduate students at the University of California at Los Angeles. The Machiguenga pie was worth about 2.3 days' pay from the logging or oil companies they occasionally work for. The UCLA pie was $160, deemed to be worth about the same to the student subjects. In other words, the monetary stakes were, for the subjects, fairly high.[3]

The UCLA mean offer was 48 percent of the pie, the modal offer 50 percent, in line with the other North American and European results. But the Machiguenga mean offer was only 26 percent of the pie, the modal offer only 15 percent (with a secondary mode at 25 percent), and offers under 20 percent were nearly always accepted.

But in similarly high-stakes experiments with the Ultimatum Game conducted by Lisa Cameron in Yogyakarta (Java), in which the stakes were worth about three months' salary, the mean offer – 44 percent – was not far from that at UCLA, while the modal offer was 50 percent, the same as at UCLA and other "developed" country locations.[4]

So are the Machiguenga anomalous? To find out, Henrich and a team of collaborators carried out the same Ultimatum Game experiment (and some other games to be described shortly) in fourteen other small-scale societies: Quichua and Achuar (tropical forest horticulturists of Ecuador), Hadza (savanna-woodland foragers of Tanzania), Ache (horticulturists and foragers of semitropical woodland, Paraguay), Tsimane (tropical forest horticulturists of Bolivia),

[3] Joseph Henrich, "Does Culture Matter in Economic Behavior? Ultimatum Game Bargaining Among the Machiguenga of the Peruvian Amazon," *American Economic Review*, 90 (2000), 973–979.

[4] Lisa Cameron, "Raising the Stakes in the Ultimatum Game: Experimental Evidence from Indonesia," *Economic Inquiry*, 37 (1999), 47–59. See also Paul Tompkinson and Judy Bethwaite, "Raising the Stakes," *Journal of Economic Behavior and Organization*, 27 (1995), 439–451; and Elizabeth Hoffman, Kevin A. McCabe, and Vernon L. Smith, "On Expectations and Monetary Stakes in Ultimatum Games," *International Journal of Game Theory*, 25 (1996), 289–301.

Au and Gnau (horticulturists and foragers of mountainous tropical forest, Papua New Guinea), Mapuche (sedentary small-scale farmers of the temperate plains, Chile), Torguuds and Kazaks (transhumant pastoralists of Mongolia), Sangu (savanna-woodland farmers and pastoralists of Tanzania), Orma (savanna-woodland pastoralists, Kenya), Lamalera (whalers of Indonesia), and Shona (savanna-woodland farmers, Zimbabwe). Henrich and his collaborators found that mean offers in the Ultimatum Game varied from the lows of 25 percent for the Quichua, 26 percent for the Machiguenga, and 27 percent for the Hadza living in small camps to 57 percent for the Lamalera, with all the rest falling between 33 and 48 percent. Rejections of very low offers were rare in some groups, but common in others.[5]

The authors of the report on this comparative study (including the ten anthropologists who carried out the field experiments) drew two general conclusions from their findings. First, their subjects' behavior violated in every case the selfishness axiom normally assumed by economists.[6] Second, the behavior observed in the experiments "often mirrors patterns of interaction in everyday life."[7] Thus, for example, the Hadza in their ordinary lives have no privacy and can rarely escape from the relentless social pressure to share, so they grow weary of this and seize any opportunity to escape it. The exceptionally low offers they make in the Ultimatum Game are perhaps a reflection of this.[8] The high offers made by the Lamlera are

---

[5] Joseph Henrich, et al., eds., *Foundations of Human Sociality: Economic Experiments and Ethnographic Evidence from Fifteen Small-Scale Societies* (Oxford: Oxford University Press, 2004).

[6] Could the offers be explained as the result of risk-averse expected utility maximizing – as purely self-interested attempts to maximize one's gains given one's degree of risk aversion and given one's estimates of the probabilities of various offers being rejected? The editors reject this possibility as requiring implausible levels of risk aversion for all groups except the Hadza and Sangu. Henrich et al., Chapter 2 of *Foundations of Human Sociality*, at pp. 26–27.

[7] Henrich, et al., Chapter 2 of *Foundations of Human Sociality*, at pp. 10–11 and 38–41.

[8] Frank Marlowe, "Dictators and Ultimatums in an Egalitarian Society of Hunter-Gatherers: the Hadza of Tanzania," Chapter 6 in *Foundations of Human Sociality*.

a reflection of the crucial importance in their lives of cooperation – in the hunting of whales. By contrast, cooperation plays a less important part in the lives of the "individualistic, independent" Machiguenga, who made very low offers in the Ultimatum Game. Michael Alvard – the author of the report on the Lamalera – suggests that where the rewards to cooperation "in day-to-day life" are high, strong norms of cooperation will be established, so that cooperators (and punishers of noncooperators) will be respected, which will dispose people to "play fair" in the Ultimatum Game.[9] This is a plausible argument (at least if it is not taken to be saying that when cooperation pays there will be cooperation). And Jean Ensminger reports that her Orma subjects immediately identified the Public Goods Game (which we'll come to next) with *harambee* – their "institution of village-level contributions for public goods projects such as building a school" – and, bringing to the experiment the normative beliefs or dispositions or habits of *harambee*, they gave generously to the public good.[10]

Public goods, common pool resource, and prisoners'
dilemma games

Another set of experiments has explored behavior in the "Public Goods Game" (PGG).[11] In a typical version of this game each player is given a sum of money (her "endowment") and invited to contribute

---

[9] Michael S. Alvard, "The Ultimatum Game, Fairness, and Cooperation among Big-Game Hunters," Chapter 14 in *Foundations of Human Sociality*.

[10] Jean Ensminger, "Market Integration and Fairness: Evidence from Ultimatum, Dictator, and Public Goods Experiments in East Africa," Chapter 12 in *Foundations of Human Sociality*.

[11] A very useful review of experiments with public goods and related games is John O. Ledyard, "Public Goods: A Survey of Experimental Research," in John H. Kagel and Alvin E. Roth, eds., *The Handbook of Experimental Economics* (Princeton, NJ: Princeton University Press, 1995). Ledyard pays tribute to the early work of the sociologists Gerald Marwell and Ruth Ames, the psychologist Robyn Dawes, and the political scientist John Orbell (beginning in the late 1970s) and of economists R. Mark Isaac and James Walker (beginning in the early 1980s) – see Ledyard's survey for references to their publications – but he does not discuss the earlier experimental work on the Prisoners' Dilemma Game (which has the same payoff structure as many of the experimental Public Goods games), in particular the pioneering work done by Anatol Rapoport and Albert M. Chammah, *Prisoner's*

some portion of it to a hypothetical public good. Each player's contribution is multiplied by some fixed amount – a dollar contributed becoming, say, two dollars' worth of the public good. This is then divided *equally* between all the members of the group: the contributions have produced a *public* good, which by definition benefits everyone whether or not they contribute. So, for example, if you start with an endowment of $10, and everyone in your group of five chooses to contribute $6, which becomes a public good worth $6 × 5 × (say)2, or $60 in total, which is then divided equally among the five of you, for a return of $12 to each of you, then your payoff will be $(10 – 6 + 12), or $16. But if you contribute nothing, while everyone else contributes $6, your payoff will be $(10 – 0 + 9.6), or $19.6. In fact, it is easy to see that you are better off (in monetary terms) contributing nothing *whatever* the others contribute. And this is true for every member of the group – even though if everyone contributes the whole of their endowment they'd all be better off than if all contribute nothing.

But when this game is played with experimental subjects – played just once, among total strangers, with no communication between the players, and with no contact after the game is over – the results are comparable to those of the Ultimatum Game: players contribute an average of 40 to 60 percent of their endowments. In other words, as in the Ultimatum Game the predictions of Rational Choice theory are disconfirmed.

Repeated public goods games have also been conducted in which, after a while, every player is informed of the contributions made by everyone else and then in subsequent games has the opportunity to *punish* those she deems to be noncooperators. A punisher can, *at a cost to herself*, reduce the income of free riders. According to Rational Choice Theory it is not "rational" to punish, and "rational" players, anticipating this, should contribute no more to the public good than they would without punishment. But in fact, in the experiments, free riders (especially if they contribute very small amounts) do get punished, and there is a big jump in cooperation as soon as punishment

Dilemma (Ann Arbor: University of Michigan Press, 1965). I'll discuss the Prisoners' Dilemma Game shortly.

is allowed, and cooperation rises further in subsequent iterations of the game until most players are contributing their entire endowment (even though actual punishment is low in later games).[12] Cooperators, it would seem, are prepared, at some sacrifice, to enforce a norm – a norm requiring everyone who benefits from a public good to contribute to its provision; or any rate they wish not to be taken advantage of. More on this later.

There is a variant of the Public Goods Game that has also been used in numerous experiments – the *Common Pool Resource Game* (or CPR Game). Whereas in the PGG the players choose how much to *contribute* to a public good, in the CPR Game they must choose how much to *withdraw* from a common resource or "common." This game is meant to model the choices available to the users of so-called "common-pool resources" (see my comment on these in Chapter 5), such as jointly used fisheries, pastures, airsheds, and so on. In any case, for both Public Goods Games and CPR Games, if played only once, Rational Choice theory tells each and every player to be a free rider – to let *others* provide the public good or refrain from using the common resource.

In fact, the payoff structure facing players in both of these experimental games is that of the famous *Prisoner's Dilemma Game*, or its n-person generalization. In its simplest version – where two players each choose between two strategies, "cooperation" and "noncooperation" – each player can get a higher payoff by not cooperating, *given* the strategies chosen by the other players (no matter what they are), but everyone would be better off if they all cooperated than if they all chose noncooperation. This was in fact the first game to be played experimentally, and it was devised in June 1950 by two mathematicians – Melvin Dresher and Merrill Flood, who do not always get the credit for it – as a test of the solution concept that had just been proposed by their colleague John Nash. This was at the RAND Corporation, a think tank for the Cold War, which seems to have been a crucible for and assured the funding of much postwar

---

[12] Ernst Fehr and Simon Gächter, "Cooperation and Punishment in Public Goods Experiments," *American Economic Review*, 90 (2000), 980–994.

research in economics and game theory[13] Dresher and Flood's initiative initially led nowhere (and the problems with Nash equilibrium as a solution concept are still not resolved, I believe), but in the decades in which game theory languished (mainly the 1960s and 1970s), one man, the mathematical biologist/psychologist Anatol Rapoport, who believed that, even in arms races and other Prisoners' Dilemmas, the players could cooperate, undertook the first extensive systematic experimental study of Prisoners' Dilemmas. (Rapoport's work – the work of a pacifist and a critic of game theory and Cold War "gaming" – is also rarely mentioned by economists.)[14] Since then, experimental Prisoners' Dilemmas have been the subject of many hundreds of studies.

What has been learned from all these experiments? The first crucial finding, replicated many times, is that, even when the Prisoners' Dilemma is played just once and every effort is made by the experimenter to ensure that the players are total strangers who will never encounter one another again, *about half of the players choose to cooperate*. Rational Choice theory predicts complete *non*cooperation (which

---

[13] For some discussion of this and other World War II and Cold War origins of game theory, see Philip Mirowski's important book, *Machine Dreams: Economics Becomes a Cyborg Science* (Cambridge: Cambridge University Press, 2002). Mirowski gives proper credit to Flood as the inventor (with Dresher) of the Prisoners' Dilemma ("arguably the most important game scenario in the entire history of game theory") and as a founder (also strangely neglected by all the economists now working on and writing surveys) of "experimental economics." Flood's earliest experiments were written up as RAND Corporation memos in 1951–52. For discussion of and references to his work, see Mirowski's book at pp. 353–360. Mirowski writes (p. 354) that at RAND, "Flood became rapidly disaffected from the game theory research program, because: (1) so-called irrational behavior was more commonplace in real-life situations than the game theorists would care to admit; (2) the individualist character of rationality had been exaggerated to an untenable degree; and (3) the Nash bargaining solution and the Nash equilibrium concept were deeply unsatisfying and implausible." Most of Flood's skepticism still applies to game theory, even to the economists who have accepted that the experiments I discuss here have shown the untenability of the standard selfishness axiom.

[14] Rapaport and Chammah, *The Prisoner's Dilemma*. For Rapoport's critical work, see, for example, "Critiques of Game Theory," *Behavioral Science*, 4 (1959), 49–66, and *Strategy and Conscience* (New York: Schocken, 1964).

is the dominant strategy for each player, so that mutual noncooperation is the Nash equilibrium).

Suppose now that this game is played a finite number of times, and this is common knowledge to the players. There is a Rational Choice theoretical argument (the backwards induction or "zip-back" argument) that concludes that, even here, the players should never cooperate, no matter how many times the game is repeated.[15] Again, experiments contradict this.[16]

The second most significant finding to come out of several decades of experimental work with Prisoners' Dilemmas is that *discussion* (and some other forms of communication) between the players greatly increases the rate of cooperation. This was verified in the statistical metaanalysis of Prisoners' Dilemma experiments conducted by David Sally.[17] He examined more than 100 articles, from which he extracted 37 studies (containing 130 distinct experimental treatments) that were sufficiently detailed, comparable, and representative. In general, the predictions of Rational Choice theory are not supported: "it is safe to say that one-trial games reveal very little rationally self-interested behavior." The principal exceptions to this generalization are that cooperation decreases with increases in the temptation to defect (which in the two-person game is the payoff gain to be had from unilateral defection from mutual cooperation) and with increases in the size of the group. The greatest and statistically most significant increase in cooperation, according to this meta-analysis, occurs when the players are allowed to *discuss* their dilemma before making their choices. In these discussions, the players generally make *promises* to cooperate, and the increase in cooperation

[15] But if a player has any uncertainty about the rationality of the other player – if in particular there is some small (nonzero) probability that she will play tit-for-tat – then this zip-back argument does not go through. See David M. Kreps, Paul Milgrom, John Roberts, and Robert Wilson, "Rational Cooperation in the Finitely Repeated Prisoners' Dilemma," *Journal of Economic Theory*, 27 (1982), 245–252.

[16] See, for example, Robyn Dawes, "Social Dilemmas," *Annual Review of Psychology*, 31 (1980), 169–193.

[17] David Sally, "Conversation and Cooperation in Social Dilemmas: A Meta-Analysis of Experiments from 1958 to 1992," *Rationality and Society*, 7 (1995), 58–92.

is especially great if promising is universal – if agreement to cooperate is consensual.[18] Neither of these – discussion (mere words) and promising (more words) – should have any effect, according to Rational Choice theory; for as Thomas Hobbes famously said (in Chapter XVII of *Leviathan*), "Covenants, without the Sword, are but Words, and of no strength to secure a man at all." Unsurprisingly, there is also significantly more cooperation when the experimenter specifically elicits promises from the players and when the players are actually told to work together or help each other, and there is less cooperation when players are directed to do better than the others – unsurprising unless, again, you are a Rational Choice theorist. In repeated games, the mere fact that players could see each other when making their choices had a significant (positive) effect on the rate of cooperation. I note also that Sally found that manipulating the entire group to create an in-group bias did not have a significant effect on the rate of cooperation. I will return to these findings later.

Some other experimental games

There are several other simple games that have been played experimentally. I'll briefly describe three that are relevant to my argument here.

The *Dictator Game*, introduced by Daniel Kahneman, Jack Knetsch, and Richard Thaler,[19] is like the Ultimatum Game but

[18] See John M. Orbell, Alphons J. C. van de Kragt, and Robyn M. Dawes, "Explaining Discussion-Induced Cooperation," *Journal of Personality and Social Psychology*, 54 (1988), 811–819, and their references to earlier work; and Norbert L. Kerr and C. Kaufman-Gilliland, "Communication, Commitment, and Cooperation in Social Dilemmas," *Journal of Personality and Social Psychology*, 66 (1994), 513–529.

[19] Daniel Kahneman, Jack L. Knetsch, and Richard Thaler, "Fairness as a Constraint on Profit Seeking: Entitlements in the Market," *American Economic Review*, 76 (1986), 728–741. And see Robert Forsythe et al., "Replicability, Fairness and Pay in Experiments with Simple Bargaining Games," *Games and Economic Behavior*, 6 (1994), 347–369, and Elizabeth Hoffman, Kevin McCabe, and Vernon L. Smith, "Social Distance and Other-Regarding Behavior in Dictator Games," *American Economic Review*, 86 (1996), 653–660.

without the possibility of rejection: an allocation is "dictated." In experiments, proposers give the recipients amounts varying from about 10 to about 30 percent of the total – less than in the Ultimatum Game experiments, as one would expect, but still in apparent contradiction to received Rational Choice theory. Of the results of the Ultimatum Game experiments, one might say: although responders who reject nonzero offers, in order to punish Proposers they deem unfair, stingy or insulting, cannot be acting "rationally," the Proposers might be making a "rational" calculation of what they can get away with given what they believe about Responders. But "Proposers" in the Dictator Game are making no such calculation, so (some would say) their behavior is a surer indicator of the human propensity to be fair.

In the *Trust Game*, introduced by Joyce Berg, John Dickhaut, and Kevin McCabe,[20] one player ("the Investor") chooses some portion of his given endowment to send to the other player ("the Trustee"). This amount is tripled by the experimenter. Then the Trustee must choose how much, if any, of the increased amount to return to the Investor. All this is common knowledge to the two players. Rational Choice theory predicts that the Trustee would return nothing. But in the experiments, Investors send about half of their endowments and Trustees return a bit less than the amount sent them.

The *Gift Exchange Game*, introduced by Ernst Fehr and his associates,[21] in which an "Employee" (or buyer) offers a wage contract with wage rate w and asks for a level of effort e. The "Worker" (or seller) then chooses whether to accept and, if she does, chooses an effort level from some range. Whatever e is actually chosen, the Employer must pay the offered w. If the Worker rejects the offer, both sides get nothing. The payoffs are such that "rational" Workers

20 Joyce Berg, John Dickhaut, and Kevin McCabe, "Trust, Reciprocity and Social History," *Games and Economic Behavior*, 10 (1995), 122–142.
21 Ernst Fehr, Georg Kirchsteiger, and Arno Riedl, "Does Fairness Prevent Market Clearing? An Experimental Investigation." *Quarterly Journal of Economics*, 108 (1993), 437–460. See also Fehr et al., "When Social Norms Overpower Competition – Gift Exchange in Labor Markets," *Journal of Labor Economics*, 16 (1998), 324–351; and Fehr et al., "Gift Exchange and Reciprocity in Competitive Experimental Markets," *European Economic Review*, 42 (1998), 1–34.

should choose minimum effort and "rational" Employers, expecting this, should choose the wage just large enough to induce workers to accept their offer. But, once again, experimental players behave differently: Employers generally offer contracts with wages well above the minimum and workers tend to respond with effort levels well above the minimum (averaging 4.4 on a 1 to 10 scale). About 30 percent of the workers always choose the minimum effort level. These experiments appear to confirm the earlier suggestion of George Akerlof that when employers pay workers more than they have to, the workers are likely to respond by working harder or doing better work.[22] Akerlof referred to this reciprocity as "gift exchange."

6.2. Doing what we ought to do, if it pays

What are we to make of people's behavior in these experiments, much of which violates the assumption of self-interest – the canonical cornerstone axiom of neoclassical economic theory and of Rational Choice theory more generally? The experiments seem to show that many people are concerned not only with their own payoff but with other people's payoffs as well; they seem, indeed, to show that many people care about the *fairness* of outcomes and are *willing to do their part*, provided that others do their parts, to bring about an outcome from which they all benefit, even though they could get a higher payoff if they did not cooperate in this way. Most interpreters of the experiments conclude that most people subscribe to a *norm of reciprocity* ("I'll do my part if you'll do yours") or a *norm of fairness*, governing participation in a cooperative endeavor or the division of the gains from cooperation. Actually, of course, reciprocity, or cooperation, generally *requires* a norm of fairness, at least in the sense of a standard for what constitutes cooperation on the part of each individual – for what is to count as a contribution, as "doing one's part."[23] We will speak, then, of a *norm of fair reciprocity*.

[22] George A. Akerlof, "Labor Contracts as Partial Gift Exchange," *Quarterly Journal of Economics*, 97 (1982), 543–569.
[23] Allan Gibbard, *Wise Choices, Apt Feelings: A Theory of Normative Judgment* (Cambridge, MA: Harvard University Press, 1990), pp. 261–262.

I feel more confident of the truth of this generalization about the widespread acceptance of norms of fair reciprocity as it applies to modern, "developed" societies, where it is supported also by a wealth of observation of behavior in more naturalistic settings.

Economists, a few of them at any rate, have recently begun to write as if they have (finally) discovered the power of norms. Some game theorists had conceded that social norms may play a crucial role in helping players coordinate on one of the many equilibria that repeated games usually have (we'll see an example of this argument at work in the next chapter); but in this role the norms themselves have no motivational power – they are just wheeled out to save noncooperative game theory from a crippling indeterminacy. Now, however, some economists seem to have become persuaded, mainly as a result of experiments of the kind described in the last section (and especially of the experiments they themselves conducted), that norms themselves, or at least norms of fair reciprocity, have the power to motivate us to act in ways apparently inconsistent with the assumption of self-interest. But in fact economists and game theorists have *not* discovered the power of norms. They are, in effect, still saying, "Yes, there are social norms, but does it pay to obey them?" They are still looking for an extraneous end that would be served, a *desire* that would be satisfied, by compliance with the norm. Normative judgments – judgments that we ought to comply with a social norm – are for them (still) motivationally inert. They are in effect treating all normative judgments as if they were prudential, which is to say as judgments that are conditional on the presence of a desire, as where my judgment that I ought (or should or must) work harder means only that, if I want to finish my book this year, then I had better work harder. The possibility that there are categorical "oughts," normative judgments that apply to someone even when she has no desire that would be satisfied by acting in accordance with the judgment, is still lost on the economist and the Rational Choice theorist. It is usually taken to be a mark of *moral* judgment that it is of this nonprudential kind. That I would not withdraw my judgment that you should refrain from gratuitously torturing animals if I discovered that such restraint would satisfy no desire of yours is part of what makes this a moral judgment.

Let us briefly examine, then, how economists and other Rational Choice theorists have responded to the findings of these experimental Ultimatum, Prisoner's Dilemma, Public Goods, and other games that seem to show that people often do not conform to the predictions of Rational Choice theory but are moved by a belief that they ought to do their part – by a norm of fair reciprocity. The main responses are of two kinds.[24]

The first approach has been simply to modify each agent's utility function, for example by *assuming* that she cares about the *difference* between others' payoffs and her own payoff, as well as her own payoff per se. (Mathew Rabin proposes a model that incorporates the other players' *intentions* as well.[25]) In one model, each player is assumed to maximize a weighted sum of her own monetary payoff and the differences between her own payoff and the payoffs of the other players – with more (negative) weight being attached to differences, or inequities, that are to her disadvantage than to differences that are to her advantage. This model (when different values of the parameters in the utility functions are plugged in) can account for, or at any rate reproduce, some of the experimental behavior found in the Ultimatum Game and the Public Goods Game.[26]

---

[24] In addition to these Rational Choice approaches, there is an approach that, though not a Rational Choice approach, has been taken up recently by some economists and game theorists (as well as evolutionary ecologists and anthropologists). The aim is to show, usually by means of mathematical models and computer simulations, how strategies (of reciprocity or "tit-for-tat," for example) or underlying dispositions (to reciprocate, or to share, say) could have evolved by natural selection on genetic variation or by selection (especially at the level of groups) on cultural variation or by both of these together. But these evolutionary models do not help us understand how norms motivate. Indeed, like the work I discuss in the text, they do not even recognize what is most distinctive about norms – their normativity – so do not help us understand how endorsing a norm – accepting that one ought to act in the way it specifies – can have motivational power.

[25] Matthew Rabin, "Incorporating Fairness into Game Theory and Economics," *American Economic Review*, 83 (1993), 1281–1302.

[26] Ernst Fehr and Klaus M. Schmidt, "A Theory of Fairness, Competition, and Cooperation," *Quarterly Journal of Economics*, 114 (1999), 817–868. Herbert Gintis has a version of this in his *Game Theory Evolving* (Princeton, NJ: Princeton University Press, 2000), pp. 258–261. He calls the actor so

Several models of this sort have been proposed, all of them assuming that the players' utilities are functions of the other players' payoffs as well as their own.[27] They are, of course, still utility-maximizing models. They "explain" the apparently cooperative or fair behavior displayed in the experimental games essentially by assuming a *preference* for fairness or equality (or in Rabin's model a *desire* to be treated "kindly," where this is defined in terms of payoff differences) and by assuming that players are willing to trade off fairness against their own (monetary) payoffs. This is of course the economists' (and Rational Choice theorists') characteristic way of proceeding: "explaining" everything by assuming preferences or desires of an appropriate form. The most charitable thing one can say about this whole approach is that it produces radically incomplete "explanations": incomplete because they leave unanswered a range of questions about *why* (and which and when) people have preferences or desires of the required form; and radically so because in assuming preferences for fairness or equality these "explanations" come close to assuming what has to be explained, and understanding the genesis of such preferences (or of any attitudes) would in fact be extremely challenging, far more so than constructing simple mathematical models that fit the observations. But the real problem with this approach is not its incompleteness. The real problem derives from its tacit presupposition that the role in individual choice of normative considerations or ideals (such as fairness) can be captured by preferences or desires.

modeled *Homo egualis*. I suggested a simple model of this kind in *Anarchy and Cooperation* (London: Wiley, 1976), Chapter 4.

[27] For three examples (in addition to the articles cited in the last two notes), see D. Levine, "Modeling Altruism and Spitefulness in Experiments," *Review of Economic Dynamics*, 1 (1998), 593–622; G. E. Bolton and A. Ockenfels, "A Theory of Equity, Reciprocity, and Competition," *American Economic Review*, 90 (2000), 166–193; and Gary Charness and Matthew Rabin, "Social Preferences: Some Simple Tests and a New Model," *Quarterly Journal of Economics*, 117 (2002), 817–869. Another example of an economist taking into account the influence of norms by merely including "the disutility from deviation from the social norm" in the agent's utility calculation – adding it, in fact, to the utility from income and the intrinsic utilities of work and leisure – can be found in Assar Lindbeck, "Incentives and Social Norms in Household Behavior," *American Economic Behavior*, 87 (1997), 370–377.

The second Rational Choice approach tries to explain norm obedience in terms of *sanctions*: people obey norms because whatever gain is to be had from not conforming to the norm is outweighed by the expected costs of being sanctioned.[28] This argument runs quickly into a number of problems. First, the Rational Choice theorist has to explain why a "rational" person would want to undertake the chore of sanctioning people or to contribute to a collective scheme of sanctioning with perhaps a specialized agency of enforcement, which itself requires the solution of a collective action problem. After all, a "rational" individual never does anything unless it pays; surely he would prefer others to do the job, and take a "free ride" on their efforts? Are those who fail to sanction themselves sanctioned? Doesn't this lead to an infinite regress?

When this point was first put to me (long ago, when I was still a Rational Choice theorist) after I had presented a paper arguing that the social sanctions available to small communities were what enabled peasants to mount rebellions (in the context of the French and Russian Revolutions), my answer was that the cost of applying such sanctions was slight and a person cannot be expected to act "rationally" in the sense required by Rational Choice theory when (among other conditions) the costs and benefits (to him or her) of the alternative courses of action are very small.[29] This argument about the domain of Rational Choice theory is, I now believe, distinctly unsatisfactory. It might be less embarrassing to Rational Choice theory if it accounted for *all* of the theory's failures. But as we have already seen (in Part One), people can fail to act "rationally" even when the material stakes are very high, because the economic considerations, which might be potent motivators in other contexts, are, for the individual in question in the choice situation in question, excluded, silenced, or

---

[28] Some Rational Choice theorists actually *define* norms as (or as including) systems of sanctions. Obviously, this leaves no room from the start for the possibility that simply endorsing a norm can itself have motivating power.

[29] The paper was "Rationality and Revolutionary Collective Action" (eventually published in Michael Taylor, ed., *Rationality and Revolution* [Cambridge: Cambridge University Press, 1988]) and the problem about sanctioning non-sanctioners was put to me by Allan Gibbard at a conference at Halifax, Nova Scotia in 1984.

demoted by some other reason or reasons. Moreover, the argument comes close to saying that people will be moved by incentives – the incentives specified in the theory – if and only if those incentives are "big" enough, which is a tautology. And if the rationale for the argument is that people will be obliged, or forced, to act "rationally" when the stakes are high because if they did not they would fail to survive, then "rationality" is doing none of the explanatory work and one needs instead an evolutionary theory showing how non-"rational" actors or non-"rational" behaviors get selected or filtered out.

Rational Choice theory has another good reason to cut off the infinite regress, namely that failures to punish norm violators are not normally punished.[30] Indeed, there are sometimes norms *against* sanctioning violators of certain norms.[31] (Totalitarian societies may provide exceptions.)

So if the sanctions are costly to apply, Rational Choice theory has a problem. Suppose, then, that the sanctions are costless. This is a plausible claim to make about the sanctions that consist of expressions of approval and disapproval by other people – perhaps true *only* of these sanctions (unless we count internal or self-sanctioning, about which more in a moment).[32] These were indeed the sanctions I had in mind when making the claim, referred to earlier, about the domain of Rational Choice theory. I also rashly assumed, like many Rational Choice theorists, that the desire for social approbation (or to avoid disapprobation) was the most important motivation after economic or material incentives.

But if someone expresses (dis)approval of another and he does so *not* just in order to avoid calling down sanctions on his own head, then presumably he does so because he does in fact (dis)approve

---

[30] This point is made by Jon Elster in *The Cement of Society* (Cambridge: Cambridge University Press, 1989) at pp. 132–133.

[31] Elizabeth Anderson, "Beyond *Homo Economicus:* New Developments in Theories of Social Norms," *Philosophy and Public Affairs,* 29 (2000), 170–200.

[32] See Philip Pettit, "*Virtus Normativa:* Rational Choice Perspectives," *Ethics,* 100 (1990), 725–755 – a Rational Choice account of norms, in which it is assumed that "people are moved in great part, though not exclusively, by a concern that others not think badly of them and, if possible, that they think well of them."

of the other's behavior – because he endorses the norm. And surely, anyone who endorses the norm – who thinks the behavior in question is wrong – and has therefore a *reason* to sanction others, has the same reason to conform to the norm himself. I will come to what I take that reason to be in the next chapter.

Are social approval and disapproval in fact effective motivators and, if so, how do they motivate? Jerome Kagan has concluded from his decades of studying child development that "A desire to avoid, or to deny, labeling the self as bad increases in intensity as the child matures; in time, it will take precedence over fear of disapproval or punishment as the primary governor of behavior."[33] This does not imply, of course, that as they grow older people come to stop caring about others' approval altogether. Most people do care about what others think of them (sometimes even for purely instrumental reasons – because it is seen as necessary for the attainment of some further end), but what most of us really want is to *deserve* their good opinion; and to feel that one deserves others' good opinion is to believe one has lived up to one's own ideals. We generally do not care much that others have a low opinion of us for failing to live up to *their* standards unless we share those standards. When we are susceptible to the disapproval of others for failing to abide by some norm, then we are susceptible also to self-disapproval for that failure; and it seems likely that social disapproval works by triggering *self*-assessment – calling us to our own ideals, telling us to be true to ourselves (the selves I described in Chapter 2).

Rational Choice theorists, if they consider such *self*-assessment, take account of it in the context of conformity to norms by assuming that the "rational" individual would count *as a cost* the prospect of feeling bad if he were to violate a norm. The emotions of self-assessment, such as guilt and shame, are simply entered into his utility function. Social disapprobation of norm violators is assumed to affect individual choice through the emotion of shame. Shame, in other words, is taken to require public exposure and the expression by others of their disapproval – to require that others engage in the

---

[33] Jerome Kagan, *Three Seductive Ideas* (Cambridge, MA: Harvard University Press, 1998), pp. 173–174.

activity often called shaming. Guilt, on the other hand, is assumed to be a private affair. Thus, Robert Frank, economist: "[W]hen a person knows he is responsible for an action that harms others, but no one else knows it, he feels guilt. If others do know, he feels both guilt and shame." And of these and other negative emotions, he says: "The desire to avoid the various unpleasant affective states . . . is the principal motivating force behind moral behavior."[34] Likewise, according to Samuel Bowles and Herbert Gintis, also economists: "Shame differs from guilt in that while both involve the violation of a norm, the former but not the latter is necessarily induced by others knowing about the violation and making their displeasure known to the violator."[35] And Bowles and Gintis proceed in their formal model simply to add these emotions of self-assessment to utility functions to be maximized along with the agent's own material payoff and her valuation of others' payoffs.

This, I submit, mistakes the nature of shame and the way shame affects behavior. The words "shame" and "guilt" are indeed often used in roughly the ways I have just quoted; but I believe "shame" should be used to mark an emotion more radically different from guilt than these definitions suggest, and one that shapes behavior more radically and more powerfully than guilt.[36] (The difference between guilt and shame on the "private" versus "public" account is perhaps merely that shame adds embarrassment to the emotion of guilt.)

The emotion of *guilt* is the more straightforward of the two. We feel guilt when we think we are doing or have done something forbidden, something that violates a rule or norm. For this, however, it is not necessary that in doing what is forbidden we cause harm to others,

---

[34] Robert H. Frank, *Passions Within Reason: The Strategic Role of the Emotions* (New York: Norton, 1988), p. 153.

[35] Samuel Bowles and Herbert Gintis, "The Economics of Shame and Punishment," paper presented at conference on *The Economy as a Complex Evolving System, III* in honor of Kenneth Arrow, Santa Fe Institute, November 2001.

[36] My view of guilt and shame derives especially from Gabriele Taylor, *Pride, Shame, and Guilt* (Oxford: Clarendon Press, 1985) and the similar views of Helen Merrell Lynd, *On Shame and the Search for Identity* (New York: Harcourt Brace, 1958). See also Bernard Williams, *Shame and Necessity* (Berkeley: University of California Press, 1993), especially at pp. 88–95.

though that is often the case. A person can feel guilty about doing things that will harm only himself, or harm nobody at all. Even if harm might result, perhaps indirectly, it is not *that* thought that makes him feel guilty but rather the thought that he has done something forbidden. And in guilt, as opposed to shame, it is the act that is judged, not the self. The act might precipitate self-reflection of a sort that leads to shame, but until that happens it is only the emotion of guilt that is felt. It is for this reason that a feeling of guilt can be erased or diminished by punishment and reparation, while shame cannot be.

A person feeling *shame* has seen herself in a different light, and what she sees she does not like. She sees that she is not what she thought she was or not what she believes she ought to be. Whatever it is that precipitates this new view of herself, it is not, as it is when she feels guilt, any particular action of hers that she judges in feeling shame, but her *self*, what she is, and her failure to live up to her ideal self. Feeling shame, then, though it may be triggered by some very specific occurrence, is not, like guilt, focused and localized: it involves the whole self, not some specific act that is, as it were, detachable from the self. It therefore cannot be removed or reversed by some act of contrition or repentance or by suffering punishment, as a feeling of guilt can be. Shame and guilt can be triggered by the same act: violating a norm, doing something wrong, causing someone harm may cause me to feel guilty, but it may also precipitate a reassessment of myself – the source of the act – and a recognition of my failure to be the better self that I had thought I was. The self-assessment that characterizes the emotion of shame can be *triggered* in all sorts of ways; the trigger does not have to be, and the emotion itself does not require, public exposure, or criticism or ridicule by others, or even the thought that others disapprove of me or my actions. For shame to be felt, there is no need, as many writers suppose, for the activity called shaming. What is necessary is a shift in the way the person sees herself, and for this to occur an actual observer, or even an imagined observer, is only a possible prop.

So the emotion of shame is truly an emotion of *self*-assessment – and as such presupposes that there is a self to assess. The self that is assessed is the ideal identity described in Part One: the self-understanding that is normative for the person.

It follows from this account of shame that shame does not work on us like a *sanction*. The prospect of the disagreeable (sometimes devastatingly and lastingly painful) feeling that is a part of shame is not something we think of as a cost, to be added to other costs and balanced against whatever material and other benefits might accrue to us from failing to do the right thing, to live up to our ideals. If this is how a person thinks about "shame," then it is not shame she is or would be experiencing.[37]

It is nice not to suffer from *agenbite of inwit* and instead to enjoy a little "sun-shine of the spotless mind" (Pope), but you are not likely to if you see these things as elements of your utility function to be weighed against other things you want.

In the end, then, all the Rational Choice attempts at explaining obedience to the norm of fair reciprocity proceed by postulating *desires*. All of them accept the model of unstructured competing desires that I described in Part One. It is this very general, and usually tacit, assumption that I wish to reject. What is extraordinary about these explanations is that not one of them recognizes what is distinctive about norms, namely their normativity, their "oughtness." Each of these explanations has, in effect, assumed tacitly that accepting or endorsing a norm, or having a normative belief, is in itself motivationally inert. Motivation comes from something else: from a desire to avoid bad consequences (material penalties, social disapprobation, the alleged costs of feeling shame), or a desire to reduce the discrepancy between others' payoffs and one's own. In this way, the economists reduce normative behavior to utility maximizing and absorb what they had initially seemed to recognize as behavior that violates the self-interest axiom into the conventional Rational Choice framework. And in this way they fail utterly to do justice to the way in which norms of fair reciprocity matter to us and move us.

---

[37] This point is made by Jon Elster in his *Alchemies of the Mind* (Cambridge: Cambridge University Press, 1999), p. 155.

7 Normativity, recognition, and moral motivation

Behavior in the experimental games described in the last chapter cannot, then, be explained by self-interested desires alone, whether the desires are for the benefits of cooperation in later periods, or to satisfy one's taste for equity, or to avoid social or other external sanctions, or to avoid the alleged internal sanctions of shame or guilt. Nor can much cooperative behavior in the real world – the world outside the experimenters' laboratories – be explained in this way. (We'll see some examples in the next chapter.) This is not to say that sanctions are never required, for example, to deter crime; but, as H. L. A. Hart said, they are not "the normal motive for obedience" to the law,[1] and I have argued that they cannot be the *only* motive sustaining cooperation.

What then is the normal motive – the motive of normally social human beings – for obeying the norm of fair reciprocity, if it is not self-interest? The short answer is that most people think it is *wrong* not to obey this norm – they believe they *ought* to obey it. But what do we mean when we say that an action is wrong, and how can a mere belief or judgment that an act is right *motivate* us to do it?

For the economists and other Rational Choice theorists (and some philosophers as well), there is no conceptual or internal connection between moral belief and motivation. They ask, in effect: "You believe or accept that you *should* do X, but is it in your *interest* to do what you

---

[1] H. L. A. Hart, *The Concept of Law* (Oxford: Clarendon Press, 1961), p. 193.

believe you should do?" For these theorists, moral belief produces
motivation only via an intervening desire: a desire to avoid the sanctions, external or internal, that would be the consequences of failing
to do what you think is right, or perhaps, most simply and directly,
a "desire" to do what you think is right. (But if the latter "desire"
really were a desire like the desire for chocolate cake, and if it were
true that action can be motivated only by desire, then there would be
no distinct category of *moral* persons. There would just be people who
were moved by sanctions or whose tastes ran to doing what they took
to be "right".) To explain a person's conformity to a norm in terms
of prudential reasons ("sanctions," broadly defined) is to ignore the
norm's normativity; it is to assume that the "oughtness" of the norm
has in itself no power over her, that her acceptance of the norm is in
itself motivationally inert.

The only argument about moral motivation that I now find persuasive – an argument that gives a convincing general account of what it
is for an act to be wrong and at the same time shows how a judgment
that an act is wrong can provide a motivating reason not to do it – is
the one developed and defended in T. M. Scanlon's *What We Owe to
Each Other*.[2] I am not going to try to do justice to this rich book, but
I hope the very brief sketch of its central idea that follows will suffice
for my purposes here. (It should be read in the light of the arguments
about ideals, desires, and reasons that were made earlier, in Part One,
Chapter 2). Then, I shall say something about the circumstances in
which those who accept the norm of fair reciprocity – who think it
wrong not to obey this norm – will in fact be moved by it.

According to Scanlon's theory, an act is wrong "if its performance
under the circumstances would be disallowed by any set of principles
for the general regulation of behavior that no one could reasonably
reject as a basis for informed, unforced general agreement." This
is an *ideal* of, in short, *justifiability to others*. And this ideal is itself
the source of the motivation – it provides a motivating reason – to
refrain from doing what is wrong. For it is a fact, says Scanlon, that
"people have reason to want to act in ways that could be justified to

---

² T. M. Scanlon, *What We Owe to Each Other* (Cambridge, MA: Harvard
University Press, 1998).

others" – they have a reason "to live with others on terms that they could not reasonably reject insofar as they also are motivated by this ideal."[3]

This ideal of justifiability to others, to which this form of contractualism appeals, is (as Scanlon says) similar to the ideal to which John Stuart Mill appeals in support of his Utilitarian principle: "the desire to be in unity with our fellow creatures."[4] Although, I believe, it exerts a powerful influence on our lives, this ideal is not something we are ordinarily conscious of while it affects our behavior. It is not to be mistaken for any ideal of harmony in our daily dealings with each other; and although it may be a necessary condition of a sense of belonging (which most people no doubt care greatly for), it is not the same thing as that either. Most people want to get along with others in their daily lives; they would like others generally to share their values and to assent to what they do; they would like their approval. This gives them a reason for wanting to be able to justify their actions to others on grounds they do actually find acceptable. But this fact does not explain *moral* motivation; the actual assent or approval of others does not in itself make an action morally right.[5] The Scanlonian ideal of justifiability is an ideal governing our relations with others; but it is an ideal, not of actual agreement or harmony, but of *moral* unity. It is an ideal of a relation with others that reflects a form of *respect* or *recognition* – I'll have more to say about these later – and failing to live up to this ideal involves a kind of estrangement from our fellow human beings.[6]

This theory, it seems to me, provides the best account of why most people are *disposed* to obey the norm of fair reciprocity. (Of course, being disposed to do something is not sufficient for actually doing it). Most people, I believe, would on reflection take it to be wrong to fail to do their part in cooperative endeavors from which they would benefit whether or not they contributed – wrong precisely in Scanlon's sense of not being justifiable to others on grounds that they could not

---

[3] Scanlon, *What We Owe to Each Other*, p. 154.
[4] John Stuart Mill, *Utilitarianism* (originally published in book form in 1863), Chapter III.
[5] Scanlon, *What We Owe to Each Other*, pp. 154–155.
[6] Scanlon, *What We Owe to Each Other*, pp. 162–163.

reasonably reject – and this ideal of living with others on terms they could not reject gives them a motivating reason to comply with the norm. They would especially take it to be wrong to fail to do their bit after they had promised or agreed to do so, or in some other way given others to believe that their cooperation could be relied upon – I'll come back to this momentarily.

This ideal is not only a motivating reason for action; it is one that for many people also has priority over other considerations in that it shapes and structures (in the ways I described in Chapter 2) the other reasons they might have for complying or not complying with this norm. It is, in other words, an identity-constituting ideal: it is a part of the self-understanding that is normative for most people, an attribute of the kind of person they think they should be. The structuring and modulating effect on other reasons that is the result of acceptance of this norm by someone for whom this is an identity-constituting ideal will be illustrated in the next chapter.

There are of course people who are not concerned to live with others on terms they could not reasonably reject – who would not experience or would not be troubled by the sense of estrangement from others that would result from their actions being unjustifiable. These are amoralists – people who are unmoved directly by considerations of right and wrong – and at some level they must be disaffected or alienated from society, unconcerned about being or willing to be "morally alone." Anyone who conformed fully to the assumptions of Rational Choice theory would fall in this category. Such a person might sometimes conform to a norm of fair reciprocity, but only because he takes it to be in his interests to.

Those who do accept norms of fair reciprocity and are disposed to be morally motivated may nevertheless sometimes withhold their cooperation. Someone who endorses such a norm is of course not obliged to contribute to a cooperative endeavor regardless of others' behavior. She must see – or expect – that enough others are doing or will do their parts, their fair shares. If this is so, then we might expect to find that a player's choices in a one-shot Prisoners' Dilemma game depend on what she expects the other players to do – though this of course would not be the case if she were a Rational Chooser. This has indeed been found in many experimental studies: if I think you are going to cooperate, I am likely to cooperate as well.[7] Some experimenters have thought this correlation results from a kind of projection, in which I think you will behave like me.[8] Others (I'll discuss some examples shortly) suggest that the players transform the game into an Assurance Game: that is the game that they really play, not the Prisoners' Dilemma they are supposed to play. (An Assurance Game has the same payoff structure as a Prisoners' Dilemma except that each player prefers to cooperate if the other player is going to.) But the experimental findings – including the observed correlation between a player's choices and her beliefs about the other player's choices – are equally consistent with the view that a person's expectation of cooperation provides (in the artificial setting of the experiment) a crucial condition for the motivation arising from her accepting the norm of fair reciprocity not to be demobilized.

Let us be absolutely clear: cooperating *conditionally* because one believes that not doing one's fair share is wrong and because one has reason, in Scanlon's words, "to live with others on terms they could not reasonably reject," is not at all the same thing as cooperating conditionally because it is in one's (long-term) interest. In Rational Choice accounts, the noncooperation of others in a repeated game (usually assumed to be the Prisoners' Dilemma), or the expectation of cooperation in a one-shot Assurance Game, triggers the "rational" choice of noncooperation – there is really only one sort of motivation in Rational Choice theory – but in the argument I am making the noncooperation of others triggers *a different sort of motivation.*

The noncooperation or nonparticipation of others, then, is one circumstance in which the person who is disposed to be morally motivated will not actually be *motivated* to do her part. But (in the real world) if someone who is disposed to be motivated by a norm of fair

---

[7] See, for example, John Orbell and Robyn Dawes, "Social Dilemmas," in G. M. Stephenson and J. M. Davis, eds., *Progress in Applied Social Psychology*, vol. 1 (New York: John Wiley and Sons, 1981), pp. 37–65, and Toshio Yamagishi, "Social Dilemmas," in Karen S. Cook et al., eds., *Sociological Perspectives on Social Psychology* (Boston: Allyn and Bacon, 1995), pp. 311–335.

[8] See, for example, John Orbell and Robyn M. Dawes, "Social Welfare, Cooperators' Advantage, and the Option of Not Playing the Game," *American Sociological Review*, 58 (1993), 787–800.

reciprocity is in fact to be motivated to do her part in a cooperative endeavor, she must, of course, believe that it is indeed a cooperative endeavor, that she is part of a group that has a common interest, a group whose members all accept this norm. She is unlikely to feel this, I submit, and unlikely to take the norm to be binding on her, if she is not fully accepted as a member of the group, if she is made to feel used, exploited, or manipulated, if she is not respected as a fully human being – if, in particular, she is treated as though she were nothing more than a specimen of *Homo economicus*: radically unsocial and therefore amoral, her behavior manipulable or in general affected only by the use of incentives and sanctions. In these circumstances, the motivation that would normally follow directly from her recognition that it is wrong not to comply with a norm of fair reciprocity is not mobilized; it is, we might say, deactivated.[9] I hope to persuade the reader of the truth of this in the next chapter by means of a series of examples.

Consider in this light an experiment conducted in some day-care centers in the city of Haifa during 1998.[10] Some parents come late to these places to collect their offspring and the teacher is obliged to stay after the official closing time. Ten such centers were observed over a period of twenty weeks. In the first four weeks records were kept of the numbers of parents arriving late. Then, in six of them, a small fine was introduced and imposed on parents who came more than ten minutes late. At the other four no fine was introduced. Economists and other Rational Choice theorists would have to predict that the fine would result in less lateness. But the opposite occurred. And when the fine was removed, at the beginning of the seventeenth week, there was no reduction from the new, higher level of lateness. (In the first four weeks, parents in the control group and the test group were indistinguishable; and the control group stayed the same for the rest of the twenty weeks.)

The most plausible interpretation of this result is that the introduction of the fine caused the parents to shift from thinking of their

---

[9] I tried out a version of this argument in the early 1990s and it appeared in my "Good Government: On Hierarchy, Social Capital, and the Limitations of Rational Choice Theory," *Journal of Political Philosophy*, 4 (1996), 1–28.

[10] The experiment is reported in Uri Gneezy and Aldo Rustichini, "A Fine Is a Price," *Journal of Legal Studies*, 29 (2000), 1–17.

choices in moral terms to thinking of them in economic terms. The moral motivation that flowed from their believing before the fines were introduced that they ought not to seriously inconvenience the teachers (who are unpaid for their uncovenanted overtime) evaporates when the fine is introduced because the fine is seen as a payment for a service rendered. The only question for the parent then is whether the service is worth the price. And once this reframing has taken place, it seems to stick even after the fine has been removed – although, since observations continued for only four more weeks, it is possible that the more moral perceptions of the *status quo ante* would have reasserted themselves eventually.

The fine imposed in this experiment was very small. It sufficed, however, to bring about the reframing of the choice situation; its effect could not have been additive, boosting whatever motivation was in play before it was introduced. No doubt a much larger fine would have reduced the amount of lateness, because, after knocking out the moral motivation (of those who framed the situation in this way to begin with and were susceptible to reframing), fewer parents would have found the benefits worth the cost: I am certainly not denying that economic sanctions can move people.

A similar result was produced by another set of experiments, this time laboratory experiments in which the subjects (students of management and business) played Prisoners' Dilemmas (or "social dilemmas," as sociologists and psychologists like to call Prisoners' Dilemma games with more than two players).[11] In two of the three experiments the subjects played the role of manufacturers who had made an agreement to reduce their polluting emissions. In some of the experimental groups, participants were told there would be no monitoring or enforcement of the agreement. In others, the participants were told that there would be inspections and those caught violating the agreement would be fined. Again, the experiments showed that the introduction of weak sanctions resulted in *less* cooperation, but strong sanctions increased the amount of cooperation. The subjects

[11] Ann E. Tenbrunsel and David M. Messick, "Sanctioning Systems, Decision Frames, and Cooperation," *Administrative Science Quarterly*, 44 (1999), 684–707.

were also asked to characterize the kind of decision they saw themselves as making. In the absence of sanctioning, about half saw a "business decision" and half saw an "ethical decision." Where a weak sanction was threatened, nearly all of them saw a "business decision." Of those who framed the choice as an ethical one, 90 percent cooperated; only 53 percent cooperated if they framed the choice as an economic one.

The demobilization or deactivation of moral motivation that I have described here has an analog or parallel in the better-known effect of extrinsic rewards on what psychologists call intrinsic motivation. An *intrinsically motivated* activity is one done for its own sake, one for which there is no other reward but the activity itself. In numerous studies, psychologists have found that people engaged without compensation in an intrinsically interesting activity will become less interested in the activity, less willing to continue with it, enjoy it less, and perform it less creatively and effectively when an extrinsic reward (such as money) is introduced and made contingent on performing well at the activity in question. In short: *extrinsic rewards weaken intrinsic motivation* (as, of course, do punishments).[12]

The main explanation given by psychologists for this effect is that it is a reaction to being manipulated for other people's ends, which occurs because (most) people want to be self-determining, in the sense of having some control over their immediate environments and of the way their lives go. Some who have written about intrinsic motivation suggest that when a person is motivated by the intrinsic rewards of an activity she is in some sense at one with the activity, immersed in it, and there is then a loss of the sense of a self distinct from the activity (and perhaps from the other people jointly involved with the

---

[12] For good accounts of intrinsic motivation and surveys of the findings I refer to, see Edward L. Deci and Richard M. Ryan, *Intrinsic Motivation and Self-Determination in Human Behavior* (New York: Plenum Press, 1985); Mark R. Lepper and David Greene, eds., *The Hidden Cost of Rewards* (Hillsdale, NJ: Wiley/Erlbaum, 1978); Robert E. Lane, *The Market Experience* (Cambridge: Cambridge University Press, 1991); and Edward L. Deci et al., "A Meta-analytic Review of Experiments Examining the Effects of Intrinsic Rewards on Intrinsic Motivation," *Psychological Bulletin*, 125 (1999), 627–668.

activity) and a loss of consciousness of self: there is what Mihaly Csikszentmihaly calls a *flow* experience.[13]

Treating someone like *Homo economicus,* inviting them to respond to monetary or other external incentives, undermines both intrinsic motivation and moral motivation. But intrinsic motivation is not at all the same thing as moral motivation, and the two effects should not be confused. In both cases, a kind of *connection* is broken by the introduction (in some circumstances) of extrinsic incentives, but the connection is of a different kind in the two cases and to different things. Moral unity and the conditions I have described for moral motivation do not describe any sort of immersion or sense of union with others or (in the case of motivation by the norm of fair reciprocity, for example) with the cooperative activity or effort itself. A sense of being part of a cooperative endeavor does not necessarily involve such union. Some sort of group identification (a murky idea I'll come to shortly) may occur, and immersion in an intrinsically rewarding joint activity may also occur, but neither of these is necessary for moral motivation.

I believe the argument about moral motivation and its demobilization provides as plausible an explanation of the findings in the experiments described earlier as any "rational choice" explanation or indeed any other explanation on offer. Let us look a little further at some alternative explanations of behavior in one-shot Prisoners' Dilemma games (and remember that the Public Goods and Common Pool Resource games used in the experiments are in fact Prisoners' Dilemmas). The economists seem to think that the Ultimatum Game is the canonical experimental game[14] – for no better reason that I can discern than its having been invented by an economist – but the Prisoners' Dilemma and the Public Goods games have been studied far longer and (recently) more searchingly and discriminatingly.

We saw earlier that the clearest finding of the experiments with one-shot Prisoners' Dilemma games (apart from the general finding that

---

[13] Mihaly Csikszentmihalyi, *Flow: The Psychology of Optimal Experience* (New York: Harper and Row, 1990), especially at pp. 62–70.

[14] See the editors' Introduction (Chapter 1) to Henrich et al., eds., *Foundations of Human Sociality.*

they overwhelmingly disconfirm the economists' assumptions about rational choice) is that when the players discuss their dilemma before making their choices, a significant increase in cooperative choices results. What the players tend to do in these discussions is to elicit from each other commitments or agreements or promises to cooperate. The effect on the rate of cooperation is most pronounced if *everyone* in the group makes a promise; and there usually is in the discussions strong pressure for everyone to promise. But there is still much cooperation even where promising is less than universal.[15] And we must remember that, even without promising or any other form of communication, the amount of cooperation is far from negligible. The economists' attempts to explain these findings fail, as we have seen; but there have been many non-Rational Choice efforts, of which all but two have been eliminated. These two have some relation to the explanation I favor; so let me say a few words about them.

The explanations remaining in the field, especially those concerning the effects of discussion on cooperation, involve something called group or social identity (or identification) *or* norms of cooperation and promise keeping *or both* of these. Besides a lack of agreement on which of these is doing the explanatory work, there is little clarity about *how* they do their work.

The argument from *social identification* derives from the work of Henri Tajfel and others, who showed experimentally that if a person defines herself as a member of a group or if her membership in a group is made cognitively salient, then she is more likely to observe the group's norms and generally to look with favor upon and to cooperate with the other members of the group.[16] There is a surface resemblance between this – as an explanation of cooperating in

[15] See Orbell et al., "Explaining Discussion-Induced Cooperation."

[16] See Henri Tajfel, "Experiments in Intergroup Discrimination," *Scientific American*, 223 (1970), 96–102; and Tajfel et al., "Social Categorization and Intergroup Behaviour," *European Journal of Social Psychology*, 1 (1971), 149–177. For further developments see Tajfel, *Human Groups and Social Categories* (Cambridge: Cambridge University Press, 1981; Tajfel, ed., *Social Identity and Intergroup Relations* (Cambridge: Cambridge University Press, 1982); and John C. Turner with others, *Rediscovering the Social Group: A Self-Categorization Theory* (Oxford: Blackwell, 1987). A good brief introduction is provided by Turner's Chapter 2 ("Social Identification

Prisoners' Dilemma and Public Goods games – and the argument I have made; so let me spell it out. In Tajfel's early experiments and in many subsequent experiments in which his findings were replicated, the subjects were divided into groups by means of some trivial test or criterion, such as those who overestimated *versus* those who underestimated the number of dots on a screen – groups that were supposed to be stripped of any psychological significance and were therefore called "minimal" groups. Much of this experimental work may have been prompted by interest in racial and other forms of prejudice and discrimination, crowd behavior, and conformity in totalitarian societies, but what the experiments show is that in the laboratory it took very little to produce group cohesion, conformity to group norms, and discrimination in favor of the members of one's own (experimentally induced) group – the "in-group" – and (it must not be forgotten) *against* members of the "out-group."

The explanation for these experimental findings, put forward by Tajfel and John Turner and generally favored by social psychologists, in what they call *social identity theory,* is that (in Turner's words) "people are motivated to evaluate themselves positively and that in so far as they define themselves in terms of some group membership they will be motivated to evaluate the group positively..."[17] In other words, progroup behavior is driven by our desire to think well of ourselves, by our "motives for positive self-esteem."[18]

Despite the accumulated mass of evidence of the ease with which cooperation (and group-conformity, in-group bias, and so on) can be produced experimentally through "social identification," I am doubtful that this is the right way to explain cooperation in Prisoners' Dilemmas (including Public Goods and "Common Pool Resource" games), as several experimenters have proposed,[19] or of doing one's

---

and Psychological Group Formation") in Tajfel, ed., *The Social Dimension* (Cambridge: Cambridge University Press, 1984), vol. 2.

[17] Turner, *Rediscovering the Social Group*, pp. 29–30.

[18] Turner, "Social Identification and Psychological Group Formation," p. 529.

[19] See especially R. M. Kramer and M. B. Brewer, "Effects of Group Identity on Resources in a Simulated Commons Dilemma," *Journal of Personality and Social Psychology*, 46 (1984), 1044–1057; M. B. Brewer and R. M. Kramer "Choice Behavior in Social Dilemmas: Effects of Social Identity,

part in cooperative endeavors in the real world (the world outside the laboratory). There is, in the first place, a question in my mind about what, if anything, in the real world corresponds to what is observed in the "minimal group" experiments. Of course, this question can be asked of all social/psychological experiments. We should not take it for granted that anything of significance in the real world is illuminated by the experiments. It seems extraordinary that the behavior observed in the "minimal group" experiments can be produced so readily in groups so recently formed (or imagined), and formed on such tenuous grounds. (It is not surprising that some have speculated that the experiments tap – not of course consciously – some deep-rooted propensity to conform with "our group," a propensity that evolved in the Environment of Evolutionary Adaptiveness.[20]) But perhaps it *is* extraordinary; perhaps in the world in which most of us now live (when we are not in a psychologist's laboratory) other capacities and mental processes (including those I mentioned earlier in this chapter and in Part One), when given a little more time than is allowed in the experiments, work to override or hold in check our propensity to "identify" with our group and conform to its norms. Perhaps this is why, in experiments with *repeated* Prisoners' Dilemma games, the high rates of cooperation that are found in the early stages of such games usually decay over time, and why, in the real world, on moving into a group (of neighbors, for example, or of departmental colleagues), our strong desire to get along with everyone in the group, and the warm feelings this produces, are eventually replaced by much more discriminating and selective attitudes and relationships.

As for the standard explanation for "social identification" and its effects in terms of self-respect or self-esteem, I think this should be rejected. Unlike many writers, I would separate these last two and

Group Size, and Decision Framing," *Journal of Personality and Social Psychology*, 50 (1986), 543–549; and R. M. Kramer and M. B. Brewer, "Social Group Identity and the Emergence of Cooperaton in Resource Conservation Dilemmas," in Henk A. M. Wilke et al., eds., *Experimental Social Dilemmas* (Frankfurt: Verlag Peter Lang, 1986).

20 See the discussion around this idea in Linnda R. Caporael, Robyn M. Dawes, John M. Orbell, and Alphons J. C. van de Kragt, "Selfishness Examined: Cooperation in the Absence of Egoistic Incentives," *Behavioral and Brain Sciences*, 12 (1989), 683–739.

say that a person possesses *self-esteem* when he approves of himself or takes a favorable view of himself, whereas a person's *self-respect* is what is damaged when he fails his identity-constituting ideals. Self-respect is what is lost when shame is experienced. Thus, self-respect presupposes a self, a self constituted by core ideals, but this is not so of self-esteem; self-respect does not require that a person look approvingly on himself (any more than respecting others requires that one think highly of them); and whereas we can say that a person can have too much self-esteem, we cannot say he has too much self-respect.[21] In any case neither self-esteem nor self-respect is something directly sought by most people. They are not the centrally important goals or goods that social psychologists (and John Rawls) take them to be. What is the case is that we have reason to want to live up to our ideals. Failure to do so can undermine our self-respect, defined in the way I define it here. Neither self-respect nor self-esteem can be had through thinking well of a group that (even though we are members of it) does not merit our favorable opinion, in the light of our ideals. Maintaining one's self-respect might require instead that one withdraw one's approval of the group, or withdraw altogether from the group (if that is possible.)

Further reason to doubt that "social identification" is the source of cooperation in the Prisoners' Dilemma and Public Goods Games is provided by some recent experimental work done mainly in Japan. First, it was demonstrated in a persuasive set of experiments that in "minimal group" settings it was not mere categorization of people in groups that produced in-group bias and cooperation, but rather that participants in these experiments had the illusory belief that others' choices depended on theirs, that their own choices would be reciprocated, and that accordingly it would pay to give to in-group members. Apparently, *only* those who had such beliefs were disposed to favor the group. These illusory beliefs – illusory because such interdependence was not a possibility in these (one-shot) experimental games – seem to be a product of the recognition that the player's *own* payoff is dependent on the others' choices. On the basis of some further

---

[21] See on this David Sachs, "How to Distinguish Self-Respect from Self-Esteem," *Philosophy and Public Affairs*, 10 (1981), 346–360.

experiments with one-shot Prisoners' Dilemma Games, it was concluded that cooperation in such games was also the product of the illusory expectation of future reciprocation.[22]

A theoretical foundation for – and generalization of – this idea was earlier provided by Alan Carling.[23] Carling asks us to suppose, in the two-person case, that each of the actors "has beliefs which make the conditional probability of a positive response from the opponent to the actor's cooperative move equal to the quantity p" (hence a probability of a negative response equal to $1-p$), and of a negative response to the actor's *non*-cooperative move equal to q (hence a probability of a positive response equal to $1-q$). By "beliefs which make the conditional probability" of a certain response I think he means beliefs that have the *effect* of creating *confidence* in that response. He interprets p and q as the *trust* and *fear* components respectively in a player's attitude toward the other player: they are the confidence she can repose in the other's positive and negative responses to her own cooperation and noncooperation respectively. It is easily shown that, if a player chooses between cooperation and noncooperation according to her expected utility, she will cooperate if and only if

$$Rp + S(1 - p) > Pq + T(1 - q)$$

where R, P, S, T are the payoffs to each player from, respectively, mutual cooperation, mutual noncooperation (defection), her own unilateral cooperation, and her own unilateral defection. One special case of this general model occurs when $p + q = 1$. This line in (p, q) space corresponds to the world of noncooperative game theory.

22 Much of this work has been published in Japanese, with only summaries in English. But we have in English: David Karp, Nobuhito Jin, Toshio Yamagishi, and Hiromi Shinotsuka, "Raising the Minimum in the Minimal Group Paradigm," *Japanese Journal of Experimental Social Psychology*, 32 (1993), 231–240; Nahoko Hayashi, Elinor Ostrom, James Walker, and Toshio Yamagishi, "Reciprocity, Trust, and the Sense of Control," *Rationality and Society*, 11 (1999), 27–46; and Toko Kiyonari, Shigehito Tanida, and Toshio Yamagishi, "Social Exchange and Reciprocity: Confusion or a Heuristic?," *Evolution and Human Behavior*, 21 (2000), 411–427. The article by Hayashi et al. (which replicated the Japanese experiments for U.S. subjects) summarizes the findings reported in (and gives references to) the Japanese language articles.
23 Alan H. Carling, *Social Division* (London: Verso, 1991).

Then, the inequality is never satisfied and noncooperation is always "rational." The illusory beliefs that were thought to be at work in the Japanese experiments correspond, I think, to the special case of Carling's model where $p = q = 1$: a single point in (p, q) space. In this case, the inequality stated previously is always satisfied and someone holding such beliefs would always cooperate.

The "illusory control" experiments have cast real doubt over the "social identification" argument, but their authors have not, I think, established their own argument in its place. On their account, the illusory aspect of the future reciprocation by others makes my cooperation *rational*. They believe that the players transform the Prisoners' Dilemma in their minds into an Assurance Game – a belief supported not only by the players' choices in the experimental games but also by their answers to a questionnaire administered after the games had been played. I have already commented on this argument. Let us grant that, for whatever reason, many players of these games think (or behave as if they think) that there will be reciprocity. But there is then no warrant for assuming that cooperation occurs because cooperation is rational (in the sense of Rational Choice theory), given this belief. If a person believes herself (perhaps mistakenly) to be part of a cooperative enterprise, then she might rather take it for granted that she *ought* to do her part, that it would be *wrong* not to cooperate when she believes the other player has cooperated *or will cooperate*, in which case she has a motivating reason to cooperate, according to the argument I made above. And in fact the results of these experiments and the subjects' answers to the questionnaire are as much evidence of *moral* motivation of this Scanlonian sort as they are of rational conditional cooperation (i.e., cooperation because it seems a good investment, given the illusory expectations).[24]

There are two other explanations involving "social identification" – explanations of the behavior observed in the experiments in which, during discussions, some or all of the players make agreements or

---

[24] I should add that even if both players are "rational" in the sense of Rational Choice theory, cooperation in an Assurance Game is not assured, as is commonly assumed. If a player's payoff when she is a unilateral cooperator represents a huge loss and all her other payoffs are very small gains, I doubt if she will cooperate.

promises to cooperate. The first of them argues that consensual promising *creates* "social identification" and hence motivation to cooperate. If, as I have just argued, we reject the hypothesis that "social identification" explains cooperation, then this argument must be rejected too. The other explanation argues that it takes "social identification" to activate norms of promise keeping – that people do not feel obligated to keep their promises *unless* they first "identify with" the group.[25]

My own argument about cooperation shares with this second explanation the view that certain conditions must be met for people to be motivated by their beliefs about right and wrong; but "social identification" or "group identity" is not, I believe, the right condition. "Group identity" might indeed be a sufficient condition for inducing cooperation in experimental games – whether by activating norms of promise keeping or of reciprocity or in some other way – but I doubt that this is what is at work in those cases in the real world (outside the psychologist's laboratory) in which people seem motivated to do their part. (The next chapter is devoted to several such cases.) Tom Tyler and Robyn Dawes, who have made the argument that "group identity" is necessary for cooperation, believe that this is why strangers and those involved in one-shot interactions (such as most market transactions) have self-interested, uncooperative motivations.[26] But, as we have seen (and as these authors are aware), in countless Prisoners' Dilemma experiments in which the game is played just once by total strangers who will never meet again there is a great deal of cooperation even without opportunities for discussion or face-to-face

---

[25] See Robyn M. Dawes, Alphons J. C. van de Kragt, and John M. Orbell, "Cooperation for the Benefit of Us – Not Me, or My Conscience," Chapter 6 in Jane J. Mansbridge, ed., *Beyond Self-Interest* (Chicago: University of Chicago Press, 1990), and Tom Tyler and Robyn M. Dawes, "Fairness in Groups: Comparing the Self-Interest and Social Identity Perspectives," in Barbara A. Mellers and Jonathan Baron, eds., *Psychological Perspectives on Justice* (Cambridge: Cambridge University Press, 1993). Tyler and Dawes have a good discussion of other work along the same lines. My argument in this chapter has much in common with the argument of Tyler and Dawes, but, again, I give no room to group identification.

[26] Tyler and Dawes, "Fairness in Groups," pp. 98–99.

interaction or anything else that could plausibly be taken as creating "group identity." Moreover, in those experiments in which "group identity" *is* said to be induced, it is far from clear that identification with the experimental group – "self-identity linked to the group," as Tyler and Dawes put it – is the source of the motivation. I would argue instead that it is an attachment not to the group but to the ideal of fair reciprocity that is the source of moral motivation. And this is confirmed by the evidence from the real world that I shall discuss in the next chapter. There we shall see how people are motivated (when conditions are right) to do their part in mutually advantageous cooperative endeavors in cases where it would be most implausible to argue that the motivation comes from identification with a group. They are, for example, willing to turn out to vote in elections in cases where their individual votes could not decide the result and to do their part in maintaining social order.

Most people, I have argued, accept a norm of fair reciprocity. They believe that failing to do their part in a fair scheme of cooperation is *wrong*, in Scanlon's sense: "its performance under the circumstances would be disallowed by any set of principles for the general regulation of behavior that no one could reasonably reject as a basis for informed, unforced general agreement." The beauty of this account of what it is for an act to be wrong is that at the same time it shows why most people are motivated (in the right circumstances) to refrain from such an act; for, as Scanlon says, "people have reason to want to act in ways that could be justified to others;" they have reason to want "to live with others on terms that they could not reject." And this ideal not only can provide a motivating reason to act but may also structure other reasons that the person may have – for example, silencing or reducing the reason-providing power of the normally operative desire for monetary gain.

Most of us, as I say, believe that failing to do our part in a scheme of fair cooperation is wrong. We surely also believe that it is even more unambiguously wrong to fail to do our part when others rely on us to do so because of an assurance we have given them, by making promises or entering (perhaps tacitly) into an agreement. It is morally wrong – it is not justifiable to others – not to keep promises when, through one's promising, others have been encouraged to do things they otherwise would not have done.[27] We can leave open the question of whether it is wrong, or a serious wrong, to break a promise on which nobody relies in any way, a promise on which nobody else's actions are conditional. In any case, in Prisoners' Dilemma and Public Goods Games, and in the situations in the real world which they are supposed to model, promises *do* encourage others – they are *intended* to encourage others – to act in ways they might otherwise not have done. So we have an explanation for why, in these games (where the conditions I discussed earlier for the motivation arising from acceptance of the norm of fair reciprocity to be deactivated are absent), a discussion period in which promises or agreements are made, or, failing actual promises or agreements, attempts are made to persuade people that they *should* cooperate, results in greater cooperation.

Most people, I believe, bring to these games their standing belief that failing to do their part in mutually advantageous cooperative endeavors is wrong – is not justifiable. If the instructions for playing the game encourage them to think of the exercise as a cooperative endeavor rather than a competitive one, they are more likely to see the norm of fair reciprocity as applicable – and this is consistent with the experimental evidence of (unsurprisingly) increased cooperation when the players are so instructed. A person's attachment to the ideal of justifiability and the moral motivation arising from the belief that it is wrong to free ride are also likely to be mobilized by discussion, or by any sort of face-to-face communication with the other player(s), and even more so by an exchange of promises, especially if everyone participates. All of these conditions reinforce the sense that each is a part of a cooperative endeavor and is not going to be taken advantage of. All of these conditions, as we have seen, increase the rate of cooperation observed in the experiments.

---

[27] See Scanlon's treatment of promises in Chapter 7 of *What We Owe to Each Other*. Like Scanlon, I do not argue (as Rawls did, following Hume) that promises must be kept because to break a promise is to fail to do one's part in a just social practice from which we all benefit.

8 Citizens and workers: the argument illustrated

8.1. We'll be citizens – if you'll let us

In our earlier discussion (in Chapter 3) of contingent valuation surveys conducted for cost-benefit analyses, we noted that many people (more than 50 percent in some surveys), when asked to choose an amount of money they would be willing to accept to forego some environmental improvement or in compensation for some environmental deterioration, respond by giving very large or even infinite figures, or by refusing to choose a sum at all, or by terminating the interview. It is a plausible argument, supported by evidence from the few studies of what people think about contingent valuation exercises in which they themselves have participated, that a central reason for these refusals is that in such contexts – when public policies are being decided – people wish to be treated not as mere consumers, acting in isolation in the market, responding only to economic incentives, but as citizens. They do not, at least in these contexts, wish to be treated as if they were specimens of *Homo economicus*, for whom the values of all things are fungible and all losses are compensable. They wish to be, and to be treated as, members of society and hence as having a part to play in the collective control of public affairs. I have also argued (in the last chapter) that, if a person is not recognized in this way, the motivation that would normally follow directly from her belief that it is wrong not to comply with a norm of fair reciprocity would not be mobilized. Let me offer another illustration of this.

The inhabitants of the United States, who make up about 4.7 percent of the world's population, generate a quarter or more of its waste. A great deal of this waste is toxic – hazardous to the natural environment or to human health. It is, to define it more fully as it is officially defined in the 1976 (U.S.) Resource Conservation and Recovery Act (RCRA), "solid waste, or combination of solid wastes, which because of its quantity, concentration, or physical, chemical, or infectious characteristics, may cause, or significantly contribute to an increase in mortality or an increase in serious irreversible, or incapacitating reversible, illness; or pose a substantial present or potential hazard to human health or the environment when improperly treated, stored, or disposed of, or otherwise managed."[1] Each of us, here in the United States, generates on average more than a ton of hazardous waste every year. And just as most of us have little or no idea of where the things we consume and use have come from, we are also fairly comprehensively ignorant about where the wastes from all this consumption go *to*. Until the late 1970s, a great deal of it was unceremoniously dumped, untreated and unsealed, or inadequately so, in unlined landfills and local watercourses, or it was shipped elsewhere, sometimes abroad. But beginning around 1980, prompted in part by a series of disasters (such as Love Canal in upstate New York), and in the context of a now highly active environmental movement, state and federal regulations were put in place, requiring toxic waste to be sent for storage to specially constructed hazardous waste facilities.

The reaction of most people living in areas where government agencies or private corporations have proposed to locate such facilities has generally been: Not In My Back Yard – although environmentalists and their organizations naturally favor a "not-in-anyone's-backyard" stance that would encourage the industrial producers to produce less waste. So powerful has the NIMBY reaction been to these LULUs – locally unwanted land uses – that hazardous waste facility siting in the United States (and Canada) has become very difficult. (And hazardous waste facilities are not the only LULUs; also unwanted, in

---

[1] See Barry G. Rabe, *Beyond NIMBY: Hazardous Waste Siting in Canada and the United States* (Washington, DC: Brookings Institution, 1994), pp. 10–11. My discussion in this section is indebted to this study. For a comprehensive treatment of all hazardous and nuclear waste siting, see also Michael B. Gerrard, *Whose Backyard, Whose Risk: Fear and Fairness in Toxic and Nuclear Waste Siting* (Cambridge, MA: MIT Press, 1994).

many cases, are prisons, half-way houses, drug and alcohol treatment centers, nursing homes, public housing, and so on.[2])

The approaches generally taken to siting hazardous waste facilities have been of two kinds. There is, first, a *public* or *regulatory* approach, in which a governmental agency, usually a state or local environmental or natural resource agency, chooses the site and the scope and character of the operation, and (characteristically) tries to impose its decision on the local community (perhaps using preemption or eminent domain), though it may contract with a private firm to build and operate the facility. And then there is a *private* or *market* approach, in which the state government, after establishing guidelines, invites proposals from private waste management firms and generally leaves it to these firms to select sites and to secure the support of the targeted local communities.

These have been the approaches, with local variations, that have been pursued by most American states and most Canadian provinces, and they have invariably met with strenuous local resistance. Moreover, when either of these approaches is adopted, the prospect of considerable economic compensation doesn't seem to help. A waste facility generates local employment of course – both directly and indirectly – which in many of the targeted communities is badly needed; the government might put in a new road and other infrastructure; and both government and waste management corporations may offer to the local communities additional economic inducements, such as a percentage of the facility's receipts. Yet these enticements generally fail to overcome local resistance, and may even stiffen it.[3]

Local citizens can, however, be won over, indeed can come to embrace such facilities with enthusiasm. An outstanding instance of this is the comprehensive waste treatment and disposal facility constructed in the mid-1980s at Swan Hills in the Canadian province

---

[2] Rabe, *Beyond NIMBY*, pp. xiii and 167.

[3] See Don Munton, "Introduction: The NIMBY Problem and Approaches to Facility Siting," in Don Munton, ed., *Hazardous Waste Siting and Democratic Choice* (Washington, DC: Georgetown University Press, 1996), and Howard Kunruether and Doug Easterling, "The Role of Compensation in Siting Hazardous Facilities," *Journal of Policy Analysis and Management*, 15 (1996), 601–622.

of Alberta. This success inspired similar efforts in the late 1980s and early 1990s in the province of Manitoba and in the state of Minnesota. A similar approach was adopted at Greensboro in North Carolina – an exception to the pattern in that state, and indeed in all the United States, of failed efforts to site waste management facilities using regulatory and market approaches. Why have the two conventional approaches met with so much resistance, while the Alberta, Manitoba, Minnesota, and Greensboro projects have found acceptance?

The crucial ingredients for success appear to be these: the siting decision is *noncoercive* – the people in the target community have the sense that they are giving their assent to the project *voluntarily*; the siting process is *participative* and *deliberative*, involving extensive open prior consultation with the local community; and the community is persuaded that there will be a wide *sharing* of burdens, which requires *assurances* to be given that there will be no uncovenanted future exploitation of the community, that other parts of the state or province will do their parts in a broader approach to managing and reducing hazardous waste (which may include recycling programs and on-site waste-reduction efforts). In the minds of the members of the community these three elements are no doubt psychologically inseparable.

Under the regulatory and market approaches, none of these conditions have typically been met. Whether the approach has been made by a government agency or by a private corporation, it has invariably been a one-sided, nonparticipative affair. The site or short-list of sites is selected by the agency or corporation. There is no prior consultation with the selected communities. Little information is provided to them. There is little discussion with them, no serious effort at assuaging their fears, no canvassing of their views, other than the minimum required by law. No detailed agreement is made with the selected communities about what wastes are to be accepted at the facility. (Of course, both government agencies and private firms are in a hurry to get a facility up and running: for governments the incentive is the prospect of job-creation and revenue; for firms, profit.) The proposed facility is not put forward as part of a larger, long-term strategy for dealing with hazardous waste, and there is no discussion of the efforts to be made or other burdens to be shouldered by waste-generators in other places. All this is bypassed and, if a private firm is involved, it is expected that, having unilaterally determined the facility's site, scope, technology, and so on, the firm will gain the assent of the community with a suitable package of economic inducements.[4]

So a targeted community has little assurance that others will do their part, little assurance that the community will not be exploited. They feel used. They do not feel part of a larger community of people who are taking collective responsibility for a problem that they collectively have produced.

So they resist. They say: not in my backyard. The siting process quickly becomes confrontational. And generally speaking the local community (with perhaps a little outside help) wins: the proposal is withdrawn.

All this is avoided in the contrasting cases in Alberta and elsewhere – the projects that have not provoked the NIMBY syndrome. The details vary, but each case is characterized by an absence of coercion: there is full disclosure of information to the public, extensive open deliberation about every phase of the project, the building of trust and the provision of assurances of burden sharing.

Of course, the prospect of economic benefits was not irrelevant to the willingness of these communities to accept a hazardous waste facility.[5] But (and this point is crucial) similar compensatory benefits have not been sufficient, in those cases where the usual regulatory and market approaches were used, to make a proposed facility acceptable to the local community and may even have had the effect of further alienating the community, of deepening its members sense of being used – of being treated as isolated individuals manipulable by economic incentives rather than as citizens, responsible members of a larger community who are willing to do their part in a fair scheme voluntarily agreed upon after full, honest, open discussion.[6]

---

[4] Rabe, *Beyond NIMBY*, p. 28.

[5] Gerrard, *Whose Backyard, Whose Risk*, pp. 125–127.

[6] Bruno S. Frey makes the strange argument that the effect of the introduction of monetary compensation is explained by the "crowding-out" of intrinsic motivation by external rewards. I described this phenomenon in Chapter 3. It certainly doesn't explain why LULUs are in certain

Moreover, the voluntary, deliberative approach that resulted in community acceptance of waste management facilities may actually have had the effect of strengthening the bonds of community, of making its members feel themselves more a part of their community.[7]

All this suggests that if people are treated respectfully and fairly, if they are included in deliberation, if they are treated like citizens – as people who are willing (without coercion) to do their part for the common good as long as they feel that others are doing their fair share – then they are likely to agree (and may even volunteer) to do their part, but if they are treated in a coercive, exploitative fashion, if they feel that they are being used for others' purposes, then they are likely to resist, to be uncooperative.

8.2.   The citizen's duty to vote

The lesson we can tentatively draw from the last section is that people want, in the appropriate circumstances, to be *recognized* as citizens – and if treated respectfully as citizens and not as *Homo economicus* they may be willing to do their bit as citizens. *Being* a citizen brings obligations – among them the obligation to vote. Are people motivated by the belief that they ought to vote?

In the United States, large numbers of eligible voters do not in fact vote, and the proportion voting has trended down over the last forty years. According to the strict version of Rational Choice theory, *not* voting is indeed the "rational" thing to do. The argument (initially anyway) goes, as it must, as follows. A "rational" person should vote if and only if the benefits that accrue to her from voting are greater than the costs to her of turning out to vote. There are two possible kinds of benefits that can result from her voting. First, there is the benefit she

conditions rejected and in others accepted, even without economic compensation. See Frey's *Not Just for the Money: An Economic Theory of Personal Motivation* (Cheltenham, UK: Edward Elgar, 1997), Chapter 8 (with Felix Oberholzer-Gee); also Frey's "Institutions and Morale: The Crowding-Out Effect," Chapter 17 in Avner Ben-Ner and Louis Putterman, eds., *Economics, Values, and Organization* (Cambridge: Cambridge University Press, 1998).

[7] Rabe, at pp. 168–169 of *Beyond NIMBY*, quotes a participant in the siting process in Alberta to this effect.

would derive from her favored candidate winning. This is a *collective* benefit, one she will obtain whether or not she votes, because it has the property (which economists call *non-excludability*) that nobody can be excluded from enjoying it. However, this collective benefit has to be discounted by the probability that her vote would decide the outcome – without it her favored candidate would lose, with it he just wins – because to the Rational Actor the only benefits that matter in making her choice are the benefits to her of *her* actions. And second, there may be *selective* benefits, which would accrue to her *only if* she votes. In the strict version of Rational Choice theory, which restricts benefits and costs to material ones, and assuming her ballot is secret so that she cannot be punished or rewarded for her vote, these selective benefits are presumably zero. Since also the probability of casting the decisive vote is very small indeed, even where the election is expected to be close, the total benefits *to her* of her voting are unlikely to exceed the cost of turning out to vote, even if this is quite small.

For example, if a voter cared so much to see her favored candidate win that she was hypothetically willing to pay $10,000 to determine the outcome of the election, then even if the odds of her vote being decisive were as high as one in 100,000, the expected benefit to her of voting would be a dime.[8] And this is most unlikely to exceed the cost to her (a Rational Actor) of turning out to vote, even if this takes only half an hour of her time. This argument about voting is of course an application of a general argument – the Rational Choice theory of collective action – which I discussed in an earlier section.

But many people *do* vote – millions of them, in fact. (And some people join or send money to political organizations, work for electoral campaigns, and engage in a variety of other political activities that are more costly or more strenuous than voting.) While it is true that about a half of the eligible voters in the United States do not vote in presidential elections, that leaves about a half who do turn out to vote. (And in other Western democracies, the turnout is substantially

---

[8] Thomas Schwartz, "Your Vote Counts on Account of the Way It Is Counted," *Public Choice*, 54 (1987), 101–121. On the general problem, see Gary Chamberlain and Michael Rothschild, "A Note on the Probability of Casting a Decisive Vote," *Journal of Economic Theory*, 25 (1981), 152–162.

higher.) This has been, I think it is fair to say, a source of embarrassment to Rational Choice theorists, who have (from the beginnings of the modern theory down to the present) devoted a great deal of energy and ingenuity to extending – or bending – the theory in an attempt to accommodate the facts. Their efforts have been of four kinds.

One attempt to find a Rational Choice explanation of voting has suggested that voters act strategically.[9] If a "rational" voter first concluded that it doesn't pay him to vote, then assumed that everyone else acted as "rationally" as he did and therefore would draw the same conclusion (and Rational Choice theory, especially game theory, standardly assumes that every player assumes every other player to be just as "rational" as himself), he should then deduce that he could determine the election outcome by voting! But shouldn't he then assume that everyone else would draw that same further conclusion? And so on. In other words, the situation facing "rational" actors has the structure of a Chicken game. In the standard, two-person version of this game, where each player has only two pure strategies available to him, each prefers to do what he thinks the other will *not* do. This preference structure can be generalized in various ways to games with more than two players.[10] The essential point about these games is that a Rational Choice analysis is radically indeterminate: by itself it cannot say what a "rational" player should do. Where there are few players – as with voting in small committees, for example, or interactions among the very small number of whaling nations – this analysis might (when the players are in fact "rational") help us to

---

9 Efforts of this sort were made chiefly by John Ledyard, Thomas Palfrey, and Howard Rosenthal. The references can be found in Donald P. Green and Ian Shapiro, *Pathologies of Rational Choice Theory* (New Haven,: CT Yale University Press, 1994), whose excellent discussion of the paradox of voter turnout (Chapter 4) I found useful in writing this section. They discuss the game-theoretic efforts at pp. 56–65. An earlier related model can be found in Michael Taylor and Hugh Ward, "Chickens, Whales, and Lumpy Goods: Alternative Models of Public Goods Provision," *Political Studies*, 30 (1982), 350–370 – but Taylor and Ward suggested its applicability to voting in committees, not to voting in large electorates.

10 For n-person generalizations of Chicken, see Taylor and Ward, "Chickens, Whales, and Lumpy Goods," or Taylor, *The Possibility of Cooperation*, Chapter 2.

understand observed behavior: precommitment to noncooperation may be "rational" in a Chicken game (or rather, in a Chicken game expanded to allow that as an option), and precommitment is sometimes observed in such situations in the real world. But reasoning of the kind called for by game theory is surely an implausible line of reasoning to impute to voters in an electorate of thousands. Either way – implausible assumptions or inability to make a prediction – this approach to voter turnout is a failure.[11]

Another way out for Rational Choice theory draws on the general argument that the approach is good only for certain problems or in certain areas. This is a tactic for holding onto some ground for Rational Choice theory in the face of local defeats. It is not a good argument. (I discussed it in section 2 of Chapter 6.) The principal part of the argument, or at any rate the one that is thought to be relevant here, is that Rational Choice theory is inappropriate when benefits and costs are very small. Aldrich has made this argument for voter turnout.[12] But in some elections many people who turn out to vote face long hours in polling lines, violence, and intimidation. As Green and Shapiro say, the way this argument is used in this context (as it is in other contexts) is an instance of "arbitrary domain restriction."[13]

Rational Choice theorists have long argued about the scope of their approach: whether its domain is universal, as the most confident imperialists of Rational Choice believe, or only partial, and if partial, whether it explains some part of every domain of social life (Green and Shapiro call this position "partial universalism") or provides the whole explanation but only in certain restricted domains

---

[11] If the indeterminacy conclusion is correct, then one could say that the game-theoretic analysis of voter turnout at least does not *contradict* observation, because it does not make any prediction at all, and from this, one could conclude, with Alan Carling, that there is no "*paradox* of voting." See Carling, "The Paradox of Voting and the Theory of Social Evolution," in Keith Dowding and Desmond King, eds., *Preferences, Institutions and Rational Choice* (Oxford: Clarendon Press, 1995), pp. 20–42.

[12] John A. Aldrich, "Rational Choice and Turnout," *American Journal of Political Science*, 37 (1993), 246–278.

[13] See Green and Shapiro, *Pathologies of Rational Choice Theory*, pp. 58 and 44–46.

("segmented universalism").[14] But the arguments I have made earlier in this book – about desires and structured reasons and the (de-)activation of moral motivation – show that none of these arguments about the domain of Rational Choice theory will do.

If we set aside the attempt to model the voter as a strategist but stay with the Rational Choice theorists who have not abandoned the effort to explain this most basic of political acts by ruling it outside the theory's domain, we are left with attempts to massage the (discounted) collective benefit and to find selective benefits – benefits contingent on turning out.

Some, for example, have argued that voters misperceive their chances of casting the pivotal vote. But it is implausible to believe that millions of voters are so deluded that they could believe their own votes to be crucial to victory. And where is the evidence of such widespread massive misperception? Others have in effect conceded that the typical voter knows perfectly well that she is not by herself going to decide the election but wishes merely to increase her preferred candidate's vote total.[15] But, no matter what end *that* serves, what difference will her one vote make to it? (Or rather, the Rational Choice theorist has to ask, what is the utility to her of that difference?) Still others have argued that the expected closeness of an election increases turnout and that this is evidence of rational choice, since increased closeness makes it more probable that each vote will be decisive.[16] But this is a bad argument for a Rational Choice theorist to make, for the only consideration is whether the voter's benefits exceed his costs, and this is not guaranteed by a close election, indeed is still highly unlikely.

So, if we are to salvage a Rational Choice explanation of voter turnout, we are left finally with finding "selective incentives." This is the tack taken in the well-known early effort by Riker and Ordeshook, in which there are "satisfactions" to be had from the act of voting (regardless of any contribution it makes to the outcome), such as

[14] Green and Shapiro, *Pathologies of Rational Choice Theory*, pp. 21–30 and 44–46.

[15] See, for example, George Stigler, "Economic Competition and Political Competition," *Public Choice*, 13 (1972), 91–106.

[16] See, for example, Yoram Barzel and Eugene Silberberg, "Is the Act of Voting Rational?," *Public Choice*, 16 (1973), 51–58.

those from "compliance with the ethic of voting," "affirming allegiance to the political system," and "affirming a partisan preference."[17] All these alleged "satisfactions" – and of course one can multiply them almost at will – are then simply *added* to the (collective) benefit derived from having one's favored candidate win, discounted by the probability that one's own vote will be decisive, to arrive at the total benefit to be had from voting! It has often been pointed out what a particularly vacuous piece of post hoc theorizing this is. I'll come back to it in a moment; but note for now that it is simply assumed by Riker and Ordeshook (as it generally is in Rational Choice explanations) that such things as "compliance with the ethic of voting" motivate like any other satisfactions.

I once thought (following John Harsanyi) that a Rational Choice analysis in which the incentives were restricted to material/economic gain and the desire for approval (or to avoid disapproval) would have explanatory power in a wide range of applications. In the case of voting, it is hard to see what selective, *material* incentives would be relevant, where political machine operatives or others don't monitor and reward voters. And indeed in the large and thorough survey done by Sidney Verba and his associates hardly anyone who voted mentioned these as a reason for doing so.[18] Selective *social* incentives might be part of an explanation for several sorts of political activity: finding friends or at any rate human company; the pleasures of joint activity – of working with congenial others; winning or enhancing the approval or even the respect of others whose good opinion one cares about or at least avoiding their disapproval; and so on. Only the last of these is a plausible candidate for an incentive affecting the solitary activity of voting.

The case for the relevance of social (dis)approbation has been made most fully by Stephen Knack[19] His central argument is that many people turn out to vote because they do not want to disappoint or

---

[17] William Riker and Peter C. Ordeshook, "A Theory of the Calculus of Voting," *American Political Science Review*, 62 (1968), 25–42.

[18] Sidney Verba, Kay Lehman Schlozman, and Henry E. Brady, *Voice and Equality: Civic Voluntarism in American Politics* (Cambridge, MA: Harvard University Press, 1995).

[19] Stephen Knack, "Civic Norms, Social Sanctions, and Voter Turnout," *Rationality and Society*, 4 (1992), 133–156.

upset friends, neighbors, or relatives who would disapprove if they failed to vote. Actually, he finds (from his own survey) that the two best predictors of turnout are "sense of civic duty to vote" and "subjectivity [by which I believe he means susceptibility] to social sanctions" – those with the latter disposition being defined as people responding affirmatively to the question, "Do you have friends, neighbors, or relatives who would be disappointed or angry with you if they knew you had not voted in this year's election?"

His evidence for the social sanctions argument comes from various surveys, including a "Social Sanctions Survey" that he himself conducted in 1990 in two counties in Maryland and Tennessee. In a 1983 ABC-Harvard poll, 37 percent of the respondents (including 41 percent of regular voters) agreed that "My friends and relatives almost always vote and I'd feel uncomfortable telling them I hadn't voted." (The same survey found that 77 percent of all respondents agreed – most of them strongly – that "no matter who wins, the more people who go to the polls, the better off our democracy will be." This, however, does not mean they are much motivated by this belief: most of those who said they rarely voted agreed with the statement.) Married persons turn out to vote more than the unmarried, at least if their spouse is educated (perhaps because she or he has a strong sense of civic duty). Knack's own Social Sanctions Survey found a small increase in the probability of voting for those who reported that they had politically like-minded neighbors who were expected to vote, who went to a neighborhood church, or who knew and occasionally talked with three or more neighbors. In the same survey he asked his respondents if, on discovering that a friend did not vote in the election they would let him or her know they disapproved. Such "enforcement" significantly increased (by 21 percent on average) the probability *they* reported that their spouses had voted. But this finding alone is not very persuasive. Knack seems to have made no effort to check for other things that might cause both norm enforcers and their spouses to vote: the norm enforcers themselves – people who presumably feel pretty strongly about voting – might be moved to vote by a sense of obligation and those whom they chose to marry and who in turn had married and lived with them might be the sorts of people who would themselves feel obliged to vote.

There is a general problem with the (Rational Choice) view that it is *sanctions* that explain conformity to norms – that people obey norms only because they are rewarded for doing so or punished for not doing so. The points I made earlier about this (in Chapter 6, section 2) apply here, to the norm of voting. Knack himself seems to understand at least that sanctions *alone* cannot explain voting, for he observes that "persons with particularly intense feelings of loyalty and obligation to society or who are especially well-socialized 'enforce' voting norms through their willingness to express disapproval at nonvoting," so those "with a low sense of civic obligation may nonetheless vote to avoid displeasing a friend or relative with a stronger sense of duty."[20] This, of course, requires that the latter associate with and care about the views of the former. But are social sanctions in fact doing any of the motivational work here?

Suppose that Knack is right (though his evidence is far from overwhelming) that social connectedness and susceptibility to the (dis)approval of others makes it more likely one will vote. Should we conclude, with Knack, that "social sanctions" significantly contribute to the decision to vote? (Informal social sanctions have played a starring role in other explanations of conformity to norms – we'll discuss some of these in the next two sections.) The conclusion is unwarranted. First, it is implausible to suppose that sanctions *alone* can explain voting – that everyone in a group of people who conform to a norm (such as a norm of civic duty) should do so *just* because they find it rational to do so in light of the expected benefits and costs, including informal (positive and negative) sanctions. It would seem that Knack agrees, for he assumes that those who both vote and *enforce* the norm of voting are not doing so because of social sanctions but because they have a strong sense of civic duty. The whole explanation, then, hinges on the existence of people motivated by such obligations, although Rational Choice theorists would have to assume that these worked as sanctions or incentives.

Second, most of Knack's evidence is compatible with, and offers as much support for, an alternative hypothesis: that association with people – in your family, neighborhood, church, or circle of

[20] Knack, "Civic Norms," pp. 137, 138.

friends – who you believe would disapprove of your failure to vote, makes you more likely to vote not because the expected social sanctions tip the cost-benefit balance but because they remind you of your ideals, including the ideal of doing your part in a cooperative endeavor; and such association – with people who presumably you believe will be doing *their* part – moreover provides the conditions in which your disposition to be morally motivated (in the way I described in Chapter 7) is mobilized.

So both Knack's argument and my alternative require that at least some voters are motivated by a sense of civic duty. There has in fact been a steady stream of empirical studies – from *The Voter Decides* (1954) to *Voice and Equality* (1995) – reporting surveys that show that many citizens are moved to vote by a sense of civic duty. The authors of *Voice and Equality* found that 93 percent of those who voted reported "civic gratifications" as a reason for voting (and 71 percent gave these as their *only* reasons), which is to say that they picked "My duty as a citizen" or "I am the kind of person who does my share" or "The chance to make the community or nation a better place" from the reasons offered to them.[21] But we should not assume that the sense of civic obligation, or the belief that one has duties as a citizen, motivates as a "gratification" or as a benefit. Such rewards – from doing one's civic duty – are the main recourse of those trying to salvage a Rational Choice explanation of voter turnout, and even the authors of *Voice and Equality* (who are not committed to this approach) seem to think of civic duty as motivating *via* (a desire for) "gratification" – they divide all the "possible motivations" for political activity (including voting) into "selective material benefits," "selective social gratifications," "selective civic gratifications," and "collective outcomes" (the last being simply "the chance to influence government policy").

But, according to the general argument about moral motivation that I made earlier, if the ideals of citizenship are part of your practical identity – if endorsing or accepting the norm that you should do your part as a citizen is a part of the self-understanding that is normative for you – then this should not only provide a motivating

---

[21] Verba, Schlozman and Brady, *Voice and Equality*, pp. 111–112.

reason to vote but is likely also to structure or shape the field of reasons you have for and against voting. The evidence supports the idea that for many people civic duty is (somehow) a motivating reason. But nobody seems to have been very inquisitive about *how* it motivates and whether in particular it has the shaping effect that I claim it should have, at least when the obligation is strongly felt. The only evidence I am aware of comes from another article by Stephen Knack, in which he asks "Does rain help the Republicans at the polls?"[22] It turns out that, for the elections he examines, the answer is: no, there are no clear partisan differences in rain's impact on turnout, contrary to semipopular wisdom. But more interestingly, he finds that those with a weak sense of civic duty are significantly less likely to vote when it rains (or snows), while those with a strong sense of civic duty are unaffected by precipitation. Moreover, of a range of factors he examines, strength of civic duty is the *only* one that has this dampening effect on rain's power to reduce turnout. (This effect produces no partisan advantage from rain because a sense of civic duty itself has no significant correlation with party.) Knack's interpretation of this finding seems to be that for those with a strong sense of civic duty the "net benefits" of voting outweigh the (for them) "relatively trivial" costs of turning out in the rain. I suggest a radically different conclusion: that those with a strong sense of civic duty do not calculate and weigh benefits and costs; their duty as a citizen provides them with a motivating reason to vote and it silences or weakens the force of competing reasons including the unpleasantness of going to the polls in the rain or snow.

We need more evidence, or rather a different sort of evidence, to test this speculation – and also to test another possibility suggested by my argument, namely that education, income, and age exert their well-known and well-established effect on turnout *via* their effect on the motivational power of civic duty, the thought being that the poor, the uneducated, and the young are less motivated by the norm of civic duty because they feel less attached to the polity and have less of a sense of being a part of a cooperative endeavor.

---

[22] Stephen Knack, "Does Rain Help the Republicans? Theory and Evidence on Turnout and the Vote," *Public Choice*, 79 (1994), 187–209.

8.3.   Workers and managers: on hierarchical cooperation

I want in this section to contrast two styles of workplace management and their implications for workers' motivation. The contrast I wish to make is in fact an instance of a quite general contrast that can be made between two kinds of hierarchy. This contrast will further help us to understand the general argument I have made about moral motivation.

Hierarchical governance in general tends to operate in one of two way, at least where its aim is to promote common interests.[23] I call the two types *coercive* and *cooperative* hierarchy. In the coercive approach, which is roughly the approach of Hobbes and is in fact a very widespread and common approach to government, hierarchical superiors try to control or regulate or determine the behavior of subordinates by one-way, top-down, individualized coercion (and by coercion I mean the use of negative *or* positive sanctions, or both together). Let us unpack this statement. First, hierarchical superiors treat individuals as isolated individuals, not as social beings who are members of communities, networks, associations, or other groups or are socially connected to one another in other ways. They make no use of, and do not try to create or foster, any capacities the governed might have to regulate their own behavior, capacities they are endowed with in virtue of such community or social networks or organization as may already exist among them.

Second, in the coercive approach subordinates' behavior is regulated by means of individualized incentives – by promising benefits or threatening penalties. These coercive efforts themselves make no use of such social connections and memberships and identifications as exist among the governed. (I'll say a little bit more about how this can happen in the following section.)

---

[23] I made this argument in "Good Government: On Hierarchy, Social Capital, and the Limitations of Rational Choice Theory," *Journal of Political Philosophy*, 4 (1996), 1–28, from which I have borrowed much of the present section and a few paragraphs of the following one. But I would not now defend everything in that article, am less enamored of the "social capital" concept, and hope that I have improved (in this book) on the embryonic argument about moral motivation that appeared there.

Third, in the coercive approach control is one-way, top-down, and leaves subordinates little autonomy or self-direction, either individually or collectively. Subordinates contribute little or nothing to the designing and planning of the common enterprise and the part they play in it. Indeed, superiors do not proceed as if they are all in a common enterprise; they treat subordinates as if they had no valuable experience or expertise to contribute; they do not solicit their participation and may not even listen to them. They tend to be remote from those they govern, having little or no regular interaction with them. As a consequence of all this, there is typically mutual distrust between hierarchical superiors and subordinates, the governors and the governed.

Under the alternative, cooperative approach, by contrast, hierarchical superiors do not govern (control, regulate, manage, and so on) their subordinates by one-way, top-down, individualized coercion but (ideally) by working cooperatively with them, working through (and encouraging) whatever capacities and dispositions for cooperation already exist among them, devolving responsibility to them, and trying to establish relations of mutual trust with them. One principle behind this approach is that wherever the governed or any subgroup of them can itself do some part of whatever work has to be done, it should be allowed and indeed encouraged to do so; and whenever possible the collective capacities that so empower such groups should be fostered.

One could summarize the contrast between the two kinds of hierarchy in terms of "social capital." Because relations between superiors and subordinates in hierarchies of the cooperative kind are characterized by repeated interaction, community, reciprocity, and trust, one might say that there is *vertical social capital* within the hierarchy. And cooperative governance also could be said to make use of and foster *horizontal social capital* – the local communities, networks, organizations, and other social bonds among the governed. So it could be said that what distinguishes cooperative from coercive hierarchy is the important roles played by vertical and horizontal capital. But there are dangers in the use of the expression "social capital": it is a catch-all term lumping together a variety of things (cooperative norms, trust, practices of reciprocity, various forms of available social organization, and in general, just about anything that facilitates cooperation), which in some contexts need to be treated separately. Moreover, in the use of the word "capital" in this context there is a danger that the forms of social capital will come to be thought of in a purely instrumental and even a cost-benefit way.[24]

A textbook example of the first type of hierarchy is the approach to workplace management found in many firms. The principal alternative to it, which clearly embodies the main features of the second type of hierarchy, has long been advocated by a small number of observers of the workplace (see above all Chester Barnard's *The Functions of the Executive*, first published in 1938) but until very recently was not seen much in practice except in Japan, where it became widely established after World War II. Richard Walton has referred to these two approaches to workforce management as the *control* strategy (in which managers impose control on workers) and the *commitment* strategy (which seeks to elicit commitment from the workforce.)[25]

[24] If, as one suspects, adoption of the term "social capital" is a tactic of argument used by political scientists, sociologists, and others to get economists (and grant-awarding bodies, and the media) to take their work seriously, then it is (as Alan Carling has suggested to me) a double-edged sword. It is somewhat akin in this respect to the tactical endorsement of cost-benefit analysis by environmentalists.

[25] See Richard E. Walton, "From Control to Commitment in the Workplace," *Harvard Business Review*, 63 (1985), 77–84. This article is an excellent short account of the two management strategies. I also found especially useful James R. Lincoln and Arne L. Kalleberg, *Culture, Commitment, and Control: A Study of Work Organization and Work Attitudes in the United States and Japan* (Cambridge: Cambridge University Press, 1990); Eileen Appelbaum and Rosemary Batt, *The New American Workplace: Transforming Work Systems in the United States* (Ithaca, NY: ILR Press, 1994); Chester Barnard, *The Functions of the Executive* (Cambridge, MA: Harvard University Press, 1938(1968); William F. Whyte, *Money and Motivation: An Analysis of Incentives in Industry* (New York: Harper and Row, 1955); Alvin W. Gouldner, *Patterns of Industrial Bureaucracy* (Glencoe, IL: Free Press, 1954); Harvey Leibenstein, *Inside the Firm: The Inefficiencies of Hierarchy* (Cambridge, MA: Harvard University Press, 1987); Gary J. Miller, *Managerial Dilemmas: The Political Economy of Hierarchy* (Cambridge: Cambridge University Press, 1992); Robert E. Cole, *Strategies for Learning: Small-Group Activities in American, Japanese and Swedish Industry* (Berkeley: University of California Press, 1989), Thomas J. Peters and Robert H. Waterman, *In Search of Excellence: Lessons from America's Best Run Companies* (New York: Harper and Row, 1982); and Ronald Dore, *British Factory-Japanese*

In the first approach, managers essentially control or coerce the workers as individuals, making use of (positive and negative) incentives. Monitoring of performance and enforcement of measured standards and explicit rules (on which there is great reliance) are hierarchical, the responsibility of hierarchical superiors, not of the workers themselves. The workers, moreover, have a negligible role in the company beyond the limits of their fixed, fragmented, narrowly defined jobs. They play no part in defining their own jobs, are given no scope for the exercise of initiative, do not work as members of teams, and are individually accountable to their superiors. They have little or no input into decisions made by their hierarchical superiors. Control and influence run in one direction only, from the top down, in a hierarchy that is taller (has more layers) and thinner (has narrower spans) than it is in the alternative approach, a hierarchy which, moreover, is emphasized by large differentials in pay and prerogatives and symbols of status. Managers typically think of workers as nothing other than a necessary cost, as people who do not need to be consulted or kept informed and who can be disposed of at short notice rather than retrained or by some other means retained.

In such a set-up, unsurprisingly, most workers are unenthusiastic about their work, do not identify with the company they work for, and are suspicious of management initiatives. They do not see themselves as engaged in a common enterprise with their hierarchical superiors,

Factory: the Origins of National Diversity in Industrial Relations (London: George Allen and Unwin, 1973). Since I first wrote (most of) this section, Truman Bewley's *Why Wages Don't Fall During a Recession* (Cambridge, MA: Harvard University Press, 1999) has appeared. Bewley's work, based on a large number of interviews with employers and others, shows that many employers are very much aware of the points about motivation that I make here and elsewhere in this book (that is why many of them do not reduce their employees' wages during a recession – as orthodox economic theory would indicate they should). Bewley writes: "Managers can promote good morale ... by idealism, that is, by making [their workers] conscious of the company's contribution to society and of their role in achieving company goals. Employees are thus made to feel part of something important outside themselves. Morale is also improved by fairness ..." (pp. 431–432). And: "What is missing [from the standard neoclassical economic model of the firm] is an appropriate theory of the firm as a community, because more than financial incentives and discipline are needed to make companies function well" (p. 436).

as sharing common interests with them. Labor relations tend therefore to be generally untrusting (on both sides) and adversarial.

This dismal approach has been widespread in the United States and other Western industrial economies. But there is another, quite different approach, long understood by a few Western firms and widespread in Japan, which is being pursued by an increasing number of firms in the United States. In this second approach, the workforce is likely to be organized in teams, and management deals with these teams, not with isolated individuals. A team is accountable for its performance as a group and to it is devolved some control over its individual members and initiative in how they organize their work. As a small group of people working closely together over a long period of time, they can and do solve the collective action problem that sometimes results from team production externalities. This is a low-cost decentralized form of social control that is unavailable to the first approach – and beyond the ken of organizational economists, who believe that shirking is inevitable in team production and can only be overcome by individualized material incentives and hierarchical monitoring.

Jobs in this second approach are typically more broadly defined (the worker taking on or circulating around what were once several separate jobs, and being involved in planning as well as executing the work) and they are more flexible and adaptive to changing conditions. Partly as a result of these two features of the second approach, there is need for fewer intermediate positions in the hierarchy: the hierarchy is flatter, hierarchical superiors have wider spans of control, and the workers and their teams are willing and able to exercise more self-control, individually and collectively.

Superiors are more concerned with facilitating cooperation between workers than with directing them. Workers are treated by management as members of a common enterprise, encouraged to contribute to shared goals, and sometimes given a material stake in the company's success (*via* profit-sharing or shareholding, for example). The management is committed to doing its best to retain workers when fewer workers are needed as a result of economic recession or of workers' own efforts to increase their productivity, by sharing the pain or retraining workers or moving into new productive activities. It reduces the distance between itself and the workforce and deemphasizes such hierarchy as remains by forgoing some of the prerogatives and symbols of its status (for example, special parking places close to its offices, separate dining facilities).

All these features of the second approach help to build and sustain trust by the workers in management, and they respond with actions confirming management's trust in them. By contrast, just about every feature of the first approach *inhibits* the growth of trust.

In firms practicing the second approach, then, there is indeed still hierarchy, but it is a quite different sort of hierarchy than that found in firms practicing the traditional approach to workforce management. It depends on, makes use of, and fosters vertical and horizontal social capital – between managers and workers and among workers.

There are many examples of companies, in various countries, that have improved productivity, product quality, and workforce morale by moving from the first type of hierarchical governance to the second. There are cases, too, of companies that have undermined worker loyalty, trust, and morale, with consequent loss of productivity, by abandoning the second approach in favor of the first.[26]

Economists interested in the firm and in regulation of the economy have generally conceived of hierarchy as coercive hierarchy. This is hardly surprising, given the premises about human motivation from which they begin. In Gary Miller's succinct characterization, their approach to the firm "views organizational control as a mechanistic problem of designing incentive systems and sanctions so that self-interested and intrinsically unmotivated employees will find it in their own interest to work toward the organization's goals."[27] Recently, it has been shown – using theorems provided by economists themselves – that this economistic program is logically bound to fail, on

---

[26] For an example of the former transition, see the interesting account by Pehr G. Gyllenhammer, "How Volvo Adapts People to Work," *Harvard Business Review*, 55 (1977), 102–113. A classic and still very instructive study of the latter is Gouldner's 1954 book about a gypsum mine in Indiana, *Patterns of Industrial Bureaucracy*. For some interesting remarks on movement in the other direction and obstacles to it, see David Osborne, *Laboratories of Democracy* (Boston: Harvard Business School Press, 1988), pp. 71–75 and 277–279.

[27] Miller, *Managerial Dilemmas*, p. 1.

its own terms: hierarchies operating in this mechanistic coercive way *cannot* deliver what economists expect of them.[28]

The person who has argued this most convincingly (Gary Miller) has, following a suggestion of David Kreps,[29] proposed that we can make better sense of hierarchies with the help of noncooperative game theory. This new political-economic account of hierarchy finds room for trust, norms and "culture," and seems to make sense of much of what was said above about behavior in the two kinds of hierarchy. But it is still built on the same (Rational Choice) assumptions about human motivation.

Consider this argument in the context of workplace management, though we could make similar arguments about hierarchies more generally. We begin by asking how the management practices discussed above contribute to a central goal of managers, namely high labor productivity. Managers, of course, want from the workers high quality work done at the highest possible rate of production, other things being equal. Workers, for their part, would like to work in the best conditions possible and to receive the highest possible wages and benefits, other things being equal. Suppose (more controversially) that the following are also true: (1) for a *given* set of management policies (resulting in given wages, and soon), workers prefer to work with less effort than more; and (2) for a *given* performance by the workers, management prefers to pay them less rather than more (where "pay" is now shorthand for wages, benefits, and conditions); but (3) both sides nevertheless prefer a state of affairs in which both productivity and pay are higher to one in which they are both lower. These preferences are of course those of the familiar Prisoners' Dilemma game (assuming the two sides choose simultaneously). This is how Harvey Leibenstein has framed the problem.[30]

If this game is not repeated and the players' choices are determined by these preferences, then the workers would choose to work at the

---

[28] Miller, *Managerial Dilemmas*. See also Paul Milgrom and John Roberts, "Bargaining Costs, Influence Costs, and the Organization of Economic Activity," in James Alt and Kenneth A. Shepsle, eds., *Perspectives on Positive Political Economy* (Cambridge: Cambridge University Press, 1990).

[29] David M. Kreps, "Corporate Structure and Economic Theory," in Alt and Shepsle, eds., *Perspectives on Positive Political Economy*.

[30] Harvey Leibenstein, *Inside the Firm: The Inefficiencies of Hierarchy* (Cambridge, MA: Harvard University Press, 1987).

lowest level of effort consistent with not being fired and management would choose to pay them the lowest wages they could get away with, despite the fact that both sides are better off when workers and managers choose higher levels of effort and pay.

One way in which managers try to get their workers to increase their productivity is by offering them a piece-rate contract. But this is likely to fail in a firm run on the lines of the first model of hierarchy. The central problem is that once management has set a piece rate for a job, the workers fear that if they were to work hard and thus earn high wages, revealing thereby that they can work much faster than the time-study engineers had established, the management would respond by cutting the piece rate and perhaps firing some of the workers. This fear is in many firms well-founded. As a result, the workers may restrict their output, applying social pressure to individuals to conform to some effort or output norm, and go to great lengths to fool the time-study people into believing that the job could not be done more quickly. Management, in response, might try to induce individual workers to defy the effort restriction norm, and, anticipating the workers' strategic misrepresentation of how fast they can do a job, would strategically make allowances for this in setting the piece rate – a response the workers would try to make allowances for when their job was being evaluated. A simple model of this situation is Kreps's "trust game," which is like a Prisoners' Dilemma game in which the two sides choose sequentially.

But as we've seen, trust and cooperation do not always fail in the real world. The argument we are examining explains why by pointing out that the Prisoners' Dilemma or "trust" game is in reality repeated, and in the repeated game, as is well known, if the players at every stage expect the game to continue with sufficiently high probability and do not discount future payoffs too greatly, then conditional cooperation (work well if you're paid well, pay well if they work well) is an equilibrium.

This does not, however, get us out of the woods, because as the Folk Theorem (referred to earlier) tells us, there will generally be very many different possible outcomes, besides mutual "tit-for-tat," that are equilibria, and the theory that produces this result unfortunately does not tell us which of these equilibria, if any, will actually result. In order to coordinate their actions so that they can converge on one of these equilibria, the players must have mutually reinforcing or correlated expectations.

Thus, cooperation in these games is made more likely by anything that (a) gives the players a stake in the future (by persuading them that they have a future in the game and/or by decreasing their discount rates) or (b) has the effect of creating and sustaining what Kreps calls *trust*, that is, expectations on the part of each player that the other player is a conditional cooperator.

It is apparent that there is nothing in the policies of managers of firms of the first (coercive) kind described earlier that would produce these conditions for cooperation. In hierarchies of this kind, the workers' lack of autonomy, the management's insistence on adherence to hierarchically determined rules and procedures, the hierarchical monitoring of performance, the worker's lack of job security, the large gap between managers and workers in pay and prerogatives and status symbols – these things, taken together, are hardly likely to give the workers a long-term view of their relation with the firm or to engender trust in its managers. In hierarchies of the cooperative kind, on the other hand, we have essentially the opposite of these conditions. In these firms, the management trusts its workers, and works in various ways to earn their trust, to foster in them the belief that their cooperation – their hard work, their sharing of information, their resourcefulness and inventiveness – will not be taken advantage of.

But Kreps and Miller now argue – the final step in the argument we are following here – that it is conventions and norms (such as the norm of reciprocity) that produce the correlated expectations that are necessary for cooperation in the repeated game, and it is the function of leaders to create such cooperative norms. This, rather than hierarchical monitoring and the manipulation of incentives, is how they can best induce cooperation.

This game-theoretical model of workplace management, which is applicable, *mutatis mutandis*, to other hierarchies, seems to me to be clearly superior to the economists' view of hierarchy as a top-down incentive system (what I have called coercive hierarchy). But notice that it too is based upon the same assumptions about human motivation. Although this view finds room for social norms and conventions, it brings them in ad hoc in order to save noncooperative game theory from the crippling indeterminacy resulting from the coexistence of many equilibria, allowing them only the very limited role of guiding the players' beliefs so that their actions can be successfully coordinated to select one of these equilibria. Their sole function is to enable "rational" egoists to achieve the best outcome they can, in terms of their preferences, in the light of what they expect others to do. Norms, then, are allowed no motivating power of their own. They have no normativity. They are not truly *norms*.

Most people do indeed accept a norm of fair reciprocity. But this does not mean that they will merely allow their interactions with others to be guided by the norm so that they may better succeed in furthering their aims. Most people believe that failing to do their part in a cooperative endeavor is *wrong* – wrong (I have argued) in Scanlon's sense, wrong in a way that shows them to have a motivating reason to refrain from doing it. They have reason to want "to live with others on terms that they could not reject." But, as I also argued earlier, if someone who is disposed to be motivated by a norm of fair reciprocity is in fact to be motivated to do her part in a cooperative endeavor, she must believe that she is indeed in a cooperative endeavor, that she is accepted as part of a group with a shared interest, a group whose members all accept this norm. And she is not likely to feel this if she is made to feel used, treated merely as someone manipulable by incentives and sanctions, with no self-determination and indeed no self. These are precisely the (commonly encountered) conditions of coercive hierarchy, and in these conditions the motivation that would normally follow from a person's recognition that it is wrong not to do her part in a cooperative endeavor is demobilized – suppressed or undermined. In a hierarchical setting, it takes conditions of the kind that characterize what I have called cooperative hierarchy – conditions that include a kind of acceptance and recognition – for the standing attachment that most people have to the norm of fair reciprocity to be mobilized.[31]

---

[31] I have discussed cooperation between workers and managers – as I discussed in an earlier section a kind of cooperative accommodation between citizens and polluters and will discuss in the next section cooperation between citizens and police – without commenting on the *contexts* within which such accommodations are made: the industrial order that produces

There is another kind of motivation, which plays no part in (indeed *could not* be accommodated by) the economists' and game theorists' accounts of behavior in hierarchies, but which, I believe, may also be a part of a good understanding of the differences between the two kinds of hierarchy described earlier. This is *intrinsic* motivation, which I introduced in Chapter 7. An intrinsically motivated activity is one done for its own sake, one for which the reward is the activity itself. As we saw, it too can be demobilized or undermined by the introduction of extrinsic incentives. (In this respect it is like moral motivation, but the two are quite distinct.)

The effect of (contingent) extrinsic rewards on intrinsic motivation (and the widespread desire for self-determination which psychologists believe to lie behind it) plausibly provide another part of the explanation for the differences of behavior in our two kinds of hierarchy. Coercive hierarchy relies on incentives, both punishments and rewards, contingent on specific performance. The incentives are hierarchically designed and administered. No use is made of any capacities the hierarchical subordinates have for collective or individual self-regulation. Subordinates contribute little or nothing to the designing and planning of the common enterprise and the part they play in it. Every aspect of this form of governance seems designed to communicate to hierarchical subordinates that the locus of control is external to them and that their reasons for acting are extrinsic.

The second kind of hierarchy works in the opposite way. It gives subordinates a sense that they have some control over what they do; they are trusted; their initiative, creativity, and learning are encouraged; and so on. While everything about coercive hierarchy seems designed to undermine intrinsic motivation, everything about cooperative hierarchy seems designed to promote it.

toxic waste, the social order (with its various inequalities) that the law is to uphold, and (here) the background structural inequalities or class divisions between workers and managers/owners (and what it is that together they produce). But this should not be taken to mean that I endorse the background conditions or that I assume that they have no effect on the particular terms on which these various actors are (variously) prepared to cooperate.

Intrinsic motivation clearly should also be included in any account of hierarchical governance. That economists in general, and the neo-classical economic approach to hierarchy in particular, have ignored it is hardly surprising: what we know about intrinsic motivation plays havoc with fundamental assumptions of microeconomic theory. But it is also ignored by those who have proposed the game-theoretical account of hierarchies, despite their recognition of the superiority of cooperative hierarchy and their desire to make theoretical sense of this.

8.4.   Social order: or why most people are not crooks

In this section I want to look at the argument that the maintenance of social order is made easier by social connections of various kinds – by community, social networks, and repeated interaction in stable groups – the argument takes various forms – and to consider what, in the light of this argument, should be the role of the state – of the police and courts – in dealing with and deterring crime. For my purpose here, *social order* means simply the security, or physical safety, of persons and their property.

Most of us take it for granted that the state should play the central role in maintaining social order. (Indeed, in the United States, those who have been most vociferous in recent decades in calling for a shrinking of central government have tended also to clamor for an expansion of police forces and the prison system.) But for most of the time humans have been on Earth, they have lived their lives in small communities, without states or any apparatus of centralized coercion. And even now, when we live under powerful states and do not live our entire lives in a single small community, community still plays a vital role in the maintenance of social order.

In an earlier work, I made the case that what makes it possible for people to maintain social order – an imperfect social order – was that relations between them were those characteristic of community.[32] By *community* I mean a group of people with durable, multiplex, and

---

[32] Michael Taylor, *Community, Anarchy and Liberty* (Cambridge: Cambridge University Press, 1982).

direct relations: they expect to continue to interact with one another for some time to come (so group membership must be fairly stable); they interact on several fronts, not in a specialized sphere; and their relations are not mediated, in particular by central government agencies. For evidence in that earlier study I drew mainly on anthropological studies of premodern societies, but the argument applies just as well to modern societies, and indeed several writers have now made related arguments about the role of community or of stable social connections in maintaining social order in contemporary societies.[33]

Although I still endorse the argument that community facilitates cooperation, I now have a different understanding of *how* community does its work in maintaining social order and in facilitating cooperation of other kinds. In the earlier work I saw community as, in effect, an *alternative organization of coercion*, one that was decentralized and more egalitarian than the hierarchical coercion of the state. The argument was essentially that community facilitates rational conditional cooperation (of the sort discussed briefly in an earlier chapter) and, if that is not enough, it makes available a range of positive and negative sanctions (most importantly, social approval and disapproval and what follows from them) that are sufficiently powerful to overcome free riding precisely because relations between people are those of community. Mutual rational conditional cooperation itself works essentially through (positive and negative) sanctions: if I cooperate, I will be rewarded with the cooperation of others, while if I fail to cooperate I will be punished with the noncooperation of others. This argument presupposes the rational actor model and (accordingly) sees the core problem for the maintenance of social order as containing free riders.

We in the West and in many other parts of the world are not now quite so dependent on communities (especially place-based ones) or partial communities, so that some of these sanctions have less power

---

[33] Some different examples are: Robert C. Ellickson, *Order Without Law: How Neighbors Settle Disputes* (Cambridge, MA: Harvard University Press, 1991); Mark Granovetter, "Economic Action and Social Structure: The Problem of Embeddedness," *American Journal of Sociology*, 91 (1985), 481–510; and the work of John Braithwaite and of Robert J. Samson and John H. Laub on crime and delinquency, which I will discuss below.

over us. But – witchcraft and sorcery aside – they still have some power. Indeed, several criminologists have concluded that crime and disorder are more likely to be deterred by informal social sanctions – especially when these are wielded by people with whom one expects to continue to interact and about whose good opinion one cares (for whatever reason) – than by formal sanctioning by governmental or legal authorities. That is especially true of authorities one does not trust or for whose office one has little respect, and especially if they are remote from and uninvolved in one's community. If this is so, then it would seem that community – even such remnants and fragments of community as now remain – matters more than the state in the maintenance of social order. There is indeed much evidence that this is so.[34] (I shall, however, question whether it is truly *sanctioning* through which community is doing its work.) For crime to be contained and deterred by informal sanctions, the offenders and potential offenders must be *connected* to others: they must be embedded in social networks, belong to groups, have continuing interactions with other people, and so on.

If this argument about the connection between community and social order is correct, then we should expect to find that most crime is committed by people who are unconnected or who are in social relations that they do not expect to last. This is indeed the case. Crime is committed disproportionately by *males* (who in patriarchal societies are expected, to a greater degree than women, to move through a period of independence from their families), by *young people* (people aged fifteen to twenty-five years, who are leaving or about to leave one set of relationships – family, school, perhaps neighborhood – and have not as yet fully established another), by people who are *unmarried*, and also by people who live in large cities, areas with high residential mobility, or families that have moved a lot, or are not strongly attached to their parents or to their school.[35]

---

[34] See, for example, L. S. Anderson, T. G. Chiricos, and G. P. Waldo, "Formal and Informal Sanctions: A Comparison of Deterrence Effects," *Social Problems*, 25 (1977), 103–114; and Charles R. Tittle, *Sanctions and Social Deviance: The Question of Deterrence* (New York: Praeger, 1980).

[35] See John Braithwaite, *Crime, Shame and Reintegration* (Cambridge: Cambridge University Press, 1989), Chapter 3 and pp. 89–94.

In a careful reexamination of the evidence, Sampson and Laub come to similar conclusions.[36] They establish the great importance of "informal social ties and bonds to society at all ages and across the life course" in inhibiting delinquency and crime. A child's relations to her parents, school, and peers are significant determinants of delinquency; and social bonds in the transition to adulthood and in adulthood itself, in the form of job stability and marital attachment, are significant inhibitors of crime, even among those with a record of earlier delinquent behavior. They show, too, that incarceration, while its direct deterrent effect on crime is negligible, makes it harder for someone to form these bonds, and in this indirect way has an important positive effect on crime. I'll return shortly to the effects of incarceration.

Although decentralized informal social controls still play a large part in the maintenance of social order – much larger in some arenas than in others – we also have police forces, courts, and prisons: hierarchical arrangements involving a division of labor and concentrated power. To these institutions of the state the general argument about hierarchy made in the last section applies. Here, as elsewhere, there are two sorts of governance, making use of hierarchy in two quite different ways. In the cooperative approach, the police and courts make use of local communities and organizations, leaving to them at least some of the work of social control and, for the rest, encouraging them to share with the police the work of maintaining social order, helping them to strengthen their capacities to do so (their "social capital"), and working cooperatively with them.

But, I think it is fair to say, policing and criminal justice in at least the countries of the West have in the recent past approximated the coercive model of hierarchy: little use is made of and there is no attempt to foster horizontal social capital, and there is little vertical social capital in the hierarchy. More recently, however, there have been efforts in a number of these countries to move the practice of policing in the direction of the second model. In the English-speaking

---

[36] Robert J. Sampson and John H. Laub, *Crime in the Making: Pathways and Turning Points Through Life* (Cambridge, MA: Cambridge University Press, 1993).

world these reforms normally go under the label of "community policing." This label covers a great variety of ideas and programs; but the core *aims* are, very briefly, these:[37] (i) Decentralization of police organization and command, to give greater autonomy to local commanders and to patrol officers. (ii) An effort by the police to encourage people to see themselves as coresponsible for maintaining social order, as "coproducers" of order with the police, and generally to help people to help themselves to maintain social order (for example, by helping them entrepreneurially to create neighborhood organizations). (iii) Opening up two-way communication between police and people, with the police working among and cooperatively with the people and accepting that they can contribute to effective policing, making themselves and their work more open and accessible to the public and allowing civilian oversight, building trust between people and police. (iv) Making use of such local community as exists and of whatever local organization is available; building these up where they are weak and even creating them where they are absent.

Bearing in mind my earlier warning about the use of the phrase "social capital," we could summarize the idea of community policing by saying that it works by making use of and building vertical social capital (between police and communities) and horizontal social capital (within the communities).

Elements of this approach have been introduced in many U.S. cities and in Great Britain and other West European countries, although for the most part there is more talk than action in all these Western countries.[38] But the clearest embodiment of the second model of

[37] See Jerome H. Skolnik and David H. Bayley, *Community Policing: Issues and Practices Around the World* (Washington, DC: National Institute of Justice, U.S. Department of Justice, 1988), esp. Chapter 1; Skolnik and Bayley, *The New Blue Line* (New York: Free Press, 1986), passim; Wesley G. Skogan, *Disorder and Decline: Crime and the Spiral of Decay in American Neighborhoods* (Berkeley: University of California Press, 1990), esp. at pp. 91–93; and Wesley G. Skogan and Susan M. Hartnett, *Community Policing, Chicago Style* (New York: Oxford University Press, 1997).

[38] Where community policing reforms in the United States have been carefully evaluated, it appears that they have had some, albeit limited success. As we might have expected, they appear to be more successful where there is some local horizontal social capital to make use of and build upon. See Skogan, *Disorder and Decline*. See also Wesley G. Skogan, ed., *Community Policing:*

hierarchy in any actual system of policing and criminal justice is to be found in Japan, which has the most developed and longest established system of community policing in the world. Japanese policing makes extraordinary efforts to work *in* and *with* communities of every kind: the officers work out of highly accessible police posts located in every neighborhood, and they make it their business to get to know everyone and every business in their jurisdiction; and the whole country is honeycombed with neighborhood associations and countless other civic associations that seek to help and be helped by the police.[39]

Policing that is as thoroughly communitarian as this may not be to the taste of everyone in the West. But there is another way in which crimefighting can make use of the facts about social connection and crime and disorder that I summarized previously, which is likely to be less objectionable. If it is true – as the evidence suggests – that community (in the weak sense in which I have defined it) plays a more effective role in the maintenance of social order than does the coercive state, and that informal social sanctions are more effective than formal legal ones, then it follows that forms of sentencing and punishing offenders that *exclude* them, or have the effect of making their acceptance and recognition by society difficult, are counterproductive. And this of course is just what sentencing and punishing typically do in America, where incarceration is often the first recourse, not the

Can It Work? (Belmont, CA: Wadsworth/Thomson Learning, 2004) and, on the (largely successful) results of the Chicago Alternative Policing Strategy, Skogan and Hartnett, *Community Policing, Chicago Style.* Where local "communities" are seriously divided along various economic and cultural lines – and genuine overall community is correspondingly weak – there may be little agreement on what social order is to begin with. See on this Adam Crawford, *The Local Governance of Crime: Appeals to Community and Partnerships* (Oxford: Clarendon Press, 1997), esp. Chapter 5.

[39] On Japanese policing I found especially useful David H. Bayley, *Forces of Order: Policing Modern Japan* (Berkeley: University of California Press, 1991), and John Owen Haley, *Authority Without Power: Law and the Japanese Paradox* (New York: Oxford University Press, 1991). See also Walter L. Ames, *Police and Community in Japan* (Berkeley: University of California Press, 1981). For a less benign picture, consult Setsuo Miyazawa, *Policing in Japan: A Study on Making Crime*, trans, F.G. Bennnett with J.O. Haley (Albany: State University of New York Press, 1992), and Patricia G. Steinhoff, "Pursuing the Japanese Police," *Law and Society Review*, 27 (1993), 827–850.

last, and where, moreover, in some states, the ex-con is disbarred by law from certain employments and from voting. (There are currently about two million people in prison in the United States – 686 in every 100,000 of the population. This is the highest rate of incarceration in the world. The rate per 100,000 is 139 in England and Wales, 96 in Germany, 85 in France, and only 48 in Japan.[40]) In America, and to a less extent elsewhere in the West, the approach to punishment tends to stigmatize the offender, makes it hard – harder than it was before – for him to think of himself as a member of society, banishes him from society for a wide range of offenses, and again upon his release from prison makes it difficult for him to find a place in society, to be accepted.[41] This approach, then, *excludes* the offender and further alienates him from society. It deals with him through assertions of power and removes from him some of the control he has over his life and his responsibility for it.

John Braithwaite has argued in his important book, *Crime, Shame and Reintegration,* that a better approach to the control of crime is to foster the social conditions that make effective shaming possible and to make serious actual use of shaming, but then also (and this is the distinctive contribution of Braithwaite's book) to try to *reintegrate* the offender into society.[42] The idea is to make it quite clear that he has done wrong – that he could not reasonably expect society to

[40] These figures, for dates around 2001–2002, are from Roy Walmsley, "Global Incarceration Rates and Prison Trends," *Forum on Crime and Society*, 3 (2003), 65–78. I thank Naomi Murakawa for this reference.

[41] For example: most states of the United States do not allow felons to vote for some time after being convicted, but in some states this ban lasts for years after their release from prison. It is estimated that in 2005 about 4.7 million people in the United States could not vote because of felony convictions. When the governor of Iowa, Tom Vilsack, recently announced his intention to restore voting rights to felons upon completion of their sentences, he said, "When you've paid your debt to society, you need to be reconnected and re-engaged to society," and an ex-con who appeared with the governor declared, "If nobody hires you and you don't feel like you're a part of anything, all you will do is feel like you may as well go back to what you know, which is doing drugs." *New York Times*, June 18, 2005.

[42] Braithwaite, *Crime, Shame and Reintegration*. See also the further development and testing of some of Braithwaite's ideas in Eliza Ahmed, Nathan Harris, John Braithwaite, and Valerie Braithwaite, *Shame Management Through Reintegration* (Cambridge: Cambridge University Press, 2001) and

accept behavior of that sort – but then to accept him back into the
community, and by doing so accord him some respect as a human
being rather than treating him as if he were *nothing but* a criminal or
delinquent and accordingly stigmatizing and rejecting him.

Here again Japan provides a model. "Reintegrative shaming," as
Braithwaite calls it, is a central aim of that country's criminal justice
system. A great effort is made to shame offenders but the shaming tries to be reintegrative. If the offender is shamed and genuinely
repents, he very often will not be further punished.[43] Furthermore,
the Japanese state, although it does of course directly punish crimi-
nals, does so far less readily and far more leniently than do Western
industrial states. Far fewer offenders apprehended by the police are
even reported for prosecution; of those who are, most are given small
fines after summary proceedings, or prosecution is suspended; and
of those actually tried, most receive suspended sentences, few are
committed to prison, and those who are jailed receive much shorter
sentences. Japanese police officers and judges want from suspects and
defendants acknowledgement of guilt and sincere repentance. They
expect and usually get from the defendant a confession, an approach
to the victim via family and friends, and payment of compensation to
and forgiveness by the victim. Again, the contrast with the American
approach is great: punishment by the state, especially incarceration, is
the last resort of the Japanese system, which seeks reintegration – the
reconnection of the offender with society – while in the United States
punishment is almost the only resort, and reconnection is ignored.[44]

in John Braithwaite, *Restorative Justice and Responsive Regulation* (Oxford:
Oxford University Press, 2002).

[43] Reintegrative shaming is no doubt more effective in Japan than it would
be in the United States because Japan is a more "communitarian" society – and not just in its villages and hamlets. The *mura* (hamlet) has served
successfully as a model for urban neighborhoods and even for firms, and
while community and informal social control have weakened in the mura
itself, they have been strengthened in the cities and in firms. See, for example, Haley, *Authority Without Power,* esp. Chapter 8; Bayley, *Forces of Order,*
esp. Chapters 7 and 8; Theodore C. Bestor, *Neighborhood Tokyo* (Stanford,
CA: Stanford University Press, 1989); and Braithwaite, *Crime, Shame and
Reintegration.*

[44] Hayley, *Authority Without Power,* Chapter 6; Bayley, *Forces of Order,*
Chapter 7.

It should be noted parenthetically that the Japanese approach to crime and punishment – which is communitarian in its policing and communitarian in its sentencing and punishing – has apparently worked (and at lower cost than crime control in the United States[45]): Japan's crime rates are much lower than those not only of the United States (the most crime-ridden of the industrial democracies) but of the other Western industrial democracies as well, and, while crime rates have steadily risen in recent decades in these other countries, they have actually fallen in Japan.[46]

Reintegrative shaming approaches the delinquent and the crooked as human beings, who may be capable of acting not merely as cost-benefit calculators, balancers of competing self-interested desires, but as moral beings who are capable of being moved by reasons provided by their own ideals of right and wrong; who, however inchoately and unsuccessfully, long to belong, to be accepted, and to "live in unity with their fellow creatures." This is what the "shaming" part of reintegrative shaming does. It reminds the wrongdoer (and examples of it remind the potential wrongdoer) of his own ideals; it calls him to live up to those ideals; it thereby allows him, and encourages him to exercise, a measure of responsibility for and control over his life. The reintegration part of reintegrative shaming then readmits the offender back into society, making it possible for him to (re-)establish those social connections and some degree of self-determination that are the conditions for him to care that his actions be justifiable to others and hence to be morally motivated in the way that I described earlier.

The general argument I made (in the last chapter) about moral motivation makes it plain why conventional Western policing and sentencing is disastrous (and where it is practiced most rigorously – in the United States – it most spectacularly fails). The lesson is: recognize people as human, as social and moral beings; don't treat them as if they belonged to another species (*Homo economicus*), to be coerced or moved as isolated individuals by rewards and penalties alone; don't ignore and even undermine, but recognize and foster their social connections, their attachments and commitments, and invite them to live

---

[45] Bayley, *Forces of Order*, p. 151.
[46] Bayley, *Forces of Order*, Chapter 1.

up to their ideals, including especially the ideal of fair reciprocity, of doing their part in a cooperative endeavor; and therefore don't alienate and exclude them from society, destroying whatever sense they have of being part of a cooperative endeavor. If you do this, the ideal of their actions being justifiable to others will get no traction with them.[47]

[47] This argument about crime-fighting, drawing on the argument (in section 3) about coercive and cooperative forms of hierarchical governance, applies broadly to *corporate* crime; for the owners and managers of business firms are humans too, and therefore generally have the distinctively human capacities and dispositions I have been insisting on throughout this book. The argument about why most people are disposed to recognize and obey a norm of fair reciprocity – to do their part in a mutually advantageous cooperative venture – and in particular to refrain from criminal activity, therefore applies to them. Whether or not this moral motivation will be mobilized depends on the way they are treated by regulators. This is the conclusion of those who, unlike the economists, with their ideological assertions about the irrelevance of moral appeals and their one-sided view of hierarchical governance as always a matter of arranging incentives, have actually undertaken empirical studies. See, especially, the work of John Braithwaite and various associates: a good brief summary can be found in Braithwaite's *Crime, Shame and Reintegration*, Chapter 9, a longer one in Ian Ayres and John Braithwaite, *Responsive Regulation: Transcending the Regulation Debate* (Oxford: Oxford University Press, 1992). They have found that very many (but not all) corporate executives care about their companies' reputations, not just because that is good for business but for its own sake, and they care about their own personal reputations. "They are also often concerned to do what is right, to be faithful to their identity as law abiding citizens, and to sustain a self-concept of social responsibility" (Ayres and Braithwaite, p. 22). If this is so, then we should expect to find that managers, like the citizens and workers I discussed above, do not like being treated as if they were nothing more than the asocial and amoral calculators of economic theory, and that, if they are treated in this way, they are more likely to *act* like *Homo economicus*. This is indeed what the empirical investigators have found. Government regulation does not have to take the coercive form standardly assumed by economists, in which the regulators assume that those they govern are movable only by incentives and sanctions, never by considerations of right and wrong, of the justifiability or unjustifiability of their actions, and that only the threat of legal sanctions, and perhaps also fear of loss of sales from bad publicity, can motivate compliance with the law – with laws that protect consumers, workers, and the public at large from (among other things) harmful products, polluted and degraded environments, and unsafe and unhealthy workplaces. Nor, of course, does it have to take the form of entirely voluntary self-regulation favored by the administration of George W. Bush. (There are, of course, corporate executives who do not

I do not of course doubt that sanctions can be effective, or that they will always be needed. But they are not (as I earlier quoted H. L. A. Hart as saying) "the normal motive for obedience." Fear of sanctions – or the cost of sanctions balanced against the economic gain – is not the reason most people refrain from stealing, cheating, and so on. For most people, normally, crime is unthinkable; it doesn't come into their heads as even a possibility. Most people do not weigh their desires or make cost-benefit calculations about whether to commit crimes. Because, for them, to commit crimes, to be a free rider on the social order provided by others, is wrong (wrong in Scanlon's sense of not being justifiable to others), the considerations that might move a Rational Chooser are for them silenced or suppressed.

accept that they should obey certain laws and do not feel they do anything wrong in flouting them, and there are those who cannot be shamed, who are not and do not wish to be part of the moral community.) The realistic alternative to coercive hierarchy is what Ayres and Braithwaite call *enforced self-regulation*, which is a form of cooperative hierarchy and is analogous to the *comanagement* regimes favored by many of those who deal with natural resource commons.

Index

Other books in the series (*continued from page iii*)

John Kane
The Politics of Moral Capital

Ayelet Shachar
Multicultural Jurisdictions

John Keane
Global Civil Society?

Rogers M. Smith
Stories of Peoplehood

Gerry Mackie
Democracy Defended

John Keane
Violence and Democracy

Kok-Chor Tan
Justice without Borders

Peter J. Steinberger
The Idea of the State